# A Clash
### *of* Transitions

PETER LANG
New York • Washington, D.C./Baltimore • Bern
Frankfurt am Main • Berlin • Brussels • Vienna • Oxford

# A Clash *of* Transitions

## Towards a Learning Society

Olga Strietska-Ilina,
EDITOR

PETER LANG
New York • Washington, D.C./Baltimore • Bern
Frankfurt am Main • Berlin • Brussels • Vienna • Oxford

Library of Congress Cataloging-in-Publication Data

Strietska-Ilina, Olga.
A clash of transitions: towards a learning society / edited by Olga Strietska-Ilina.
p. cm.
Includes bibliographical references.
1. Knowledge management—Europe, Eastern.  2. Knowledge
management—European Union countries.  3. Information society—Europe,
Eastern.  4. Information society—European Union countries.  I. Strietska-Ilina, Olga.
HD53.C563    303.48'33094—dc22    2006023219
ISBN 978-0-8204-7476-2

Bibliographic information published by **Die Deutsche Bibliothek**.
**Die Deutsche Bibliothek** lists this publication in the "Deutsche
Nationalbibliografie"; detailed bibliographic data is available
on the Internet at http://dnb.ddb.de/.

"Towards the European Society—Challenges for Education and Training Policies
and Research arising from the European Integration and Enlargement" has been
funded by the European Commission, DG Research, Framework Programme 5

Cover design by Sophie Boorsch Appel

© 2007 Peter Lang Publishing, Inc., New York
29 Broadway, 18th floor, New York, NY 10006
www.peterlang.com

All rights reserved.
Reprint or reproduction, even partially, in all forms such as microfilm,
xerography, microfiche, microcard, and offset strictly prohibited.

# Table of Contents

Acknowledgments ............................................................................. vii
List of Abbreviations and Acronyms ............................................... ix

Introduction .......................................................................................... 1
    **Olga Strietska–Ilina**

A Clash of Transitions. Towards a Learning Society ..................... 11
    **Olga Strietska–Ilina**

The World's Trader, the World's Lawyer:
Europe and Global Processes ........................................................... 61
    **Göran Therborn**

Is a "Learning Society" a Credible Concept in
Central and Eastern European Countries? A Literatue Review ..... 81
    **Liliana Voicu**

Human Capital and Benefits of Education and Training.
European Challenges and Strategies towards
a Learning Society ............................................................................ 117
    **Manfred Tessaring**

Lisbon Process and a Knowledge Europe:
A Policy Perspective of Central and Eastern
European Countries .................................................................................. 145
    **Juraj Vantuch**

Learning Challenges for Social Inclusion
in Transition Economies ........................................................................... 173
    **Adela–Luminita Rogojinaru**

Guiding Learners in the Learning Society:
The Situation in Nine Central and East
European Countries .................................................................................. 205
    **Ronald G. Sultana**

Vocational Education and Lifelong Learning
in Tomorrow's Europe ............................................................................... 243
    **Burkart Sellin**

Contributors ............................................................................................... 269

# Acknowledgements

Grateful acknowledgment is hereby made to Sage Publications Ltd for permission to reprint the following copyrighted material: Therborn, Göran. The World's Trader, the World's Lawyer: Europe and Global Processes, *European Journal of Social Theory*, Volume 5, No. 4, pp. 403–427, Sage Publications, 2002.

# List of Abbreviations and Acronyms

| | |
|---|---|
| CAP | Common Agricultural Policy |
| CD | compact disc |
| Cedefop | European Centre for the Development of Vocational Training |
| CEE | Central and Eastern Europe |
| CEECs | Central and Eastern European countries |
| CIPS | Vocational Information Counselling Centre |
| CIS | Commonwealth of Independent States |
| CJEC | Court of Justice of the European Communities |
| CMEA | Council for Mutual Economic Assistance |
| DSL | digital subscriber line |
| EC | European Commission |
| EEA | European Economic Area |
| EEC | European Economic Community (the former name of the European Community) |
| EIU | Economist Intelligence Unit |
| EMU | European Monetary Union |
| ESF | European Social Fund |
| ETF | European Training Foundation |
| EU | European Union |

| | |
|---|---|
| EUR | euro (European currency) |
| EURES | European Job Mobility Portal |
| EURONE&T | project "Towards the European Society: challenges for education and training policies and research arising from the European integration and enlargement" |
| Eurostat | Statistical Office of the European Communities |
| GDP | gross domestic product |
| GDR | German Democratic Republic |
| GNP | gross national product |
| HRD | human resource development |
| IAEVG | International Association for Educational and Vocational Guidance |
| IALS | International Adult Literacy Survey |
| ICT | information and communication technology |
| IFP | International Futures Programme |
| ILO | International Labour Organisation |
| IMF | International Monetary Fund |
| IPTS | Institute for Prospective Technological Studies |
| ISCED | International Standard Classification of Education |
| IT | information technology |
| LFS | Labour Force Survey |
| n.a. | not available |
| NAFTA | North American Free Trade Agreement |
| NAPE | National Action Plan for Employment |
| NATO | North Atlantic Treaty Organisation |
| NDP | National Development Plan |
| NGO | non–governmental organisation |
| OAED | Greek Manpower Employment Organisation |
| OECD | Organisation for Economic Cooperation and Development |
| OSI | Open Society Institutes |
| p.c. | per capita |
| PES | Public Employment Service |
| Phare | originally "Poland and Hungary: Assistance for Restructuring their Economies", later covered other CEECs |
| TACIS | Technical Aid to the Commonwealth of Independent States |

| | |
|---|---|
| CARDS | Community Assistance for Reconstruction, Development and Stabilisation |
| PLOTEUS | Portal on Learning Opportunities throughout the European Space |
| PPP | purchasing power parity |
| R&D | research and development |
| RPE | real public expenditure |
| SME | small and medium–sized enterprises |
| UCLA | University of California, Los Angeles |
| UK | United Kingdom |
| UNDP | United Nations Development Programme |
| UNESCO | United Nations Educational, Scientific and Cultural Organisation |
| UNICEF | United Nations Children's Fund |
| UOE | joint UNESCO/OECD/Eurostat data collection |
| US | United States |
| USA | United States of America |
| USD | dollar (USA's currency) |
| USSR | Union of Soviet Socialist Republics |
| WB | World Bank |
| WTO | World Trade Organisation |

## Country codes

| | |
|---|---|
| AT | Austria |
| BE | Belgium |
| BG | Bulgaria |
| CH | Switzerland |
| CY | Cyprus |
| CZ | Czech Republic |
| DE | Germany |
| DK | Denmark |
| EE | Estonia |
| ES | Spain |
| EU–15 | 15 old member states of the EU |
| EU–25 | all 25 member states of the EU |
| FI | Finland |
| FR | France |
| GR | Greece |

| | |
|---|---|
| HR | Croatia |
| HU | Hungary |
| IE | Ireland |
| IT | Italy |
| LT | Lithuania |
| LU | Luxemburg |
| LV | Latvia |
| MT | Malta |
| NL | Netherlands |
| NMS–10 | 10 new member states of the EU |
| NO | Norway |
| PL | Poland |
| PT | Portugal |
| RO | Romania |
| SE | Sweden |
| SI | Slovenia |
| SK | Slovakia |
| UK | United Kingdom |

• OLGA STRIETSKA–ILINA •

# Introduction

The idea of this volume came into existence when the map of Europe looked quite different. On the 1$^{st}$ of May 2004 ten new states became members of the European Union (EU). Among those were eight countries of Central and Eastern Europe which have been undergoing major reform of their societies and economies since 1989. Czech Republic, Estonia, Hungary, Latvia, Lithuania, Poland, Slovakia and Slovenia joined the EU in a time of demanding changes. An oft–used metaphor of jumping into a train going at full speed well depicts the EU enlargement. In addition, the final destination was not quite known even to the "old passengers", and the newcomers naturally had an even vaguer idea and no say on the shape of the destination prior to the embarkation.

The Lisbon strategy, agreed by the European Council in March 2000, set out an ambitious goal, "to become the most competitive and dynamic knowledge–based economy in the world, capable of sustainable economic growth with more and better jobs and greater social cohesion." Somewhat lacking in feasibility of achieving such a twofold objective of competetiveness and social cohesion, the Lisbon agenda required major reforms from the EU member states. It put a special emphasis on innovation, research and development, and thus on the "learning economy". This major reform was launched at the time of EU enlargement—a demanding and challenging reform in itself for new member states but also for old members and EU institutions and decision making.

The European dream project, the transition to this new and widened Europe, and the capacity of the socieities and individuals to cope with these multiple transitions became the subject of the research project "Towards the European Society: Challenges for Education and Training Policies and Research Arising from the European Integration and Enlargement"[1]. The project aimed at investigating the impact of the European integration and enlargement processes on policies related to learning in the European Union and in the accession countries. Such discourse involved a much broader range of issues and could not be limited to education and training, or even to human capital. The contextual issues of globalisation and the development of the "ideology" of the learning society and knowledge economy could not be limited to Europe alone, and thus the discourse involved much of the international debate and comparison widely presented in other volumes resulting from the project[2]. This publication focuses on the angle of countries in transition, i.e., countries of Central and Eastern Europe some of which have already entered the EU, while others are expected to join in 2007, but certain transition issues touch upon a broader spectrum of countries and thus concern the entire EU.

The first chapter of the volume provides a general insight to the subject. The discussion is developed around various transition contexts, such as the transition to a New Europe, transition to democracy and a market economy, and transition to a knowledge–based economy as far as the Lisbon strategy is concerned. The horizontal issues in all transition contexts are accession to the EU and the particular role of education and training in all transitions. The gap in understanding of the concept of the European project between old and new member states contributes to different expectations from EU membership. For CEECs "coming back to Europe" has a very idealistic and nostalgic meaning. For them, Europe is not so much a project as a memory, a freedom once lost and now regained. For Western Europeans, Europe is far more a project which is still to be shaped and implemented. The Idea of Europe somehow has to incorporate both understandings in the process of identity building. The traditional values of democracy, human rights and the rule of law have to be firmly tied to the Lisbon strategy and the Idea of Europe as a world economic hegemony with a socially cohesive society. This may help to build a genuine European political identity which would encompass East and West. It is, however, important that the Lisbon objectives are clear to citizens and the possible costs of transition to competitive Europe are clearly stated, even if some sacrifices are to be made on the social side of the agenda.

The Lisbon agenda was formulated and accepted at the time when CEECs were still in the process of negotiations over acceptance of the *acquis communautaire* and the continued reform of their economies. The completion of the transition to a market economy was a priority. This "double transition" along with the accession process on the top of it pushed countries to tackle the most urgent issues rather than strategic ones. The objectives set out in the Lisbon strategy were not on the CEECs' priority list. On the other hand, there was a realisation that any delay in the "second" transition would widen the gap between old and acceding member states and that CEECs will have more difficulties to catch up later. The challenges brought to CEECs by the knowledge revolution are dramatic. The Lisbon transition costs may turn to be the highest for CEECs.

The chapter by Göran Therborn looks at Europe's position in the world, whereby Europe stands out as the central point of global flows of trade and capital and as the region of transnational normativity. While Therborn recognises Norman Davies's arguments against writing a Western European history of Europe, his own global perspective preserves the focus on that part of Europe which historically, and currently, has been most influential. For Therborn, today the major Eastern European project is absorption into Western Europe. He highlights the historical background and interrelation of foreign trade and international law within Europe, both in early modern social theory and in post–World War II institution building as well as the spread of European law onto other continents. On the other hand, "there are good reasons not to stay basking in the sunshine, but to dwell on the dark sides of Europe". The advantageous historical and current position of Europe in the world is hardly expressed in the roles which contemporary European leaders want to play and in contemporary formulations of European heritage and identity. This is due partly to "a nostalgic misjudgement by ex–great power politicians, but largely because of the delimited position of conventional trade and law in Europe".

Liliana Voicu in her chapter looks at the concept of a learning society in CEECs. She tries to answer the questions of whether the concept is credible and viable in the region and to what extent it is inspired and affected by the process of EU accession, and what the major controversies of the debate are. She produces the analysis by comparing literature reviews produced for ten CEECs, including Bulgaria and Romania, for which the accession process is still under way, and the Russian Federation. The latter served as "a litmus paper" in the comparison, as a country whose historical experience of a communist past and transition processes is very similar to those of CEECs but which has not been affected by EU enlargement and therefore EU policy rhetoric. Although CEECs are considered here as a homogenous region with a necessary degree of simplification for the comparative reasons, Voicu well appreciates the diversity in economic development, social cohesion and cultural backgrounds of countries of the region. She asks whether the diversity brings differences in the national discourses on the learning society.

Voicu found that the process of EU integration strongly affected the learning society debate, making the general tone of the argument and the concept itself very much policy–driven and normative by nature. In–depth conceptual reflections on the concept of a learning society are very rare in CEECs, if indeed they exist. This is the case in spite of the deeply rooted tradition on the role of learning and the "cult" of education in these countries. The regions which gave the world "the teacher of nations" Jan Amos Komenský (in Latin, Comenius), Janusz Korczak, Konstantin Ushinsky, Lev Vygotsky and Anton Makarenko mostly develop their current thinking around information society with the emphasis on information technologies and policies aiming at their development. This attitude is well reflected in another interesting but alarming controversy relating to the permanent stress of harsh competition and the constant change, "which may surpass human limits". The pace of change during the period of transition and the subsequent requirement for "the learning citizen" to constantly adapt to the change raises a fundamental but frightening question of whether "a learning society is a desirable society after all".

An answer to the latter question is partially provided in the following contribution by Manfred Tessaring, which offers an important general insight on the benefits from and returns on investments into education and training. The material and non–material benefits of education and training for individuals, companies and the whole society are discussed in the context of the recent debate in Europe on the significance of investments in training triggered by the strategy set out at the European Council in Lisbon. Although research on the impact and benefits of education and training for individuals, enterprises and society confirms the importance of the human capital in contributing to economic growth, social cohesion and many other benefits at all levels, current investment is not sufficient and the Lisbon targets will not be achieved by 2010 without a significant increase of investment in education and training. Institutional settings and education and training systems, as well as their capacity to incorporate the interests of various sectors and actors, are equally important. Cooperation, consensus and public–private partnership may be a key to the successful implementation of the Lisbon strategy.

Juraj Vantuch also focuses on the Lisbon strategy but within the framework of the EU accession process. Without trying to undervalue the importance of the key objectives of the Lisbon agenda and its role in emphasising the role of education and training in European policy making, Vantuch points to several important gaps. First, the strategy presents important and appealing ideas but does not elucidate how they can be implemented and whether it is feasible at all. Second, the strategy is largely designed for reform on the part of old EU member states and therefore deals with their "transition". New members of the EU are still very much in the process of their primary transition, that is the transition to democracy and a market economy, and have to deal with the newly demanded transition to the knowledge–based economy on the top of it. Here the question of priorities comes into view and brings us to yet another gap revealed here: the gap in the understanding of what exactly is an appropriate policy mix—depending on the country and the policy perspective.

By analysing new member states' response to selected targets of the Lisbon strategy, Vantuch comes to the conclusion that the still weak economies of new member states and acceding countries face a serious challenge in meeting various policy requirements and commitments, especially against the background of other fiscal pressures and requirements of the EMU and the need to satisfy the Maastricht convergence criteria. Under such conditions the importance of investment in human capital becomes merely declarative, whereas the actual budget allocation to education and training, and research and development are based on the residual principle. The unpopular decisions on the necessary cut–offs in other policies, such as Common Agricultural Policy, might be needed. The Lisbon agenda would pay mere lip service to the importance of investment in people for the promotion of the knowledge–based economy, unless some, possibly unpopular, yet highly vital, prioritisation is made.

Adela–Luminita Rogojinaru continues the debate on the benefits of education and training for the society and individuals started in the chapter by Tessaring. She analyses social cohesion through all forms of learning and skills acquisition in the context of transition in CEECs. After the collapse of the communist regime CEECs faced a new social phenomenon of exclusion. CEECs found themselves on the path of transition from an egalitarian to a meritocratic society. In a society where wealth and access to power is based on merit, the role of education and training becomes the pillar for the definition of the social status. The question of equality of access to learning and to information and information technology therefore becomes crucial for the provision of social cohesion in society. At the same time higher levels of education do not always guarantee better chances for employment and wealth distribution in transition economies. It is not only the knowledge but also its quality and specific competences acquired that play a role here. CEECs have not so much suffered from inadequate levels of education, but rather they have been affected by a skills mismatch resulting from structural changes.

The invisible hand of market distribution does not bring about social justice. As a result of economic transformation some social groups found themselves below the poverty level, which proves a crucial factor leading to exclusion. This particularly concerns young people and young families, as well as ethnic minorities. Some groups are characterised by an accumulation of factors that determine exclusion. Education and training measures alone cannot bring the solution here. The question of a broader social, cultural and political participation should be addressed and eventually incorporated into the learning society discourse.

Ronald Sultana, in his analysis, critically readdressed the prevailing discourse about the learning society, and particularly the role of guidance within that society. In this context again, the EU agendas for both the learning society and for lifelong guidance are marked by two logics, the economic and the social. The "chameleon concept" changes its ideological colours according to the context in which it is applied. By and large, the essence of the concept is economistic, and only the rhetoric is social. The submission to economic imperatives leads to the mobilisation of individuals in a very particular way. "Individuals must remain engaged in learning, ever flexible and ever nimble, constantly re–shaping and re–inventing themselves in line with unpredictable changes in the labour market. They must be ever ready to enter and re–enter learning, training and working routes, and, given the "European dimension", to move to wherever such training and employment opportunities exist." Frequent job changes caused by restructuring are presented in the lifelong learning/guidance discourse as exciting and stimulating opportunities. There is, however, little acknowledgment that the loss of lifetime employment contracts leads to precarious lives and insecurity, and to the deterioration of socially important work–based communities.

According to Sultana, in CEECs, countries that are much poorer than the old EU member states, the economic logic behind the "mobility agenda" of the EU is clear: the availability of skilled labour from economically depressed countries could be used either as comparatively cheap sources of labour, or/and to drive down wages for "mainstream" European workers, making the old continent more competitive. Little however is acknowledged on what the response to the needs of European enterprises and the economy brings to the CEECs region, to mobile workers themselves and to their families. The most vital transition at the individual level— the one between education, training, and employment throughout one's lifetime—is largely mediated by economistic, neo–liberal, argumentation. Sultana suggests that more should be done to "unmask" the presumed innocence behind the lifelong learning debate, "where we examine not only the way we, as social actors, use the discourse, but more importantly, the way the discourse uses us".

The final chapter of the volume by Burkart Sellin is based on the findings of a research project which attempted to elaborate scenarios and strategies for future vocational education and training and lifelong learning in Europe. The likely scenarios for the next decades in response to current and future challenges are selected and analysed in the attempt to overcome short–termism in policy making and to take into account some longer–term consequences with particular attention to the specific situation of CEECs. The scenarios were formulated in three different contexts: business and technology, employment and the labour market, and training, skills and knowledge. The first important finding was that the basic trends and the likelihood of their occurrence did not principally differ between old and new EU member states. However, the question of economic renewal was the focus of attention especially among CEECs. It would however be overly simplistic to say that there was a clear trend towards neo–liberal development. The reform pressure in the CEECs is certainly and naturally much greater than in the old EU member states. Furthermore CEECs did not wish to see their newly acquired freedom of movement jeopardised, but they did fear that the emigration of highly–

qualified skilled workers will cause a brain drain to the West and thus delay the necessary modernisation of their own economy. CEECs also often noted increasing inequality between different target groups, regions and economic segments during the reform process.

A prospering economy alone is not realistic, nor tolerable. It needs a serious social backup, especially under the condition of profound social transformation. Three major scenarios were discussed and selected as overarching ones: "Europe on the edge" where everything is uncertain and major current problems are not resolved, "protective and incremental Europe" where some problems are solved but many still remain, and "sustainable and competitive Europe" where lifelong learning is important, networks are common, workers mobility increased, unemployment reduced, training actively provided, but social inequalities likely to remain. Most of those involved in the European level debate favoured the "sustainable Europe" scenario. However, it is characteristic that the issue of inequality did not find a scenario where it is likely to be resolved. It seems that the very question of the feasibility of achieving competitiveness and social coherence posed at the beginning was answered in the negative.

The authors of this volume did not aspire to come to a mutual agreement, and although a number of gatherings and discussions took place prior to the creation of the volume, the discourse was meant to be a debate rather than an accord. Naturally the contributions are polemic and consider quite different perspectives of transitions. They might not therefore depict a straightforward picture and lead to a clear conclusion. Nor do they pretend to present an exhaustive picture. There are certainly many aspects of transition processes not touched on in this publication. Nevertheless, we hope that the contributions are thought–provoking. They certainly do not intend to leave the reader with the impression that there is no way out. In many instances we find positive examples where economic competitiveness and social cohesion have been reconciled in the multiple transition processes and did not cause major impairment for societies and individuals. Such examples were found among the Baltic countries of CEECs and in old Nordic member states of the EU. Perhaps these are particular cases to look with much greater attention in the future.

We hope that it is possible to learn a lesson for future policy–making in a time of profound change and better understanding of certain parts of

• *Introduction* • 9

Europe, their policies, choices and systems. What contours and meanings Europe will bring in the future depends vitally on this understanding.

## Notes

1. It is important to note that the project was a so–called "thematic network" which means, in EU language, a network of people who gather and share research findings and ideas on a certain theme. That is to say, the project did not conduct primary research but rather tried to get the most out of what was available from various sources.
2. Other volumes resulting from the work of the project are: Kuhn, Michael and Sultana, Ronald (eds.) *The Learning Society in Europe and Beyond*, 2006; Kuhn, Michael and Sultana, Ronald (eds.) *Homo Sapiens Europeus? Creating the European Learning Citizen*, 2006, and Kuhn, Michael (ed.) *The European Learner — a New Global Player?*, 2006.

• OLGA STRIETSKA–ILINA •

# A Clash of Transitions. Towards a Learning Society

## Introduction

I had an interesting discussion with a publisher about the title of this publication. I was told that "a clash of transitions" is not a suitable expression because "transition" can only be from one state to another and that for a native English speaker it is hard to imagine what is hidden behind the title. I was recommended to call the book "*A Difficult Transition to a Learning Society*". I realised however that this would be an oversimplification. We had many discussions with other authors and colleagues who happened to be involved into the EU accession and learning society debates, and while I recognise that we all got somewhat "lost in transition", the agreement about the multiple transitions taking place was unanimous as was the agreement about mutual contradiction and incompatibility of some aspects of transition processes.

What I will try to do in this chapter is rather simple and straightforward. I will try to identify and explain various transitions which new EU member states and Europe in general encounter and their characteristics. I realise however how difficult the task is. Almost certainly I will be blamed for not covering the subject fully, and there always will be dozens of other transitions to discuss. Therefore, I would like to make sure that

I do not pretend to "cover" the subject but merely to "uncover" some important aspects of it.

It is important to define the geographical area we will be talking about. One American scholar mentioned to me how interesting such a perspective might be: some years back "transition countries" for him would have meant predominantly countries of Latin America. When we speak about "transition countries" nowadays we mostly mean countries of Central and Eastern Europe and former Soviet Union republics, although these are as heterogeneous as their transition processes. We would predominantly speak about Central and East European countries (CEECs)—and not all of them but only those which became members of the EU on 1 May 2004, i.e., Czech Republic, Estonia, Hungary, Latvia, Lithuania, Poland, Slovakia and Slovenia, and those which are expected to enter the EU in 2007, i.e., Bulgaria and Romania.

It is however impossible to narrow down the discussion to CEECs alone, as indeed many processes they undergo concern the EU as a whole, or even the wider Europe. Europe itself is very much in transition trying to confront the challenges dictated by a global transition. Therefore we do not only speak about multiple transitions but also multiple layers and actors of the same transition processes.

I would also like to delimit our discussion to some specific transitions. If transition to a learning society alone would be too narrow a subject, we need nevertheless to talk about this particular aspect when it comes to other types of transition. Speaking about "learning," one can avoid too narrow a focus on education and training, as other types of knowledge and skills acquisition, distribution, production and use, as well as related policies, are also matters of our interest. So, what we shall be speaking about here is not the narrow meaning of a learning society but a much broader approach to a Learning Society as a major European project. Naturally transition to this type of a leaning society involves a profound change of values and identities and thus these aspects will also be considered.

The discussion here will be developed around various transition contexts, which sometimes overlap, sometimes contradict: transition to a New Europe, transition to democracy and a market economy, and transition to a knowledge–based economy as far as the Lisbon strategy is concerned. The horizontal issue in all transition contexts, however, will be accession and integration to the EU.

The EU is a champion in dubious policies and politics. It is supranational and at the same time respectful of nations and states. It designs major European strategies to be implemented by all member states in fields which have been traditionally considered as national responsibilities. In the economy it employs social model slogans but liberal actions. It has enlarged and pretends to become an "ever closer" union but the membership is still regarded in terms of 15 plus 10.

Its ambiguity is of long standing and inherited from the cultural tradition of the Western civilisation and its divisions: "between Rome and Byzantium, between church and state, between monarchs and feudal lords, between self–governing town and surrounding country, between Protestants and Catholics, between each and every nation…, between the old world and the new" (Garton Ash 2004, 11). Although disunity may be indeed its "deepest unity" (Garton Ash 2004, 12), the argument here will be that for the project of a cohesive and competitive Europe to succeed, genuine unity is essential. This cannot be achieved by half–actions and hypocritical proclamations. Even unpopular decisions have to be challenged and discussed openly. It is not so much a problem of wrong strategies as such but rather an attempt to sell them disguised as more popular, or even populist, ideas.

## Transition to a New Europe

We should start our discussion here with an attempt to understand what Europe actually is, as a construct, and how its identity is formed. One could wonder however why should we concentrate on the question of identity at all. The reason is simple. For any major project it is essential that those who build it identify themselves with that what they are trying to build and with other "builders". If this is not the case, the commitment to decisions and their implementation is vague, the solidarity with others who built the project is low and thus low too are the empathy and the preparedness for losses in the name of others, and the prospects of the project's success become gloomy. If the European "Dream Project" does not intend to remain limited to the dreams of its citizens, or rather of European elites, and actually aspires to implementation, at least a certain level of identification should exist.

Geographically speaking, Europe is a subcontinent or a large peninsula which spreads between the Atlantic and the Ural mountains, although the borders have been conceived differently throughout history.

What ancient Greeks called *Europa* was only the Greek mainland, Hellas, and the lands around the Aegean Sea. For Herodotus, however, Europe did not have precise natural frontiers and was something that Asia and Africa were not. The term itself comes from the Greek mythology where *Europa* was a Phoenician woman kidnapped by Zeus and brought to Crete[1]. The Phoenicians were a Semitic–speaking people who inhabited what now is roughly the northern part of Lebanon, a territory which may hardly be considered European nowadays[2].

The eastern border of Europe has always been defined vaguely, and in modern times its limits have been pushed back and forth between the Black Sea and the Ural mountains for centuries. The recent discussion about the Europeanness of Turkey in fact well continues the tradition. Indeed, if Istanbul is claimed to be not a European city, would one recognise Constantinople as a European one? Not only were the origins of Europe not entirely European, but also no one could establish precisely where Europe stopped and Asia and Africa began (Pagden 2002). The disputes about European borders are as old as Europe itself. What Europe is or is not has always been a geopolitical question.

A recent survey of perceptions of the European Union (Optem SARL 2001) demonstrated that although Europe can be defined geographically, in the opinions of its citizens this is of a secondary importance. What makes Europe Europe, in their view, is its culture and history. What is alarming here however is that this identity of Europe and the feeling of "being European" are very exclusivist. According to the same survey, in CEECs Europe was defined in cultural and humanistic values as what Russia was not. EU citizens also mostly excluded Turkey on the same principle. Culturally Europe was defined as opposed to the US.

There are two problems here. First, the cultural definition of Europe may turn out to be geopolitically defined too and it very much depends on a person's perspective. For my Japanese colleague, the Russian far eastern city of Vladivostok is very European. She could see and feel it immediately after landing there, and this was in spite of the fact that the city is nine times farther from Moscow than from Tokyo. Everything depends on perspective and there are probably at least as many cultural perceptions of what is European inside Europe itself as there are member states. Cultural is therefore clearly not a stable definition and does not provide good grounds for identity construction.

A second, and even more important problem here, is that in searching for its identity Europeans undertake the easiest but rather dangerous and not very reliable path, trying to identify themselves in terms of what they are not. Such an approach was traditional for nationalism movements of the 19h century in their attempts to build nation–states. The national identity was built around inclusivity of the "we" definition against exclusivity of the "them" definition. Europeans, often failing to explain their identity of "we", identify themselves as who they are not, and here they are as a rule "not Americans"[3].

The disagreement between Europe and the US over Iraq allegedly gave birth (or "rebirth" according to Derrida and Habermas) to Europe (Garton Ash 2004, 54). The European powers united against the expression of power by the US. Indeed, the most pronounced European unity in post–modern politics was against power rather than the construction of its own power. There are good reasons for this and the very *raison d'être* for the EU was balancing powers inside Europe. It is however symptomatic that inside Europe there is still much opposition, especially expressed by large countries, and the only real unification takes place as opposition to external powers—mostly the US. Although all basic Western values are widely shared by the EU and the US, the opposition to power is one of several dissimilarities over which the division is formed. As Robert Kagan put it "Americans are from Mars and Europeans are from Venus: they agree on little and understand one another less and less" (2003, 3). Kagan's well–known book is however very valuable, not as much for its very good explanations of differences between Europe and the US, but for the excellent clarification of reasoning behind this or that political decision and behaviour. Not only does the US have good reasons for its foreign policy actions but European countries also have reasons to support or not these actions.

It is not our aim here to discuss US policy. It is however important to understand that it was unavoidable that the impulsive praise of European unification in its disagreement with the US (the "rebirth" of Europe) was soon followed by disagreement and subsequent splits within Europe herself. In spite of a long–claimed (and certainly objective) reason for the US to support European integration, in certain questions—and for the sake of the support and/or approval—they seek partners now, and they will do in future, to support decisions which might not be too popular around the EU but which might find sympathy in some countries (traditionally the UK, but also Poland and other CEECs). Similarly Russia will continue negotiations with selected EU powers, such as Germany, France and even the UK, in a mode of "divide and rule"—so far well-employed (e.g., on the energy question). Constructing a European identity on the basis of opposing what Europe is not (i.e., not the US) is therefore not sustainable.

The reasoning behind certain choices of CEECs is important to apprehend. These countries were helped as much by the US as by the EU on their path to democracy, especially at the early stage of transition. CEECs associate democracy and humanistic values with the West in general rather than with Europe in particular. The CEECs' communist past is too recent to forget and interventions in other totalitarian regimes in the cause of democratic values and human rights may find a warm welcome for some time. It is very important to fully realise that this political behaviour might last for a considerable time until the CEECs attain a deeper feeling of association with the rest of European countries, or indeed it might persist even in the longer run. Western European countries which do not share a similar past have difficulties in appreciating such political choices, hence the arrogant patronising of some politicians, such as Chirac, who argued that CEECs should be thankful and silent. With such patronising, "coming back to Europe"—the sense in which EU accession is largely seen in CEECs—might end up being a great disillusionment.

What is accession for CEECs and how does it influence their identities? Recently I had an interesting discussion with a Czech politician who referred to the region as: "what used to be called 'Central Europe' before its accession to the EU". I wondered later whether this is an indication of the identity change as a result of the EU accession. Or perhaps Central Europe is not an objective paradigm at all, is it just a mental construct? What is it—Central Europe?

*Mitteleuropa* has always been a geopolitical concept and exclusive by nature—lands in between the East and the West and between their superpowers. The very concept of *Mitteleuropa* was developed by such powers, Germany in particular. The book *"Mitteleuropa"* by Friedrich Naumann published in 1915 was the culmination of the German political thought about the region and aimed to demonstrate how the region belonged culturally to the German enclave. For Jan Masaryk however the same term meant something that does not belong to the German enclave. For Poland the definition of Central Europe served as something that was not part of either Prussia, Habsburgs or Russia. Culturally (from the *Gemeinschaft* point of view) and geographically the region includes Germany and Austria to the same extent as the Czech lands or Hungary. Coming to the region one would find many genuinely distinctive features in the architecture, cuisine, habits and in many other respects. But politically Central Europe is a patchwork of the smaller states between empires, a "buffer zone" between Germany (or formerly Prussia), Austria and Russia, the region constantly partitioned between European superpowers, after World War I *cordon sanitaire*. Geopolitically too the region was very important, a Heartland, in the sense that whoever ruled it ruled the world (Pocock 2002). Interestingly Donald Ramsfeld's label "the New Europe" was the title of a magazine devoted to Austro–Hungarian topics at the beginning of the 20$^{th}$ century (Davies and Moorhouse 2002). In historiography the term was used in the post–Versailles period to characterise the newly independent countries which emerged from former empires.

The post–Yalta division of power in Europe strongly affected the region for several decades, which might not be very long in a historical perspective but it had an enormous impact on the history of the region and the formation of its identity. It underlined the opposition of systems, values and polities of the East as opposed to the West. Suddenly Central Europe, or *Mitteleuropa*, ceased to exist, and the region was incorporated to the East.

According to Göran Therborn (in this volume) "the major Eastern European project is absorption into Western Europe". Indeed, Milan Kundera called the region "a kidnapped West". For the CEECs coming back to Europe is adhesion to the values of democracy, human rights and free market economy of the West. Does this mean however that Central and Eastern Europe is a mindset without any objective grounds? Politically speaking it probably is, but culturally speaking the region still has a rather distinct identity and it may take decades before CEECs will die away as a distinctive region. Speaking of Central Europe a distinction should be made between Central Europe as a cultural phenomenon relying on a common past and Central Europe as a new political entity. (Pehe 2003, 129). Coming "back to Europe" has always been understood in CEECs as an institutional and legal integration with the West, and not as a confirmation of their cultural belonging to Europe. Most Central Europeans never doubted their European identity (Pehe, 2003). According to empirical surveys, people in CEECs feel more European than their counterparts in Western Europe: 60% of Poles and 40% of Czechs believed that their European identity was as strong as their national one far prior to the EU accession—in the late 1990s (Dunkerley et al. 2002).

If CEECs "come to the West", however, what they find there is largely politically and socially scattered landscape and the very concept of the West in crisis. The fall of the Soviet Union in a way eliminated the need for geopolitics (Kagan 2003, 25). With the disappearance of the communist East, the "West slowly descended into crisis." (Garton Ash 2004, 8). Indeed, the objective reality of the West has always been doubtful in the sense of blurring definitions and boundaries. What exactly is the West? Certainly it is something defined mostly in terms of certain commonalities in the political culture and values. But the West has always existed in terms of the binary opposition West/East. Both concepts, of the West and the East, are relative. In Greece, which is considered a cradle of Western civilisation and which is self-identified by its own population in the same terms, the Greeks still discuss the westernisation of their society as a result of the entrance to the EU and closer ties with Western Europeans. As long as the East can be clearly defined, the West has a chance too. With the end of the Cold War, with the fall of the Iron Curtain and the Berlin Wall, certain geographical areas vanished from the East, suddenly being promoted to "Central Europe", later "New Europe", "new Member States" and so on. If the "Cold War West was a reality" (Garton Ash 2004, 8), the post–1989 West is at least uncertain. If it is something what CEECs have been striving for, it needs at least a better definition.

Divisions between Europe and America over the world politics are more a result than a cause of the crisis within Western civilisation. The union between Europe and the US had existed to a large extent due to a common enemy which used to be the Soviet Union. International terrorism has so far been a divisive rather than a unifying factor, as there has been more disagreement than common strategy.

At the same time, what is traditionally considered basic European values and grounds for identity, the emotional glue, is common for Europe and the US, and in fact nowadays applies to the US more so than to Europe. Indeed both share the destiny of Greco–Roman roots, Christendom, and the eighteenth–century Enlightenment but Americans preserve traditional values even more strongly than Europeans, particularly when it comes to the role of Christianity in the everyday life of the whole society, penetrating even into the work of the government and other high–level institutions. In Europe, where most of countries are highly secularised and religious beliefs plural, especially with fast-growing Muslim populations, Christianity can hardly serve as emotional glue for European identity. Here again our argument about culture-based identity formation, meaning here any aspect of the culture—including religion—is valid: an exclusivist conceptualisation of identity is not suitable for such a diverse society.

What can serve well are in fact traditional values of democracy, the rule of law and human rights—the traditional attributes of Western values. Francis Fukuyama's thesis about *"The End of History"* argues that the progression of human history as a struggle between ideologies is largely at an end and proclaims the eventual triumph of political and economic liberalism. Even accepting part of the criticism of the thesis, including one by Samuel Huntington and his "Clash of Civilisation", one should recognise that values of Enlightenment are widely shared at least in what can be broadly defined as a western civilisational enclave. As Göran Therborn put it, Europe is "the world's lawyer" in the sense that it gave the world the value of law and its rule as well as respect for democracy and human rights. There are only two points which emerge here as a sort of scepticism. First, Europe fails to protect these traditional values on a world scale, relinquishing its place to the US, which is more willing to sacrifice the lives of its citizens and the money of its taxpayers for international military operations, including those in Europe. The EU emerged out of conflicts and Europeans are not inclined to involve themselves in new conflicts. This is understandable but the question arises of how far Europeans really care about their own values, if even in traditionally European territories, the Balkans, they easily give way to Americans to defend them? The second point of scepticism is that the traditional democratic values and the rule of law are indeed attributes of the West in general, and they are not distinctive enough to provide sufficient grounds for formation of a unique European identity. Something much more distinctively European is needed.

As the founder of the European Community Jean Monnet once said "Europe has never existed... one has genuinely to create Europe" (Rifkin 2004, 200). The myth, something that Eric Hobsbawm called "the invention of tradition", is still to be written for Europe. It has to be created for the EU as a political entity and an economy, but it has to take into account the traditional European values as well as merits and worths as they are valued by Europeans. It is important to realise that national identities still surpass the European identity, although there is no real identity conflict as we speak of multiple identities here[4]. But more important here is the fact that the European identity surpasses that of the EU.

"Geographical Europe", wrote Norman Davies (1996), "has always had to compete with notions of Europe as a cultural community, and in the absence of common political structures, European civilization could only be determined by cultural criteria." When it comes to the question of identity, according to empirical studies, emotional identification with Europe does not translate into identification with the EU. The EU is however nowadays a real political and economic entity and, according to the most recent Eurobarometer survey (2006), it is seen to be of genuine worth and a symbol of cooperation between member states. What citizens prize most about the EU are the aspects of economic cooperation and development, such as the single currency, free movement of people and the Single Market. EU citizens spontaneously associate the EU with cooperation, unity, equality, common decisions, rules and legislation, and these seem worthwhile, "a good thing" for one third of Europeans. EU membership is valued by almost half of the population. This is something to build on.

One should remember that the EU is not congruent with Europe, and while European identity could be culture based, the EU identity must be built around a concept which could be as inclusive, pluralistic and overarching as possible. The EU as a political entity includes regions and peoples whose cultures and languages are exceptionally diverse, and therefore the construction of the EU identity must provide for unity and solidarity of all its integral parts. The EU identity can be built based on the overarching categories of statehood and citizenship, as opposed to the established categories of nationhood and nationality[5] more typical of old–fashioned nation–building and of 19th century nationalism. If we accept Ernest Gellner's idea of nationalism which created nations (Gellner 1992), perhaps "supranationalism" can create a "supranation". The EU should built a belief that the common origin of the group of states that became members of the union resides in civic commitments, i.e., a belief based on attachments that are more instrumental than sentimental (Herrmann and Brewer 2004). No matter how European identity is constructed and what cultural and historical narratives are used there, for the European Union as a political entity identity must be developed on the basis of statehood and citizenship, post–national and supranational aspirations. This does not mean however that the EU should not use its own narratives, invent its own myths and traditions, to reinforce the process of statehood identity formation. Indeed, parting from 19th century nationalism does not mean completely rejecting its methods. The awakening of national identities at the end of the 18th and 19th centuries was a process from which much can be learned. Nationalism created nations but it was not a self–sustaining process. The grand narratives were (re)discovered and (re) invented, and national elites played a great role in the awakening of the nationhood, in the same way that European elites may play a role in the awakening of the statehood. The process is already taking place but it should become much more proactive.

According to public opinion polls, comparisons of the systems of values between Europeans and Americans demonstrate that the people of the US value work much more, they are more prepared to work extra time and to move to other places if needed. Europeans place a higher value on their social life, they place their private life ahead of their job, they spend more time on vacations and value a good quality of life. Although they earn less than Americans, they prefer to have more free time at the expense of higher wages (Rifkin 2004). Of course, this all is valid only to a certain extent, as for instance in the UK and in CEECs populations are more receptive to liberal market values, flexibility and mobility of labour, etc. But overall, their societies are still far more pro–social than that of the US. On the whole Europeans are welfare oriented.

The Lisbon European Council in 2000 set a new strategic goal for the EU for the next decade: "to become the most competitive and dynamic knowledge–based economy in the world, capable of sustainable economic growth with more and better jobs and greater social cohesion" (2000, 2). The comparison of the European economic indicators with the US and Japan—unfavourable to the EU—and growing competition from new world powers—India and China, pushed European policy making to take on more pro–liberal objectives but with an attempt to preserve the so–called *European social model.* The latter has often appeared in the discourse of recent years as *the* feature of Europe, something that Europeans are prepared to identify with. The Lisbon strategy, which strives to push Europe economically to the top of the world *and* claims to preserve the social model, may therefore augur well for a modern "grand narrative" of the EU statehood, providing some good grounds, a social glue, for loyalty to the EU and for the identity building of its people. Europe has articulated a new vision for the future which is not only based on the traditional Western values but is also "different in many of its most fundamental aspects from America's" (Rifkin 2004, 15).

In the statehood–awakening process, the role of education and training is very important. It is important not for teaching the common European origin, the cultural myth which may turn out to be a course on the history of wars, but more importantly about common European values of democracy and the rule of law. Also, Europeans today know very little about each other. Eurobarometer surveys demonstrate a very low level of awareness about other members of the EU. Learning more about the history and traditions of all EU countries might prove useful. It is important to explain why EU was created and how it happened that a number of countries were "excluded" from Europe and pushed into the Eastern enclave, the communist camp, for decades. European diversity is no doubt very important but it will do good to Europe only if differences in cultures, traditions, habits and even policies are well explained to all EU citizens from the historical and political perspectives, especially to young Europeans.

One of the narratives, in the case of the EU, is the history and the reasoning of its creation as such. One would argue however that the objectives put forward by the founding fathers of the EU are not only complete but that EU integration is much more advanced by now than initially expected. There is peace, economic cooperation and stability, a Single Market, a single currency and free movement of people in Europe. On the other hand, the founding fathers of the union included an objective of a much tighter political union. The ultimate goal of creating a United States of Europe and federalist ideas altogether have somehow been abandoned in favour of an economic union and a pseudo–bureaucratic alliance[6].

For a statehood identity however the EU should become a State, rather than an intergovernmental and supranational union as it is now. For this, the EU as a State needs to take over a number of responsibilities. EU citizenship, for instance, is now granted exclusively by member states, and thus the process appears to be an obstacle in the formation of the European people—a conglomerate of European citizens as opposed to nations and nationals of the EU member states. Citizenship may rather be granted by a centralized process or at least there should be a centralized EU–level procedure alongside national ones. Also, in spite of the fact that the EU identity should not be built around cultural categories, one must not underestimate the uniting role of the language, not only for a nation but also for a State. In the history of Europe first, due to the role of the church, Latin played the role of the unique means of communication, followed by Italian and finally, thanks to the Enlightenment and international diplomacy, French, which remained dominant until the end of the 18$^{th}$ century. It is also true that educated European elites have always been multilingual. In the age of ICTs and intense information exchange and communication it is however hard to expect that all EU languages (soon to become 21 and later 23) will play an equal role. This is simply very expensive and administratively demanding. For statehood a state language must be chosen. The absence of a common language in the EU contributes to the democratic deficit, being one of obstacles to an open and direct political discourse with the EU public. Nowadays only English can play this uniting role at least as a working language, but this has to be acknowledged and accepted by all member states. On the other hand, while the objectives and decisions have to be clear and pronounced for the future, the implementation process should be cautious and gradual.

One may wonder whether such level of integration is something desired by EU citizens. First, this is one of the objectives of elites to make such ideas more popular around the EU and among the citizens. Let's call this process "EU statehood awakening". Second, if we look at the results of the most recent Eurobarometer survey (2006), although EU citizens recognise a number of achievements in cultural and economic integration, a far from negligible proportion of them considers that a lot still remains to be done, in particular as regards political unification. Europe still has this transition process in front of it.

Identity building in the EU is certainly an on–going process and there is a steady growth in numbers of those whose European identity surpasses their national one. This is especially the case with young people, the "Erasmus generation"[7], which is much more European, multilingual and cosmopolitan.

Various political processes help to develop identity, such as the enlargement process itself (see Sedelmeier 2003). Countries which entered the EU had to fulfil the requirements of the membership criteria which were laid down at the June 1993 European Council in Copenhagen. The membership requirements included that the stability of the candidate country's institutions guarantee democracy, the rule of law and human rights. The very formulation of the requirements and subsequent legislative processes helped to develop the EU's self–perception of an entity which guarantees its citizens respect of these criteria. The formulation of the requirements also helped to specify to the outside world what is required for membership. Due to the absence of clearly defined geographical criteria and the fact that whether the country is or is not European is regarded as a subject for a specific political assessment, the fulfilment of the requirements of democracy, the rule of law and respect for human rights appears much more important. Indeed, Cyprus is geographically Asian but due to its deep historical and cultural ties with Europe and its fulfilment of the Copenhagen requirements, it was accepted into the EU. Perhaps one day EU citizens will realise that Europe represents overly tight boundaries as cultural glue and that the EU as a political entity may well pass these boundaries with membership instituted solely on the basis of the respect for democracy, the rule of law and human rights.

The effect of enlargement on identity building, however, has not been purely positive and not all the related processes were smooth. The level of solidarity among citizens throughout the EU is still very low. Enlargement engendered many fears among Europeans, especially the fear of waves of migration of a cheap labour force from CEECs to old member states. After the enlargement and the immediate rise in the support for EU membership, there was a subsequent drop in this support (Eurobarometer 2005). The ratification of the EU Constitution failed in France and in the Netherlands. 2005 in general was considered a year of EU crisis.

One of the reasons was negative public opinion about migration issues, although several recent studies showed that the labour migration was not as significant as initially feared. The free movement of persons is one of the fundamental freedoms guaranteed by community law and an essential element of European citizenship. However, the transitory measures allowing the retention of restrictions in the access to the labour markets of old EU member states, and obliging workers from new member states to still seek work permits—in the same way as prior to accession—was introduced by most old member states, and only three countries (Ireland, Sweden and the UK) opened their borders for free movement of labour for CEE citizens of the EU.

The initially high waves of migration for work right after enlargement, slowed down significantly in subsequent months, and many of those who migrated opted to come back home after several months of working abroad. The Commission's February 2006 report found that very few citizens from the new member states actually moved to the EU–15 countries. According to the report, EU–10 citizens represented less than one percent of the working age population in all old EU member states except Ireland (3.8%) and Austria (1.4%). The countries, such as Ireland where proportionally the in–coming labour migration was the highest, have low unemployment rates and migration from the East helped to fill labour shortages in their markets. Thus, the effects have been rather positive for these old member states. The fear of waves of cheap labour are especially high in countries neighbouring the new member states (Germany, Austria) where even cross–border labour commuting may dump down wages and push out some of the local labour force. The effects of migration however are no less important for new member states. If in the current economic situation labour emigration may ease unemployment hardship in some CEECs, in the longer run it may cause more negative than positive effects. First of all, qualified people leave their countries to find a job that often requires lower skills and qualifications than they possess. This causes not only a braindrain for the CEE economies but also a *brainwaste* on a larger scale of the European labour market. Second, and even more important, people who tend to move out from their countries for work are mostly young. In the current demographic situation in CEECs this also causes *youthdrain* (Traser and Venables 2005). Third, in CEECs the process of institution building is not complete yet, and their young democracies badly need highly qualified administration and civil servants at all levels. It is often the case that it is these few who move to other EU member states and, by no means in the last resort, to the Brussels institutions. All in all, intra–EU East–West migration helps to solve problems in some countries, often at the expense of the others, whereas both positive and negative effects are reciprocal. The Europeans fail to see such issues from a European perspective. The effects of intra–EU migration have not yet been sufficiently discussed and measured for the EU as a whole. Both politicians and peoples still tend to think and count in terms of individual countries' gains and failures.

The low level of solidarity manifested itself not only in the migration issues and negative public opinion about "the Polish plumber" on western European labour markets but also in budgetary issues. The French farmers do not wish to give up the generous subsidies they get in favour of CEE farmers, whereas France insisted that the UK rebate to be abolished, the UK on the CAP reform and thus cuts in subsidies for French farmers etc. Further on–going tensions took place during the discussion of the "Frankenstein Directive", a nickname that says much about the "popularity" of the EU Services Directive which aimed to introduce free–market competition and equal treatment to all economic services operating within the EU. Among many arguments against the Directive, mostly expressed by the European Trade Union Confederation, there were several which simply manifested the fear of migration of cheaper services from CEECs, as well as the fear that these services might be of a worse standard and quality due to lower professional and qualification requirements there. What is symptomatic here is the lack of trust in co–citizens' systems (education, professional standards, quality of services, etc.) and almost xenophobic fears. Such lack of trust, empathy and indeed solidarity can hardly provide for cohesion within the EU and may eventually bring "the wall after the wall" effect on the European scale.

The transition to the New Europe project has not been smooth for its participants and the change in identity, although taking place, still does not provide for the necessary level of cohesiveness inside the EU. These transitions are still very much on the way and the inside tensions are still to be solved.

## Transition to Democracy and a Market Economy

The countries in question had a four–decade history of communism before 1989. In all countries of the region, vital changes have occurred since then, the lasting importance of which should not be underestimated. A shift to market economy, open society and democratic polity has been a unique socio–economic experiment in itself, the accomplishments and failures of which still have not been analysed and evaluated in their entire complexity. From the perspective of our analysis it is important to understand the interconnections, the factors of influence and the special mission that arise from the social, economic and political transitions for the area of learning.

It is important to bear in mind that the progress made by the CEECs during the period of transition varies markedly throughout the region. All CEECs advanced economically and experienced steady economic growth. According to Eurostat figures, average real GDP growth in the region has stabilised at 4.5% since 2000 and reached 6.3% in 2005 varying between below 3.2% in Poland and over 10% in Latvia. By the time of accession to the EU the most painful transition period was behind the CEECs, whereas the acceding countries of Bulgaria and Romania were still seen as needing to make some further progress. The completion of transition to a full market economy in all countries of the region will however still take some time and involve further social and economic changes.

All CEECs have experienced profound changes in employment patterns. Employment levels continued to fall throughout 1990s across the region, and only recently started to rise in Latvia, Hungary, Slovenia and Bulgaria. At the beginning of the economic transition from a planned to a market economy, in most CEE countries there was an immense drop in employment in state–sector industry, followed by a steady decline. Whilst there has been a net creation of jobs in the private sector, it could not absorb the entire labour shift from the state sector. This resulted in continually increasing unemployment.

Unemployment appeared an entirely new paradigm for the region whose previous experience was full employment under the communist state–run economy. Unemployment affected especially some regions where structural economic changes seriously affected industries which had been major employers in the territory. While the average unemployment rate among old member states continued to decrease from 1996, dropping to an average of 7.9% in 2005, in new member states it increased till 2000 and has remained almost at the same level since then— 13.5%. Unemployment continued to grow throughout the period of transition, reaching 16.4% in Slovakia and 17.7% in Poland in 2005. Only in the Czech Republic, the Baltic States and Bulgaria has unemployment slightly decreased recently. The difference in the unemployment situation between old and new member states is especially high among young people (under 25 years old): the rate in new member states is twice as high as among old ones and it reached 30.4% in 2005. The structure of unemployment has been changing in all CEECs, manifesting growth of long–term unemployment and an increasing proportion of young people, new graduates, people with low or no qualifications, elderly, ethnic minorities and people with disabilities.

The countries have tackled the problem of unemployment through specific employment and training measures, the effectiveness of which has been measured only in some countries, providing a useful benchmarking perspective for the others. CEECs have gone through a process of harmonisation of employment policy under EU guidelines trying to tackle both the priorities set as a common European agenda and particular challenges arising from the specific features of the socio–economic transitional situation. These measures, together with the accession of CEECs to the EU have had some positive effects on the employment situation: the unemployment rate has dropped by about 1% for the whole population as well for the young cohorts.

In all transition countries unemployment and income decline have brought rising poverty and demographic crisis. The demographic situation has been characterized by a sharp fall in birth rates and a rise in mortality in a few CEECs. The ageing of the society has many implications for social policies and a further burden on the public budget.

At the same time the opening up of the economy and the subsequent pressure from competitive markets pushed the transition process into adjusting to global changes. Although the basic pattern of the employment shift and the restructuring of output and trade was the same in CEECs as in the whole EU and in global markets, the excess of manpower in industry and, in some countries, in agriculture (Romania, Poland, Lithuania and Bulgaria) on the one hand, and the underdevelopment of the service sector on the other, demanded an even higher rate of adjustment.

The characteristics of employment have changed dramatically since 1989: in majority of countries there has been an immense shift from the industrial and agricultural sectors to services. The agricultural sector had been overstaffed in the whole region under the previous regime, and there have been substantial shifts in employment from agriculture to services. Despite the extensive job losses in industry, the proportion of employment in this sector is still above the EU average. The opening up of CEE markets also introduced an important qualitative shift in the restructuring of the industrial sector, featuring a move from heavy industry and labour–intensive production to sophisticated manufacturing and technology and knowledge–intensive production. This shift has brought about quickly changing skill requirements in the industrial sector.

Employment in the services sector has risen throughout the entire region since early 1990, although it is still below the EU average. The absorption capacity of the services sector still has the potential to compensate for job losses in industry and agriculture, especially for the less–qualified in the labour force. Taking into account the lack of vocational preparation for it during the pre–transition period, the shift in labour towards the services sector often occurred without any specific vocational preparation and large–scale re–training activities (this is especially true for less–demanding occupations).

The shift in employment from large to small and medium–sized enterprises (SMEs) followed the pattern of EU countries but saw a greater rate of change due to the restructuring of large state industrial enterprises. In spite of the significant employment shift towards SMEs, the proportion of those employed in large industries in CEECs still remains larger than in old member states. Given that this trend will continue, it is important to take into account the special skill requirements of SMEs, where highly adaptable manpower with multiple qualifications and the ability to learn throughout their working life signifies focal challenges for the learning society. The latter change is closely related to changes in the organisation of work, with flexible job definitions, greater responsibility and independence of employees, more emphasis on team working and adaptability to quickly changing new technologies with the ability to undertake a variety of tasks at the shop floor.

In addition to the specific problems of transition economies, the CEECs face the same challenges as old EU member states, such as demands imposed by the globalisation of the economy, technological change, and the rise of the information society. The very processes of transformation from a centrally planned to a market economy and from a closed to an open, globally competitive economy do not yet cover the whole picture. Catching up with developments in the global economy also implied the need to pursue flexible and innovative production models emphasising knowledge creation and utilisation over simple resource exploitation, developing the knowledge intensive service sector, and strengthening the potential of local and regional economies.

The crucial challenge faced by the counties of the region was to complete the transition to a competitive market economy while at the same time creating sufficient jobs to avoid excessive rates of unemployment or inactivity, especially among the risk groups. A "double transformation" in CEE, in which the countries of the region experienced not only the single transition from a state to a market economy, but also underwent (and to no less an extent) a global transformation, involved shifts in employment towards SMEs, de–industrialisation, shifts from the Fordist–type production to a flexible organisation, changes in the world of work with a focus on information technology, knowledge–intensive industries, and a major transformation towards the learning society.

The political transformation to a democratic society not only touched on the reform of the electoral systems and institutions but also included a shift to the civil society and a new mode of participative polity. These processes in themselves imply a large scale of change in the culture and mentality of the population. The economic transformation brings changes in social structures, the emergence of new types of elites, the middle class and changes of the role and the nature of the political and intellectual elites in the society. The societies have been affected by the transformation not only at the level of the society and the economy (macro), but also at the level of the institution and the individual. Changing roles, rights, obligations and responsibilities have profoundly affected values, cultures, and identities.

The years of a communist regime have distorted many basic socio–economic parameters in CEECs. Many democratic values widely recognised in the Western States are not taken for granted or are differently understood in CEECs. The role of learning therefore becomes essential in promoting democratic and civil societies in these countries. Lack of democratic tradition however impacts on mentality, reciprocity and procedural habits in the CEE societies, often directly affecting the pace and the shape of policy formulation and implementation, including policies in the field of education and training. Lack of ownership over policy development partly results from the mode of polity in CEE which is not sufficiently participative. For instance, the role of social partners in the definition of learning needs is still not adequate in many cases. Other important actors in the learning process also play an insufficient part in the consultation and planning processes. Often the only efficient thrust towards the "sharing" approach and consensus building comes from the EU in the form of formalised requirements (e.g., ESF planning, etc.). The systems are too centralised on the one hand and unable to accommodate faster and more flexible changes at the local/bottom level on the other. Regionalisation in education and training often occurs without the effective application of the principle of subsidiarity and therefore takes the form of formalistic devolution. The role of the informal and voluntary sectors in lifelong learning is limited. The role of individuals as key players in the learning society is undervalued.

Such features are sometimes manifested in the failure of certain well–established Western methods, policy approaches and systems when used in the CEE conditions. Therefore the question arises whether some of the EU–pushed policies and methods are applicable in CEE and whether these countries should not rather seek for alternative measures and methods to achieve the same universal goals in the European Project. Unfortunately, there is not only a lack of a participative approach in policy development but above all a lack of political emancipation owing to the direct borrowing of policies and methods.

## Profound Changes in Income Status and Social Consequences of Transition

The period of transition is characterised by a combination of the egalitarian heritage and social status inconsistency with evolving new social differentiation. The state communist social system was totalitarian and anti–meritocratic where frequent social status inconsistencies were typical and were caused particularly by imbalances between education, work complexity and the cultural level of life–style on the one hand and earnings level and power position on the other hand. Under the communist regime the better qualified strata were in an unfavourable situation, being discouraged by their income status inconsistency.

The increase in social differentiation during the transition period has been connected with the intensification of intergenerational vertical social mobility among the economically active population. This mobility has been prevailingly upwardly oriented and has had a largely structural character. The society has been becoming more open, although still with a tendency to closeness of social groups along the lines dividing manual and non–manual occupations (Machonin, Tuček et al. 1996). Mobility processes among the economically active were combined with a wide–ranging decline of a section of the economically active population into economic non–activity, be it in the form of unemployment, retirement, or child and family care. The upwardly oriented mobility along with the improvement in social positions of those who remained at the top, led to an increase in social inequality. In spite of the systemic and relatively successful attempts of some governments to hinder a mass increase in poverty, the group of people at risk increased along with the downward mobility of lower strata.

These processes have been typical of all countries of transition from the state–planned to market–oriented economy, but the level of the social differentiation varied to a great extent. More stratified societies enjoyed professional and educational factors in relative harmony with the income and life–style, unlike others where professional, educational and income factors still showed significant discrepancies. For instance, in Romania the unemployment rate among those who completed secondary education was until recently higher than among those with only compulsory educational attainment and is now only insignificantly lower. Little difference in the (high) rate of unemployment between qualified and non–qualified people remains the case in several CEECs (e.g., the Baltic States) and is evidence of continuing social status inconsistency along the axis of education. Very high rates of unemployment among those with upper secondary educational attainment (Poland, Slovakia, Bulgaria, the Baltic states) might however result from the quality and types of qualifications provided inadequate for the needs of the transforming economy.

Under the communist regime the remuneration maintained extremely small wage differentials for decades, and the estimated rate of return on education was very small and invariable. At the level of individual and household incomes, these effects translated into the most egalitarian distribution of income in the world. The transition from the centrally planned to a market system resulted in a major increase in the rates of return on education gradually reaching those in Western Europe. It is however important to note that wage differentiation increased not only along the axis of educational attainment but also along other categories such as age and gender. In some countries the differentiation between the private and public sector was also high, as it was between types of industries. In particular, those working in the primary sector and in mining and quarrying lost much of their former wage premium, while those working in trade, financial intermediation, transport and telecommunications gained the most (see Munich et al., 2000). It is therefore a question of what paid more—a higher level of educational attainment or a job in a lucrative business. A widespread tendency in the relatively more deprived countries of CEECs during the period of transition was the so–called brain–waste, where highly qualified personnel withdrew from the state and public sector, including universities and research institutes, preferring to occupy positions with lower qualification requirements but higher pay.

The reverse side of the healthy differentiation processes, increasing returns on education and formation of human capital value were raising inequalities: the greater the life success of the educated, the fewer the chances received by those without qualifications. Although many CEE countries still enjoy relative social stability, overall income decline, continuously rising unemployment and increasing differentiation in CEE societies have become major pitfalls of transition and put disadvantaged groups at a high risk of social exclusion. These processes may further deepen under the pressure of competitiveness. Some analyses show growing inequality in access to education in the CEECs (e.g., Matějů

2000) and predict that it will deepen further. The growing importance of education for life success on the one hand, high intergenerational reproduction of educational qualifications on the other hand, and finally insufficient participation in higher education in a number of CEECs will contribute to rising social inequalities.

According to a Eurobarometer survey in most CEECs in 2001, an unequal distribution of the economic cake and a vaguely threatening future was the general impression that prevailed, particularly by those in the middle to lower socio–professional categories. The population reported deterioration over the last decade with a gap between the privileged few and the great mass of the population, the disappearance of the safety net of the State, and growing uncertainty about the future. The citizens of these countries also note the dissolution of social ties, the disintegration of the social fabric, a rise in crime, corruption among politicians etc. The observation in CEECs of a gap between themselves and the countries of Western Europe, and the idea that this has not been narrowed, also adds to the pessimism.

Social exclusion appeared to be a new, or undisguised, problem in CEECs. Under the communist regime the existence of social exclusion as well as poverty was not admitted; marginalisation was perceived as a social choice. That is why the issue of social exclusion was not adequately addressed—scientifically or empirically. In the early transition period, with the rapid growth in poverty the primary focus was on studying poverty, though with a certain reduction of the concept of poverty to measuring income and consumption–based definitions of poverty, and insufficient focus on the educational and occupational aspects of poverty (also criticised by Szalai 1999). UNDP focused on studying poverty in transition economies in 1997, where limitations of the income–based perspective were realised and the Human Poverty Index was introduced, which included indicators of different dimensions of deprivation, including lack of education (UNDP 1997). The latter report revealed the enormous social cost of transition, which in most CEECs, particularly in the early transition period, led to a decline in income, the highest–ever growth in income inequality, crime growth, loss of social protection, decrease in life expectancy and a sharp decline in the birth rate.

The UNDP research (1999) also revealed that in the process of globalisation and the rising importance of the development of information and communication technology and biotechnology, the race to lay claim to knowledge becomes inevitable. The lack of access to knowledge (PC skills, language skills) and to information tools (the Internet), widens the gap between "knows and know–nots" as well as between "conventional" "haves and have–nots" (UNDP 1999).

The role of education and training in the promotion of social cohesion has only recently been recognised in the region as a tool of "systemic inclusion of the generation of youngsters in ...all forms of education and training...those related to jobs and those not directly related" (Trbanc 1999). The results of extensive studies on vocational education and training against social exclusion in the CEECs initiated by the European Training Foundation (ETF)[8] demonstrated that social exclusion has several tendencies common to CEE countries: it occurs in the case of an accumulation of a number of disadvantagous characteristics (e.g., low skills, long–term unemployment, membership of a national minority); there is a spatial accumulation of risk factors (deprived regions) and it has an intergenerational reproductive tendency.

The profound changes in social stratification and changes in social status affected social values of education and employment. Education started to be seen by the population as not only a value in itself and a matter of social prestige but also as a private investment in the individual's future. At the same time the above mentioned persistence of social status inconsistencies further diminishes the economic value of education and CEE societies tend to ascribe a much broader value to education than the purely economic one. The reduction of the value of learning to the knowledge–based economy as a concept therefore might not find too perceptive grounds in CEECs.

Research into work and job values demonstrates considerable differences between CEECs and old EU member states with regard to a number of variables, e.g., independent and interesting jobs are scored higher by Western Europeans, while CEECs primarily appreciate higher rewards (Večerník 2003).While people in old member states' value initiative, responsibility, interest and promotion more, CEE workers prize the economic aspects of work, such as pay, hours, vacations, etc. At the same time CEECs often demonstrate a greater readiness to work extra hours, more favour competition, demonstrate higher flexibility and more often place work ahead of the family and other life values (Večerník 2003). The change towards post–materialist values of post–modern society (Inglehart 1990), where the values of starvation are replaced with the values of security has perhaps not yet fully occurred in CEECs. In the period of transition and economic hardship alongside the globalisation process, where much unskilled and semi–skilled work was moved to CEECs in the form of foreign direct investments, with the rise of unemployment and poverty in CEECs, workers in the region appear less satisfied with their jobs, as compared to their Western counterparts, owing first and foremost to unsatisfactory salaries (Večerník 2003). Job insecurity in the region in the period of transition exacerbated the effects of globalisation. As Ralf Dahrendorf put it "from being a burden, work has become a privilege." (1990, 144)

# Education and Training in CEECs: Challenges of Reforms and Transition

Virtually all CEECs had an advanced system of education that had developed in pre–communist times and during the communist period. Under the communist regime, elementary and lower secondary education was provided on a compulsory basis by state–run schools. Upper secondary education (ages 14–16 up to 18) was provided in the three main streams of general, technical and vocational education and was also virtually compulsory in some countries (as in the former Soviet Union). General education was provided mostly for a small cohort of potential enrolments into higher education, the capacity and selection of which was rather limited. The republics of the former Soviet Union represented an exception, where vocational training had very low prestige, general education enjoyed higher participation rates and access to higher education was somewhat better. Vocational education and training in other CEECs were traditionally broad, enjoying high participation rates and relatively high prestige.

Under communist rule, the region maintained its membership of CMEA[9], which involved a division of labour between the countries, with specialisation in the production of certain goods. Therefore the countries were specialised in particular industries and agricultural products. Vocational training, being closely linked to state enterprises, and education in general, was provided in accordance with a meticulously calculated manpower supply for the state planned economy, repeated the pattern of overspecialisation of the economy itself, with narrow branches of specialisation in education and training. Training was directed towards lifetime jobs. The nature of the centrally planned economy was reflected in an under–representation of market–oriented branches, for instance in the service sector. The school system and the content of education were defined by the state and its structures, neglecting what are considered modern innovative methods of curriculum development, teaching and learning.

Schooling in CEECs prior to 1989 has been mostly criticised for passive learning and encyclopaedic knowledge along with an old–fashioned mechanical mediation of the knowledge defining teaching methods (e.g., Parkes 1999). The criticism mostly came from the Western perspective, where learning was considered a more creative process and finding a clever solution to a question has always been valued more than just knowing the answer. Such an approach valued the process of learning more than a conventionally understood result of learning, i.e., knowledge. Provision of "encyclopaedic knowledge" as a teaching approach has become almost a negative characteristic. During the post–1989 reform period this resulted in devaluing explicit knowledge as a learning outcome at the expense of tacit knowledge and core competences (from "know what" to "know how"). The traditional value of knowledge has always been very high in CEECs and such a reform approach demanded a certain change in mentality[10].

The transition period had other implications for education and training in CEECs. The lack of flexibility in training, overly narrow specialisation, overproduction of semi–skilled and skilled workers and underproduction of a highly qualified labour force were features of the systems in CEE at the beginning of the 1990s, at which time education and training began to find itself increasingly irrelevant to the quickly changing demands of the reforming economy.

The weakening of state–based enterprises and the process of restructuring the economy worked to fracture the links between enterprises and vocational schools, and as a result the danger of vocational knowledge and skills remaining irrelevant to labour market requirements has increased. Companies, concerned with their own survival on the market have ceased to operate on–site schools and have lost interest in making contracts with vocational schools for the practical training of apprentices. This has led to a situation in which the system of vocational education and training in CEECs is predominantly school based (the case of the Baltic republics, Romania, Bulgaria). In some countries, elements of partial, enterprise–based apprentice training have been preserved, but the extent of this continued to diminish (Czech Republic, Slovakia, Poland), and only in two countries (Hungary and Slovenia) was the dual system of apprenticeship training either preserved or re–introduced to a certain extent. Economic hardship and short–sightedness among enterprises have also depreciated training and development in human resources, and participation in continuing training in some countries has been decreasing over the past decade.

The process of democratisation and the transition to a market economy presented the education and training system with challenges and instigated the need for substantial reform. The reform process in CEE featured diversification of the education offer, the introduction of private education, and an improvement in access to comprehensive upper–secondary education programmes, especially in general education, and subsequently in higher education. Higher education has undergone the process of significant diversification where non–university tertiary education was introduced.

In all CEECs the reform has been supported by EU–funded support programmes and other international aid. In the pursuit for quick and immediate solutions, and being under time and financial constraints, experts and practitioners in CEE often tended to look for ready–made answers, which came into being in the form of the models adopted from the West. A thorough systematic analytical work into verification of the feasibility, adjustability and impact of such adoptions was not in place. In spite of the invaluable input of international expertise into the process of reform, the role of national expertise in the reform process was often neglected. It is important to note that although the systems of education in CEECs had a number of similarities, they also differed to quite a great extent, reflecting the longer–term tradition of these countries prior to the period of communism. The reforms, however, featured a number of similar measures offered by the Western experience and applied for all CEECs without a thorough verification of their relevance to specific circumstances.

The modernisation has attained a new significance challenged by the learning society agenda. Making the systems more flexible, integrated and accessible for learning by all and throughout their lifetime introduced a new dimension to the reform process. The countries stressed an objective of focusing on the development of human capital, prepared to compete on global markets. The CEECs competitiveness at a global scale so far was based on low costs alongside the relatively high quality of the labour force. The countries however started to realise that this is not a solution in the longer term as the costs of labour will inevitably grow. The CEECs realised the need to concentrate on investment into human resources, on the diversification of the training offer, on an increase in the appropriateness of given qualifications to the new competitive requirements.

The consequences of globalisation have had an ambiguous impact on education and training. On the one hand, the increasing importance of knowledge–intensive industries, accumulating new technologies and ICT in the production process, and the employment shift to the service sector and SMEs, increased the demand for up–skilling and multi–skilling. On the other hand, globalisation trends have led to more severe competition, which, under the conditions of the turmoil of transition economies, made access to training increasingly difficult, especially after the completion of the initial training. All CEECs enjoy very high rates of educational attainment at upper secondary level, where the percentage of the population aged 20 to 24 having completed at least upper secondary education varies between 75.2% in Romania and 91.5% in Slovakia and is much higher in all CEECs than the EU–15 average (74.5% in 2005). However, participation in lifelong learning among adult population (25–84 years old) is much lower in CEECs than in the rest of the EU, varying between 1.1% in Bulgaria and 7.6% in Latvia, and only in Slovenia is the participation rate 17.8% which is above EU–15 average of 11.9% (Eurostat 2005). Similarly participation in higher education in CEECs is lower than in old member states, although the dynamic was very positive demonstrating high growth of participation throughout the 1990s. The initial education still needs to enhance access and capacities at higher levels of education and provide a broad basis as a primary incentive for lifelong learning.

The opening up of economies to the highly competitive global markets introduces a dilemma of a need for ever–higher standards of skills and competencies (up–skilling) and at the same time a lack of training provision by enterprises as a result of severe competition on the market. The role of education and training in preventing and combating the negative consequences of transformation has additional accountability in CEE. The role of the state in providing initial education and re–training for adults under these conditions becomes indispensable, but even more so is its role in the systemic re–organisation of training provision in such a way as to allow for alternative methods and sources of financing the system, better access to training among all age cohorts, and increasing the relevance of learning to the needs of the labour market. The education and training systems are undergoing tremendous changes, trying to meet the challenges of both ends of the double transformation.

At the same time CEE governments are trying to make ends meet within the public budgets, trying to prioritise between hard and soft investments. CEECs inherited from their communist past poor infrastructure, housing and transport networks, as well as a number of structural problems in the economy. Reforming "on all fronts" meant also investment to all ends, where prioritisation between what is of vital importance now and what is of strategic importance in the future, is obviously difficult to make. Expenditure on education and training, considered a key to the success of the Lisbon strategy, has been rather stable in the last decade varying between 4% and 6% of GDP among new member states, and 3.5% in Bulgaria and Romania. Although the difference with the average EU public expenditure on education and training (5.2% in 2002) was not high, it is important to take into account the differences in the amounts of actual expenditure. Economically CEECs are still much poorer than old EU members. GDP per capita in PPS in 2004 in Latvia was only 42.8% of that of the EU–25 average, whereas even the most affluent of the new-comers—Slovenia—enjoyed only 79% of the EU average, while acceding Bulgaria and Romania show only 30 and 32% respectively. Under such conditions it is difficult to push through reform processes and increase participation rates substantially without alternative financial sources. Access to and efficient usage of EU cohesion funds are therefore vital for CEECs. There will be a need for financial solidarity within the EU to prevent an education gap growing between the old and new members. (Reiter 2003, 143)

Learning does not only contribute to labour capital but is also otherwise meaningful for individuals, contributing to the human and social capital, and to human development in general. Due to the long tradition of formalised education rooted in the Middle Ages, learning has traditionally had a value in itself in the countries of the CEE region. The recent economic turmoil and the rate of change, however, have imposed a market–driven perception of learning. In the transition from a state to market economy, under conditions of economic hardship, CEE societies become liberal and utilitarian, in some respects to a greater extent than many old member states. It is however important to preserve the traditional, non–utilitarian, values of learning and knowledge so widespread formerly in the region, as these are culturally intrinsic for the CEE societies.

## Accession to the EU

The EU had undergone four successive enlargements, the experience of which was invaluable for the 2004 enlargement. However, the last enlargement was unprecedented in terms of scope and diversity: the number of candidates, the area (an increase of 23%) and population (increase of 74 million), and the cultural diversity.

From the point of view of basic economic and political conditions, in order to join the EU, the candidates needed to fulfil the requirements known as the Copenhagen criteria, according to which a prospective member must:

- be a stable democracy, respecting human rights, the rule of law, and the protection of minorities;
- have a functioning market economy;
- adopt the common rules, standards and policies that make up the body of EU law.

The challenges arising from EU accession were twofold: first, there were formal requirements (*acquis communautaire*) necessary to fulfil in order to enter the EU; second, and more importantly, there were broader issues that arose for the CEECs from the virtual objective of a successful entry and minimised costs of accession.

The formal requirements limited the process of negotiations which determined the conditions under which each applicant country could join the EU. Applicants were expected to accept the *acquis communautaire*. The latter represent laws and rules adopted on the basis of the EU's treaties. The negotiations focused on the terms under which the applicants adopted, implemented and enforced the *acquis*, and, particularly, the granting of possible transitional arrangements which must be limited in scope and duration and phase the compliance with certain laws and rules by a date agreed during the negotiations.

The EU discourse on the dimensions of EU social policy is relatively broad, encompassing not only the rather limited *acquis*, but also the wider principles of European social policy (in its broad meaning), i.e., the soft *acquis*. Therefore, apart from the EU legal regulation, other strategic and policy documents needed to be taken into account. Whereas *acquis* was a minimum requirement for accession, a wider spectrum of strategic and policy instruments served as a guiding mechanism for the member states to meet the requirements of the European Project. The acceding countries needed to catch up with those requirements in order to be able to become successful full–rate members of the enlarged Europe.

Such requirements (either formalised in a form of a document or not) arose mostly from the challenges of global changes and the knowledge–based economy, the Lisbon strategy being among the most important ones. The principle of the learning society appears as a major and a primary instrument for new member states to achieve a status comparable to that of the old members of the EU. Therefore, to meet the formal requirements of the *acquis* appeared minor compared to the challenges imposed by the global developments, greater role of new technologies and knowledge economy. Lifelong learning attained an entirely new significance in this respect.

CEE countries still have to tackle a major challenge of becoming equal and competitive partners of the old member states after the entrance to the EU. This involves the issue of economic competitiveness, labour productivity, knowledge–intensive investments and development of the productive processes, the role of science, research and developments in the CEE countries.

Although the EU acknowledged the strategic importance of the enlargement project from the very beginning of the transformation in the CEE, in practice, during negotiations period it followed a "non–strategic" approach (Inotai 2001). "Europe agreements" between the EU and CEECs were signed in the early 1990s, implying a virtual objective of accession, and therefore the transition process from its early stage was heavily linked and in many respects driven by the process of preparation for accession to the EU. In their striving to "go back to Europe", the countries demonstrated a very high rate of preparedness to accept the conditions laid down by the terms of the *acquis communautaire*. Not too experienced in EU integration and perhaps not always entirely comprehending the "kitchen" of the decision–making process in the EU, being dependent on the EU funds, CEE governments were ready to accept the requirements as they had little or no influence on contents of the decisions undertaken in the EU.

As the result, the process of accession was not understood as an opportunity to reform the countries in a steady, efficient and thoughtful manner, using the funds and the expertise available from the West, but rather as a "golden carrot", and the need to comply with all the demands of the EU—both *acquis*–type and soft—was seen as a "stick" and thus an obligation. CEECs lacked political and expert emancipation and tended to accept what was offered as a ready–made receipt from the West. This resulted in automatic copying of Western systems and approaches and in throwing away the baby with the bathwater when it came to reforming well–developed aspects of systems in CEECs. The transition process itself was very much accession driven and thus copied the pattern.

CEECs' specific Dream Project was returning to Europe. For them this meant complying with certain criteria and values based on democratic principles and fair treatment—as opposed to their previous experience of the communist camp cooperation. There was "an unrealistic belief in the idealism and goodwill of West" (Schöpflin 2004, 32). The accession negotiations, however, introduced them to a rather different practice. The EU obliged them to accept all regulations, the implementation of which is quite expensive. There was no room for serious national discussions with the involvement of the national decision making, experts and the civil society of the adopted Western systems, laws and approaches and their possible impact. In fact there were no *negotiations* to the extent that the term might be understood by old member states, as CEECs could never effectively discuss the rules whose application was a lot more flexible for old members (Schöpflin 2004). An adequate understanding of differences in the mentality and political cultures of CEECs was missing from the process of negotiations. The adoption was therefore formalistic and superficial and may eventually lead to damaging and even counterproductive results. As George Schöpflin accurately depicted, "the failure to engage the post–Communist states in a political, as opposed to technocratic, process has had the paradoxical result of exporting the democratic deficit eastwards" ( 2004, 37).

Only after the finalisation of negotiations did talks on the EU after–accession funding start. Due to procedural limitations over budget negotiations in the period right after the accession, the new members ended up being net contributors. After experiencing such a result of "negotiations", the leading politicians from the CEECs then had to go and sell the EU to their voters (Dahrendorf 2003, 224–225). An additional problem was that poorer than expected EU funding in the initial after–accession period alongside the on–going implementation of the *acquis* and other post–entrance adjustments caused a budget deficit in most CEECs which diminished and postponed their chances to enter the Eurozone, which had been widely expected to boost their economic growth. The EU budget adjustments occurred in a later period preventing such a "loss" situation on the side of the new entrants, who are expected to benefit particularly from the forthcoming financial period of 2007–2013. Much depends on their ability to efficiently absorb the funding and to take strategically wise decisions in the allocation of funds.

A proper political debate is something still to be put on the EU agenda after the accession. Overcoming the democratic deficit of the (pre)accession period largely depends on the ability of old members to apprehend the specific features of the political culture of CEECs as well as on the ability of CEECs to become decision–makers rather than decision takers and to treat the policy debate with a mature and strategic approach on equal footing with other EU members.

To make the accession a success, it is necessary to realise the expectations from accession by the actors. Here we need to come back to the question of identity and of understanding of Europe. For CEECs "Europe" is a very idealistic and emotional notion. For them "coming back to Europe" meant parting from communism, i.e., parting from lack of personal and collective freedom and coming to democracy, parting from an economically poor lifestyle and gaining economic affluence. Personal and national gains may therefore be expected as immediate rewards of accession. The EU accession is, in one way, a delusion. There is an ideal image of Europe among CEECs which is much more liberal, democratic and affluent than Europe is in reality. Its liberal capitalism is restricted and regulated by interventionist state policies and by a strong role of the welfare state. Its democracy suffers from deficit, especially when it comes to decisions taken by the EU institutions, not well trusted by and not even quite familiar to EU citizens. European affluence is relative, as compared to other world powers, and the redistribution of its affluence is limited by a lack of solidarity among EU countries and citizens. Altogether, accession to the real Europe may turn out to be a bitter disillusionment for CEECs. Acquaintance with the real face of Europe and its policies as well as a direct debate with all citizens and governments, including those in CEECs, is, therefore, of exceptional importance.

The CEECs' European identity building is an on–going process, not because they do not feel European (as mentioned before, the opposite is the case), but because they still feel different from their western counterparts. What Piotr Sztompka (2004, 488) called an "East–European syndrome" still prevails, with "an inferiority complex towards the West". This is exacerbated by the reserved acceptance of their Europeanness by others. The entrance to the EU does not automatically mean that CEECs would feel at home and would be treated by other Europeans as "one of us" (Sztompka 2004). The opposition to labour migration from CEECs to western countries of the EU right after the accession—a question already discussed earlier in this contribution—clearly demonstrated the low level of solidarity. Patronising in the process of accession negotiations and mistrust to the CEECs' much–reformed and relatively developed systems deepens the gap in cohesiveness inside Europe. How smooth and fast people from CEECs will transform from "Homo Sovieticus" to "Homo Europaeus", however relative the two labels may be, depends largely on the understanding of tensions which arise from the transition. CEECs in general do not trust ideology and politics. They expect much from membership while understanding little of the costs of adjustment. Their motivation as EU members depends greatly on the ability of the EU to explain, to welcome, to help and to encourage their new members avoiding patronising, ideology and bureaucratised politics, and preserving these nations' feeling of sovereignty and freedom. If this does not occur, an unfortunate comparison of the EU to the former Soviet regime will be inevitable[11].

## Transition to a Knowledge–Based Economy (Lisbon Transition)

How the European Union stands in the globalised world and how it manages to take on the opportunities offered by globalisation while avoiding the high costs is very important. These questions have been a major concern of European politicians in last decade. In a sense, the transformation which is going on in the economy and society nowadays is of comparable importance to the 20th–century "Great Transformation" as described by Karl Polanyi. With its networking governance, the economy of scale, expanding single–market and single–currency zone, the EU provides a remedy for globalisation. On the other hand, economic growth in China, the exodus of knowledge intensive services to India along with lower labour costs in both economies, provide firm grounds for unease among political elites and push Brussels institutions to search for alternatives in the European policy.

As discussed earlier, the Lisbon agenda may serve to satisfy aspirations of Europeans to be economically competitive in a world–wide scale and at the same time to retain the social model. The Lisbon agenda opened a path to something that Jeremy Rifkin called "the European Dream". It is not "just a glib political catchphrase. There are profound changes occurring in Europe at the personal, institutional, and even metaphysical level. Even most Europeans, when pressed, aren't exactly sure what they've gotten themselves into." (Rifkin, 2004, 84).

Here I do not intend to argue that such reforms are unnecessary. The question of "how best to streamline the entrepreneurial spirit without sacrificing the social well–being of the EU workforce is a critical concern". (Rifkin, 2004, 55). A combination of the liberal economic strategy and the social model is an unprecedented policy experiment, and there is no direct evidence that it is possible at all. As one of the greatest economists of the 20$^{th}$ century Ludwig Von Mises put it at the end of the 1950s (!), the idea that there is a third system—between socialism and capitalism, a system as far from socialism as it is from capitalism but that retains the advantages and avoids the disadvantages of each— is pure nonsense (1995). So, the idea is not new, although it is of course much more sophisticated at present, but the trouble is that its sophistication comes in the disguise of essentially the same principles. The question at the heart of the Lisbon dilemma for most EU member states and the union in general still remains of how much the union is prepared to fall behind the growth rates of other economies in order to preserve its social model, or how much it is prepared to trade off its social model for economic growth (Garton Ash 2004). As Jeremy Rifkin put it, "the European Dream is compelling but seems a bit utopian and out of reach" (2004, 267).

Even at the European policy level itself it became clear that the Lisbon strategy tried to approach too many and too different targets and that a better focus was necessary. A Wim Kok report (2004) came close to abandoning the social dimension altogether. In 2005 the strategy of the Barroso Commission put more emphasis on competitiveness implying that a competitive economy will bring a higher growth and thus will provide better economic grounds for social cohesiveness and welfare security. Complete abandonment of the social agenda would have been too unpopular, and thus the pro–liberal economic targets and policies which require evermore flexibility and mobility from the citizens remained disguised under the social label.

In reality there is nothing like a genuine "European social model". André Sapir (2005) distinguishes at least four models in Europe— Nordic, Anglo–Saxon, Continental and Mediterranean—all more or less more social than that of the US. The Mediterranean model has rather strict employment protection legislation and low unemployment benefits. The Continental model provides generous unemployment benefits and quite strict legislation on employment protection. The Anglo–Saxon model has relatively lower employment protection and relatively high unemployment benefits. Finally, the Nordic model provides generous unemployment benefits but soft employment protection legislation (Sapir 2005, 4).

Both Anglo–Saxon and Nordic models are efficient in economic terms, but only the latter manages to combine both social cohesiveness and economic competitiveness. From this point of view, the Nordic countries provide little experience in the combining aspects of liberal and social economic approaches, the new "Third Way" in the socio–economic policy, demonstrating at the same time the best socio–economic performance indicators in the EU. Although the approach is characterised by high social spending, it is liberal when it comes to employment protection legislation. The model promotes measures to support security in employability, i.e., finding a new job, changing jobs, maintaining social security benefits while changing employment, retraining, etc., rather than job security which frequently prevents employers from restructuring their enterprises, i.e., hiring and firing. Such an approach provides for necessary flexibility in the economy and security for the labour force, and thus it has attained the name "flexicurity" (see Schubert and Martens 2005). The high level of security is confirmed by the Eurobarometer data (2005) where the Nordic countries demonstrate a very high level of life satisfaction and optimism in both employment situation in their country and their personal job situation.

The security of the labour force in their mobility in the flexible labour market in the flexicurity Nordic model is only possible thanks to the quality and the versatility of the labour force. Finland, Denmark and Sweden demonstrate very good results in the OECD study of functional literacy. The participation rates in education and training among the adult population are also the highest in these countries. The learning society therefore is already in existence and functional there. It is however also a question of investment and wealth. The three countries demonstrate the highest investment in education and training, research and development and innovation policies. And while governance and innovation systems are very important factors of investment success, the presence of resources remains a primary concern. The benefits come at a high cost and viability depends on the citizens' commitment to the system and their willingness to pay for it (Hultin 2005). This is relatively easier to achieve in rather small, homogenous and rich Nordic countries than in most other EU member states.

It is important to realise that the transferability of the flexicurity model to other countries is highly questionable for a number of reasons. First, as already mentioned, such an approach is quite expensive and assumes a certain level of affluence of the society. Poorer economies have budgets that are too tight for them to implement generous flexicurity measures. Second, high levels of taxation assume high levels of solidarity and not all societies demonstrate the levels of solidarity necessary for the approach[12]. Third, in some countries employment security in the sense of security of keeping one's job is *the* face of the social model, and people might not feel ready for constant change in their employment situation, the need to retrain and/or even move to an entirely new field of work over and over again during their lifetimes for the sake of finding a new job. In France the government's attempt to fight youth unemployment by introducing flexibility measures for employers in the firing policy of young people caused a two–month crisis on a national scale. In Germany, due to the long tradition of the dual system in training, occupation (*Beruf*) and work are closely linked to qualification attained and constitute an important part of an individual's identity. Endless changing of jobs and lifelong retraining may eat away at the very foundation of an individual identity and societal values.

When it comes to CEECs, it is important to bear in mind that the Lisbon agenda was formulated and accepted at a time when these countries were still in the process of negotiations over acceptance of *acquis communautaire* and continued to reform their economies. The objectives set out in the Lisbon strategy were not on CEECs' priority list. The completion of the transition to the market economy, economic restructuring and decentralisation were still on–going and were seen as a priority. The "double transition" along with the accession process on the top of it pushed countries to tackle the most urgent issues rather than strategic ones. Additionally, the Lisbon strategy was initiated from above and gave a poor sense of ownership even among citizens of old member states. The new members of the EU have just completed negotiations over accession and were still in the process of implementation of the *acquis*—a gigantic task in itself and also superimposed from above. Therefore there was a feeling among CEECs that the Lisbon strategy was something designed for old members, whereas their primary task was limited to the *acquis* implementation. On the other hand, there was a realisation that a delay in the "second" transition would widen the gap between old and acceding member states and that CEECs will have more difficulties in catching up later (see, e.g., Piech 2004).

The new member states entered the Lisbon process later and were asked to draft programmes and action plans. This happened around accession in 2004, i.e., at the time when the initial enthusiasm about Lisbon's ideas was fading and the implementation record by other EU member states was considered poor (Telička 2005). This was the time when it was becoming clear and publicly accepted that the initial objectives of the Lisbon Council to become the most competitive and dynamic knowledge–based economy in the world and to overtake the US economy by 2010 were unfeasible. The future of the strategy was gloomy. The unrealistic rhetoric reminded CEECs of communist times (Telička 2005).

CEECs started to have a feeling of ownership in the formulation of future reform priorities only after EU accession and especially after the mid–term review, and the need for further reforms got recognition. There could be a certain level of readiness among CEECs to accept a more pro–liberal strategy set in a later version of the agenda under the Barroso Commission. Although CEECs' economies still look significantly more pro–social than in those of the UK, Ireland or the US, their economic reform has been more liberal than in mainstream continental Europe. Economic hardship and the need to reform the economy are nothing new in these countries and they may simply keep the reform ball rolling and "transit" to the "Lisbon society".

"Reform fatigue" (Telička 2005) may, of course, cause certain dissatisfaction, in particular with the government and the EU membership as such. According to the recent Eurobarometer survey (2005), there is a substantial difference in the perception of satisfaction with life between old and new member states: in the former EU–15 82% are generally satisfied with the life they lead, while only 69% share the same view in new member states. There are fears of further restructuring amongst the population of the new member states, particularly under conditions where the safety nets and unemployment benefits cannot mitigate the adverse effects of change (EC 2004). To a certain extent this is the case and might partially explain results of elections in several CEECs where anti–EU slogans found support among the population. Still the CEECs have been in a process of a constant change for more than 15 years and change has become inherent in these societies. Continual change therefore will still be accepted there more easily than a sudden requirement to reform in the stable democracies and well-off societies of western Europe, where the need for change might be difficult to appreciate. New member states with their more liberal and dynamic economies represent a fresh push much needed in the EU (Ackermann 2003). In any case the reform strategy needs to be clear and even unpopular measures have to be publicised, explained and discussed with the citizens.

The challenges brought to CEECs by the knowledge revolution are dramatic. The Lisbon transition costs may turn to be highest for CEECs, given their weak technological base, higher share of labour intensive industries and services, and competitiveness built so far on lower labour costs rather than other factors. CEECs face an additional burden of weak institutional capacity, limited resources and the legacy of a centrally planned economy. If the accession to the EU does not bring more knowledge intensive activities, research and development capacities and innovation to CEECs, and if instead it accelerates braindrain, brainwastage and youthdrain, the accession may eventually widen the knowledge economy gap. In the global competition and the evermore rapid change of the information age the ability of nations, companies and individuals to adapt, the gap between those who respond to the challenges aggressively and those who do not is likely to increase.

The success of building of the knowledge economy and learning society in CEECs, their economic competitiveness with minimised social costs of various transitions, depend on several issues. First and foremost, this is investment into knowledge production, meaning education, training and lifelong learning, but also research, development and innovation. This concerns primary investments in continuing training and support mechanisms which would encourage alternative, private, investments into training. This also concerns further investment in higher education to make it more accessible. Development of primary and applied research, and innovation systems are also on the priority shopping list for CEECs.

Labour markets are still insufficiently flexible to support the mobility and effective allocation of human resources that are so vital for a rapidly changing knowledge economy (WB/EC 2002). It is however important to realise that in CEECs, where budgets are tight, solidarity is limited by the poor economic situation of households and job security remains a value inherited from the communist past[13], the flexicurity model can hardly be implemented, at least not in the short run.

Resources are poor and thus important decisions are to be made in terms of budget reallocation and strategic, long–term investment choices. The dependency of CEECs on funds coming from the EU budget will not diminish in coming years. There is a question of efficiency in terms of financial absorption and system viability. It is, for instance, often more important how far the innovation system is developed and prepared to put innovations into practice than the actual degree of investment into science and technology. The capacity to integrate "foreign innovations" to the national systems is also very important.

Finally, CEECs need to adopt a strategic approach in policy design. The oft–cited success story of Estonia may be demystified if their experience of active public discourse, which included politicians, experts, business and civil society, on key strategic policy issues in the early transition period, is taken into account. The pro–active, strategic role on the part of the government in dialogue with private sector and civil society is a key to success (WB/EC 2002).

How far the Lisbon priorities can be incorporated into the decision–making process and into political affairs in new member states is limited by the lack of a socio–economic axis in the party politics of CEECs. The main cleavages along which parties are polarised in these countries are still more conventional left–right[14] and nationalist unlike the post–industrial, post–modern politics of the West. The knowledge–based economy, investments in human capital, innovation, research and development do not necessarily come into the party agenda, or at least not as a factor for political choice and behaviour of the electorate. It is thus difficult to contest the Lisbon agenda in the electoral process and to verify the direct support of the population. The dialogue with the public should therefore be more technocratic than political and should be initiated by the government.

Having said all the above about what CEECs need urgently to do in order to avoid widening the gap between them and old member states and so to avoid remain "second–class passengers" on the EU train, most of these apply to most old member states too, if they want to avoid widening the gap between them and other world powers in the globalisation contest.

The Lisbon process and the Idea, the European Dream project which is linked to it, have so far been very "bureaucratic". The common objectives and benchmarks are not set out in connection with national programmes and strategies. Top–down European initiatives are unlikely to be successful if they fail to take into account diverse cultural and systemic contexts (Livingston 2003). The EU concentrates more on Decisions, Communications and Laws than on a dialogue with its citizens. Here we come back to the question of identity. For the success of the project, those who are to implement it need to commit themselves to the implementation. The Europeans need to identify themselves with the Idea. Only then can the Lisbon agenda, the European Dream project, succeed as a grand narrative of the building of European statehood. No matter how many legislative arrangements, action plans and road maps, indicators and benchmarks, committees, councils and task forces will be set up, if "the personal sense of accountability and responsibility is not deep enough and thick enough to weather the inevitable storms that will accompany the new journey, then, all of the legislative and executive actions and intellectual support notwithstanding, the European Dream will fail". (Rifkin 2004, 384).

Now we come to the key point of the discussion—the learning society. Conceptualisation of the learning society and knowledge–based economy largely preceeded the formulation of the new European policy agenda. It was realised and widely accepted that the capacity to learn increasingly determined the relative position of individuals, firms and national systems (Lundvall 1996). The approach to education and training in the Lisbon strategy inherited this understanding and the role it assigns to learning thus is highly economistic. The strategy strives for competitiveness based on the knowledge economy and expects citizens to learn through their lives, reacting flexibly to the needs of the labour market. But as we have seen, in Europe and for the sake of the project of building united, cohesive and competitive Europe, learning is no less important for identity building, for solidarity among countries and citizens and to support the very grounds on which Europe is built. Moreover, the context of technological change and pressures coming from globalisation push for changes towards the knowledge economy, although the overall change taking place is as much economic as social and even societal. When treated as purely a commodity, knowledge may reinforce systematic social inequalities rather than contribute to solidarity and social cohesiveness. Education and training are not an exclusive panacea against increasing global competition. Only universal and accessible provision of learning along with other systemic social protection measures and with a substantial investment in the knowledge production and innovation systems, can increase European chances for success. Fulfilment of the European Dream project, or putting it bluntly—addressing a common European interest—will require substantial redistribution of wealth in the European society as a whole.

Having said all the above, I do not intend to say that economic competitiveness is not important and that a liberal agenda must be abandoned. On the contrary, it might be necessary to put a greater focus on the pro–liberal strategy and be prepared to lose some of the qualities offered by European social models. Or, if the flexicurity model is the answer, as in any case it seems to be the only viable solution offered by present practice, then its adaptability to other national economies should be seriously contested, and specific measures and conditions of its implementation in each national context have to be defined. The European Dream Project should become a pragmatic, down–to–earth programme, undisguised by populist slogans and seemingly trouble–free proposals. In a way, the ratification of the EU Constitution was a test to the EU reform strategy as well as to the enlargement. A test which the EU failed. The failure was mostly due to low awareness on the part of the population of what is going on and what is expected to occur in the future in the union. Democratic deficiency has been recognised and a more efficient debate with the EU citizens is being established. It is however crucial to recognise that hypocritical catchphrases in the most efficient dialogue may be counterproductive, especially among citizens of countries where hidden meanings had been long covered by ideological propaganda promising paradise. In short, whatever it is, the real transition to better economic competitiveness, for the very sake of the project, needs to be openly discussed.

## Conclusion

A major clash of transitions appears at the level of understanding of what the European project is by Eastern Europeans and their Western counterparts in the EU. For CEECs "coming back to Europe" has a very idealistic and nostalgic meaning. For them entrance to the EU is also going back to the Europe of the very brief inter–war period, to a democratic and independent past. In this past there was no unity at a European level nor the need for economic cooperation and network–type governance to the extent dictated by the globalised presence. For CEECs, Europe is not so much a project, but rather a sweet memory, a reality once lost and now regained. For Western Europeans, Europe is far more a project which is still to be shaped and implemented. (Plesu 2003) The Idea of Europe somehow has to incorporate both understandings in the process of identity building. The traditional values of democracy, human rights and the rule of law have to be firmly tied to the Lisbon strategy and the Idea of Europe as of a world economic power with a socially cohesive society and the quality of life preserved. Such an approach may not only integrate different perceptions of Europe but will also provide grounds for the building of a statehood identity in a highly diverse society with pluralistic values. This may help to build a genuine European political identity which would encompass East and West.

The idea of Europe, however, should not be reduced to the adjustment of benchmarks and indicators and to the fulfilment of certain political and economic conditions. The European identity cannot be reduced to such a perception (Drakulic 2003). It is important to avoid too much of "a bureaucratised ideology" in the idea of Europe. The greatest fear among CEECs is that European reunification could be transformed into an ideology— "yet another ideology". (Plesu 2003, 150) There is no trust in ideology in CEECs. The same concerns European institutions. The most pervasive legacy of communism at a mental level appears to be widespread distrust (Moxon–Browne 2004). In this sense, the deeds will do more than pay lip service to any strategy or agenda. Solidarity in EU decision making and budget allocation as well as empathy at an individual level will be the best demonstration of the commitment to the project of a unified and democratic Europe. For this, a common European interest should be recognised and emphasized. Without such recognition, it is very hard to envisage proper legitimacy for the transfer of resources eastwards (Schöpflin 2004).

Accession to the EU is a ticket to get on a train which is going at full speed. The destination is very ambitious, not clearly defined and, in any case, not determined by CEECs. The European Project is much more a process than a clearly identified destination. But how far the train will go depends greatly on the success of all passengers in apprehending, sharing and finally getting to the designated destination.

## Notes

1. According to Herodotus, *Europa* was kidnapped by the Minoans—the pre–Hellenic people of Crete.

2. Phoenicians spread rapidly as they were successful traders and sailors.
3. I am not the first to reveal this European inclination. For instance, Timothy Garton Ash has written about this (2004) and many other authors (e.g., Citrin and Sides 2004). The point here is however to demonstrate why it is important to find explanations and definitions which may help Europeans to identify themselves as Europeans and as citizens of the EU—not based on the exclusivity characteristic but on the inclusive identification.
4. According to empirical surveys the strengthening of European identity over time does not threaten or weaken national identities (see Ruiz Jimenez et al. 2004)
5. For more about the categories see Roger Brubaker (1992, 1996), as well as an earlier conceptual work on civic and ethnic nation by Antony Smith (1991).
6. Furthermore, peace and stability in Europe are only partially a contribution of the EU, and result mostly from the end of the Cold War. The primary objective of European unification was to protect Europe against itself. Many territories outside the EU remain unstable (Balkans, CIS, parts of Russia), and potential conflicts are not prevented by tightening the markets and policies of all nations in Europe in such a way that war will become a virtual impossibility. Victor Hugo in the mid–19th century said: "The day will come when you France, you Russia, you England, and you Germany, when all you nations of the continent, without losing distinctive qualities or your individual glories, will bind yourself tightly together into a single superior entity, and you will come to constitute a European fraternity, as absolute as Brittany, Burgundy and Alsace are now bound together with France." (*Douze discourse*, Paris, 1850, quoted from d'Appollonia 2002, 176). European integration thus should not stop at incorporation of the territories in the centre of Europe, the patchwork of "countries in–between". The ultimate stability and peace in the continent may be achieved only with the eventual binding of all powers of the continent—including Turkey in the Balkans, and Russia in the east. While immediate inclusion of such powers might be self–destructing for the EU, it is still important to realise that this inclusion is in the common interest of Europe and thus ever closer economic and political cooperation with these countries is in the interest of the EU, at least as much as in the interest of the applicant (Turkey) or even if the interest in membership is not expressed by the country (Russia).
7. After the European university students' exchange programme "Erasmus".
8. The studies were carried out in all CEECs mostly in 2000. See more the contribution by Rogojinaru in this volume.
9. Council for Mutual Economic Assistance was established in 1959 and included Albania (until 1962), Bulgaria, GDR, Hungary, Poland, Romania, USSR, Czechoslovakia. Yugoslavia had a status of associated partner in

CMEA, underlying its independency in the communist path. The latter was a member of the Non–Aligned Countries.
10. I still have considerable doubt that the provision of encyclopaedic knowledge should be entirely eplaced by more process–oriented and creative learning. The ideal would be a combination of both. Some years ago at the beginning of the 1990s in the class of students at a university where I taught it was always Easterners who knew the answer whereas Westerners were very good at guessing and solving. Instead of substitution of one method for another, mutual enrichment would probably benefit both systems.
11. In 1994 Vaclav Klaus, the current president of the Czech Republic, then prime minister, compared future dependence vis–à–vis Brussels Eurocracy to the old totalitarian rule from Moscow, saying: "Finally we are an independent nation and we would not like to lose this freedom for new dependence on the community institutions of Brussels" (Kinsky 2003, 138, translated by the author). Such comments are quite typical among the central and eastern European eurosceptics.
12. Canada might be another useful example of a combined social approach with a competitive economic performance, but the level of solidarity of the Canadian society is very high and thus their approach may not work in other, less cohesive societies.
13. The value of employment security does not contradict the fact that a high percentage of the population had to change their jobs and occupations after 1989. The high inter–occupational mobility was a price of the transition period and not always a choice of individuals.
14. It is important to note however that the left–right cleavage in the party politics of CEECs is not conventional in the connotation of "left" and "right". The "left" is often associated with post–communist parties, rather than genuine European–type social democracy, and the "right" with pro–liberal, and thus more radical pro–reform, parties. Party politics in CEECs is still in transition and is steadily developing along the axes more typical of western European politics.

# References

Ackermann, J. "Desperately Seeking Europe". In: Stern, S. and Seligmann, E. (eds.) *Desperately Seeking Europe*. Alfred Herrhausen Society for International Dialogue. Archetype Publications. London. 2003. pp. 9–20.

Von Mises, L. *Economic Policy: Thoughts for Today and Tomorrow.*, Free Market Books, San Francisco, California, 1995.

Brubaker, R. *Citizenship and Nationhood in France and Germany*, Harvard University Press, Cambridge Mass., London, 1992.

Brubaker, R. *Nationalism Reframed. Nationhood and the National Question in the New Europe*. Cambridge University Press, Cambridge, 1996.

Citrin, J. and Sides, J. "More than Nationals: How Identity Choice Matters in the New Europe". In: Herrmann, R.K., Risse, T., Brewer, M.B. *Transnational Identities: Becoming European in the EU*. Rowman & Littlefield Publishers, Inc. 2004, pp.161–185.

Dahrendorf, R. *Modern Social Conflict. An Essay on Politics of Liberty*. University of California Press, Berkeley, 1990.

Dahrendorf, R. "Workaday Europe, Soapbox Europe: Who Will Close the Gap?" In: Stern, S. and Seligmann, E. (eds.) *Desperately seeking Europe*. Alfred Herrhausen Society for International Dialogue. Archetype Publications. London. 2003. pp. 225–234.

Dunkerley, D., Hodgson, L., Konopacki, S., Spybey, T., Thompson, A. *Changing Europe: Identities, Nations and Citizens*. Routledge, London and NY, 2002.

d'Appollonia, A.C. "European Nationalism and European Union". In: *The Idea of Europe. From Antiquity to the European Union*. Woodrow Wilson Center Press and Cambridge University Press. 2002, pp. 171–190.

Davies, N. *Europe: A History*. Oxford University Press, Oxford, 1996.

Davies, N., Moorhouse, R. *Portret miasta środkowoeuropejskiego*. ZNAK, Krakow, 2002.

Drakulic, S. "Europe Tastes Better". In: Stern, S. and Seligmann, E. (eds.) *Desperately Seeking Europe*. Alfred Herrhausen Society for International Dialogue. Archetype Publications. London. 2003. pp. 21–27.

EC. *Report of the High Level Group on the Future of Social Policy in an Enlarged European Union*. DG Employment and Social Affairs, 2004.

Fukuyama, F. *The End of History and the Last Man*. Free Press, 1992.

Garton Ash, T. *Free World: Why a Crisis of the West Reveals the Opportunity of our Time*. Allen Lane, Penguin Books. London, 2004.

Gellner, E. *Nations and Nationalism*. Oxford, Blackwell, 1992.

Herrmann, R.K. and Brewer, M.B. "Identities and Institutions: Becoming European in the EU". In: Herrmann, R.K., Risse, T., Brewer, M.B. *Transnational Identities: Becoming European in the EU*. Rowman & Littlefield Publishers, Inc. 2004, pp. 1–22.

Hultin, G. "Learning the Lessons of the Nordic Experience". In: Schubert, C.B., Martens, H. *The Nordic Model: A Receipt for European Success? EPC Working Paper*, No.20, September 2005, pp.66–74.

Huntington, S.P. *The Clash of Civilizations and the Remaking of World Order*, New York, Simon & Schuster, 1996.

Inglehart, R. *Culture Shift in Advanced Industrial Society*. Princeton University Press, Princeton, 1990.

Inotai, A. "Some Reflections on Possible Scenarios for EU Enlargement". *Begegnungen/Crossroads*, Europa Institut Budapest, No. 16, 2001, pp. 89–104.

Kagan, R. *Paradise and Power: America and Europe in the New World Order*. Atlantic Books, London, 2003

Kok, W. et al. *Facing the Challenge: the Lisbon Strategy for Growth and Employment*. Report from the High Level Group. Luxembourg: Office for Official Publications of the European Communities, 2004.

Kundera, M. "The kidnapped West", *Granta*, no.11, 1984. The version in *the New York Review of Books,* 26 April 1984–"The Tragedy of Central Europe".

Kynsky, F. "L'élargissement de l'Union face à la civilisation européenne en crise". *L'Europe en formation*, 2003, No. 4 pp. 137–149.

Lisbon European Council. *Presidency Conclusions.* 23 and 24 March 2000.

Livingston, K. "What is the Future for National Policy Making in Education in the Context of an Enlarged European Union?" In: *Policy Futures in Education*, Vol. 1, No. 3, 2003, pp. 586–600.

Lundvall, B.-Å. "The Social Dimension of the Learning Economy", *DRUID Working Paper,* No. 96–1, April 1996.

Machonin P., Tuček M. et al. *Česká společnost v transformaci. K proměnám sociální struktury.* Prague, SLON, 1996.

Matějů, P. *Lidské zdroje, lidský kapitál a funkční gramotnost.* 2000.

Moxon–Browne, E. Eastern and Western Europe: "Towards a New European Identity?" In: Moxon–Browne, E. (ed.) *Who are the Europeans Now?* Ashgate, 2004, pp.193–202.

Munich, D., Švejnar, J., Terrell, K. "Returns to Human Capital under the Communist Wage Grid and During the Transition to a Market Economy". *Discussion Paper Series*, IZA DP No. 122, March 2000.

Optem S.A.R.L. *Perceptions of the European Union.* A qualitative study of the public's attitudes to and expectations of the European Union in the 15 member states and in 9 candidate countries. Summary of results. The European Commission. 2001.

Pagden, A. Europe: "Conceptualising a Continent". In: Pagden, A. (ed.) *The Idea of Europe. From Antiquity to the European Union.* Woodrow Wilson Center Press and Cambridge University Press. 2002, pp. 33–54.

Parkes, D. (ed.) *A Cross Country Analysis of Curricular Reform in VET in CEE.* ETF. Luxembourg: EUR–OP, 1999.

Pehe, J. "Central Europe Returns to the Fold". In: Stern, S. and Seligmann, E. (eds.) *Desperately Seeking Europe.* Alfred Herrhausen Society for International Dialogue. Archetype Publications. London. 2003. pp. 123–132.

Piech, K. (ed.) *The Knowledge–Based Economy in Transition Countries. Selected Issues.* School of Slavonic and East European Studies, University College London, 2004.

Pleşu, A. "Between Musk and Must: Europe of the Eastern Europeans". In: Stern, S. and Seligmann, E. (eds.) *Desperately Seeking Europe.* Alfred Herrhausen Society for International Dialogue. Archetype Publications. London. 2003. pp. 148–157.

Pocock, J.G.A. Some Europes in their History. In: In: Pagden, A. (ed.) *The Idea of Europe. From Antiquity to the European Union.* Woodrow Wilson Center Press and Cambridge University Press. 2002, pp. 55–71.

Reiter, R. Eurocivic Pride. In: Stern, S. and Seligmann, E. (eds.) *Desperately Seeking Europe.* Alfred Herrhausen Society for International Dialogue. Archetype Publications. London. 2003, pp. 141–147.

Rifkin, J. *The European Dream: How Europe's Vision of the Future is Quietly Eclipsing the American Dream*. Polity Press, Cambridge, 2004.

Ruiz Jimenez, A.M., Gorniak, J.J., Kosic, A., Kiss, P., Kandula, M. "European and National Identities in EU's Old and New Member States: Ethnic, Civic, Instrumental and Symbolic Components". *EIOP*, Vol.8, No. 11, 2004.

Sapir, A. *Globalisation and the Reform of European social models*. Bruegel Policy Brief, 2005/01, November 2005.

Schöpflin, G. "Sixth (?) Enlargement". New Europe and European Identity. In: Gough, R. and Reid, A. (eds.) *The Perfect Union? New Europe and the EU*. Policy Exchange Ltd. 2004, pp.30–53.

Schubert, C.B., Martens, H. "The Nordic Model: A Receipt for European Success?" *EPC Working Paper*, No.20, September 2005.

Sedelmeier, U. "EU Enlargement, Identity and the Analysis of European Foreign Policy: Identity Formation through Policy Practice". *EUI Working Papers*, European Forum Series, RSC No. 2003/13.

Sirovatka, T. *Marginalizace na procovnim trhu*. Brno: Masarykova univerzita, 1997.

Smith, A.D. *National Identity*. London, Penguin, 1991.

Svetlik, (ed.) *Kakovost zivljenja v Sloveniji*. Ljubljana: Fakulteta za druzbene vede, zbirka Teorija in praksa, 1996.

Szalai J. "Recent Trends in Poverty in Hungary". In: Atal Y. ed., *Poverty in Transition and Transition in Poverty*, UNESCO publishing, Paris, New York—Oxford: Berghahn Books, pp.32–76, 1999.

Sztompka, P. "From East Europeans to Europeans: Shifting Collective Identities and Symbolic Boundaries in the New Europe". *European Review*, 2004, Vol. 12, No. 4, October, pp. 481–496.

Telička, P. "The Lisbon Strategy and the Union's Newest Members". In: *What Future for Europe's Economic and Social Model? Challenge Europe*, No.13, EPC, Brussels, 2005, pp. 113–116.

Traser, J., Venables, T. *Report on the Free Movement of Workers in EU–25: Who's Afraid of EU enlargement?* Brussels: ECAS, 2005.

Trbanc, M. "VET Against Social Exclusion: The General Picture and Some Experiences from Slovenia". In: *Transition, Reconstruction and Stability in South—Eastern Europe: The role of VET*, ETF, pp. 35–38, 1999.

UNDP. *Human Development Report: Globalisation with a Human Face*. New York: Oxford University Press, 1999.

UNDP. *Human Development Report: Poverty from a Human Development Perspective*. New York: Oxford University Press, 1997.

Večerník, J. "Skating on Thin ice: A Comparison of Work Values and Job Satisfaction in CEE and EU Countries". *International Journal of Comparative Sociology*, December, 2003, pp. 444–470.

Večerník, J. "Úvod do studia chudoby v Československu". *Sociologický časopis* 27, pp. 577–602, 1991.

Wessels, W., Maurer, A., and Mittag, J. (eds.) *Fifteen Into One? The European Union and its Member States*. Manchester University Press, Manchester and NY, 2003.

World Bank / European Commission. "Building Knowledge Economies: Opportunities and Challenges for EU Accession Countries". *Final Report of the Knowledge Economy Forum.* Paris, 2002.

• GÖRAN THERBORN •

# The World's Trader, the World's Lawyer: Europe and Global Processes

## Introduction

Many, if not all, of Europe's positive contributions to modern world history can be summed up in foreign trade and international law. True, this would then leave out the scientific breakthroughs, the Enlightenment, and popular revolution, but since the Dark Age of the European 1930s the frontiers of science have moved westwards, popular revolution left the world agenda in the 1990s, at least for the time being, and the Enlightenment is rather aged, part of the *ancien régime* as it was.

From a world perspective, "Europe" has almost always meant Western Europe. Western Europeans were what Arabs, Africans, Americans, and Asians of South and Southeast Asia, the Japanese, Australians and Pacific islanders encountered. The Chinese, and later the Ottomans, the Persians, and the Afghans also had to cope with the Russians, but mainly within the parameters of inter–state power politics. And the famous Sino–Russian Treaty of Nerchisk/Nipchu in 1689, which fixed the border between China and Russia was negotiated in Latin with Portuguese Jesuit interpreters (Spence, 1990:65–6). In the early 20th century the Polish lands produced some of the shrewdest observers of world culture, Bronislaw Malinowski and Joseph Conrad. For a while, in the second half of the Cold War, the Soviet Union provided a world model of development, particularly in Africa. But, in the end, Russian imperialism, Soviet modelling, and Polish writing remained episodes of world history and today the major Eastern European project is absorption into Western Europe.

So, while duly recognizing that Norman Davies (1996) has given us 1365 pages of arguments against writing a Western European history of Europe, a global perspective may warrant a focus on that part of Europe which, for good and for bad, currently as well as historically has been most influential.

On other occasions, there are good reasons not to stay basking in the sunshine, but to dwell on the dark sides of Europe. However, after these caveats I want to concentrate here on two features which very much define what is actually going on in Europe, and which provide the bearings of Europe's position in the world, i.e., on trade and on law.

## Beyond Spatiality: Unpacking Globalization

In social thought and discourse, the 1990s was a moment of space, of spatiality. "Globalization" was the buzz word world–wide, and Europe was set afloat with spatial programs, the "Single Market", German "Unification", the Eastern "extension" of the EU, and from Brussels and Paris notions were spread of *espaces européens*, a European "economic area", a "culture area", and, in the 2000s, a "research area".

Let us reflect briefly on the implications of a spatialization of social thought. Above all, an exclusive or predominant focus on social space means that the actors and their non–spatial social condition are taken as given. In the spatial mode, the characteristics of actors, their inequality and possibly conflicting interests are flattened out and submerged, and the quality of social conditions/relations and their transformation are thrust off the table. The game and its rules are given; the only question is the extent of the field and the number of players.

While non–geographers neglect space at their peril, and we shall soon see that social distance has in some ways gained a rather increased importance recently, a spatialization of general social discourse literally means superficiality.

The notion of "globalization", which has both a connotation of extension, from the local and the national, and of finitude, of planetary limitation, is a big bag which needs to be unpacked and specified into a set of global processes.

## Five Global Processes

This set consists of five major kinds of processes. One of them is a cultural process, with a mental referent, pertaining to the extension of social awareness. It may be subdivided into a global consciousness of worldwide variability and interconnection, and a planetary awareness of human and ecological finiteness and vulnerability. Socially, it is a discursive process.

Another is historical, acting out the path dependence of contemporary economies, polities, and cultures. In the world distribution of national income in 1820 and in 1999 there is a strong correlation, for instance, among ten major countries and regions, a Pearson correlation of 0.85 (calculated from Maddison, 1995: table 1–3, and World Bank, 2000: table 1.)

Thirdly, there are the global flows, perhaps the most visible and dramatic of the global processes. That is, the flows of trade—or of goods and services, of capital, of people, and of information, in the broadest sense, values, scientific knowledge, music, etc.

Fourthly, there are entanglements of sovereign states in trans–national networks of policies and of norm–generation. Through such inter–locking of the national and the trans–national, the latter affects the former by, agenda setting, policy prescription, policy review, and institution modelling. The post–World War II proliferation of independent states has been accompanied by such imbrications of state organization and state policies with international institutions.

Traditional inter–state clientelism, which has not disappeared, apart, these entanglements are of three major sorts. Truly global are those of the UN machinery, with its sectoral agencies, agenda–setting conferences, and its conventions, and of various attempts at a global legal order on the planetary environment, on particularly destructive weapons, on war conduct and war crimes, on world trade. Quasi–global are the powerful inter–state economic organizations of conditional aid and credit, the IMF and the World Bank, mainly affecting poor and/or indebted countries. The functioning of the IMF and the World Bank in relation to their dependencies has many resemblances with the imperial and colonial operation of individual states or small groups of states a century ago. Thirdly, there are regional orders of trans–national entanglements.

Finally, global processes include worldwide action. This may, in turn, be divided into global concert, the rare moments of really United Nations, and global reach, once the pride of the Royal Navy of the United Kingdom, later the goal of Soviet Cold War parity, now, to the envy of some Western European politicians, the monopoly of US missiles and bombs.

## The Location of Europe in Global Processes

Where do we find Europe in these global processes? To begin with, there is not much of it in global action and in global consciousness, whereas the European footprints on global history are still very visible, particularly outside Europe.

The current terms of global action were aptly captured by a January 2002 cartoon in the conservative German newspaper *Die Welt,* featuring a huge American soldier in front of a target named "Saddam", looking down on a bunch of dwarfish European politicians, and saying to the latter: "I suggest the usual division of labour. I shoot, and you clap when I hit."

From the soft evidence of personal experience, in Asia and the Americas particularly, but also in Africa, it seems to me that "Europe" does not have a major place in global consciousness, or in the consciousness of the world. The West and the rest, or the North and the South appear much more salient. On the other hand, humanitarian and environmental concerns indicate a relatively high planetary awareness among Europeans

Global history, primarily in the form of colonial heritage, assures Europe a major influence in the contemporary world. Most strikingly, colonial background still determines the language of states and elites. The very names of many states tell of their colonial history. Legal systems, sports preferences, trade and migration routes are still following deep historical furrows of colonial provenance. Bygone colonial supremacy has left fewer traces in contemporary Europe, although the direction of aid, concern, and of moral hectoring, as well as the sources of overseas immigration still largely follow the old colonial command lines.

While the marks of global history do not leave the face of Europe, it is in some of the global flows, in those of trade and capital particularly, and in normative trans–national entanglements that we find Europe standing out in the current world.

Having been a region of out–migration for four and a half centuries, Europe became a destination of net immigration in the early 1960s. Today the proportion of foreign–born residents in Sweden, which in the 19th century was one of the most vigorous emigration sources, is about the same as in the US. But the major flow of migrants of the current world is not destined for Europe. Like a hundred years ago, the major destination is USA, though now coming from the South and from the Western Pacific, rather than from the Eastern Atlantic.

A comparative size of information flows is very difficult to get at. But clearly, the most important flows of scientific knowledge and of entertainment run from the US into the rest of the world, although foreign student recruitment and music sales, for instance, show a continuing secondary centrality of Western Europe. In the setting of literary taste and of the literary canon, London and Paris, and Stockholm, respectively, may even still be taken as the prime centres of the world (cf. Casanova, 1999).

## The Centre of Trade and Capital Flows

But it is, above all, in the international flows of trade and capital, that Western Europe is still <u>the</u> centre of the world, even if less so than by the end of the *Belle Epoque*. In 1913 one third of world trade was intra–European, and trade between Europe and the rest of the world made up a good half of all international trade. Exchange among non–European regions only amounted to a seventh of all world trade (Zacchia 1976: table 1).

In 2000 a good fourth of all global foreign trade, 27 per cent, takes place within Western Europe, almost a third (29 per cent) within all Europe, and forty per cent of world exports originate in the countries of Western Europe. US exports, including commercial services, amount to fourteen per cent of the world total, and Japanese to seven (WTO 2001: tables III.1, III.3, and III.5) Intra–EU trade is twice the size of intra–NAFTA trade (WTO 2001: table I.9).

The direction of capital flows around 1900 was mainly out of Europe, of Britain above all, into the European settlements of the New Worlds. Britain held a good forty per cent of all long–term foreign investment in 1913–14, and two thirds of British overseas investment 1907–13 went to the New Worlds (Zacchia, 1976:573; O'Rourke and Williamson, 1999:211), while the two next largest foreign investors, France and Germany, together smaller than Britain, directed their capital mainly to the peripheries of Europe (O'Rourke and Williamson, 1999:229). By 1914 about half of the world's foreign investment was located in the New Worlds, and the rest was almost equally divided between Europe (with a slightly larger share) and, on the other hand, Africa and Asia (Woodruff ,1973:710–1).

In 2000 Western Europe still owns more than half of the world's stock of foreign direct investment, 57 per cent, while the US owns a fifth, and Japanese investors barely five per cent (4.7). Western Europe is also the largest host of foreign investment, holding almost forty per cent of the world stock in 2000, while USA harbours twenty per cent, and Japan less than one per cent. In flow terms, the countries of Western Europe sent out more than two thirds (71%) of global foreign direct investment in 2000 and received half of it (UNCTAD, 2001: Annex tables B4, B3, B2, and B1, respectively). US firms accounted for only one eighth of the outward flow of foreign direct investment.

In sum, while no longer the richest part of the earth and no longer the prime economic model of the world, Western Europe is till the central node of global flows of trade and of capital. While the US has become the prime producer and the prime owner of global wealth, Europe is still the main mover of economic flows.

Generally speaking, and contrary to what might seem implied in the word "globalization", in the last third of the 20th century there was a tendency towards a greater regionalization of trade, which while not dramatic was nevertheless significant. Europe has been a forerunner in this respect, but it is by no means a unique achievement, and the formal, institutional integration of Europe has played at most a secondary or tertiary role in this.

In Western Europe (including non–members of the EU), intra–regional (merchandise) trade was 64 per cent of all exports in 1963 and 68 % in 2000. The share of intra–regional imports grew from 56 to 65 per cent. (WTO, 2001:table II.4) In North America intra–NAFTA exports rose from 28 to 50 per cent, while intra–regional imports remained at its old level. The difference is due to a surge of Asian imports, and the US import surplus. (WTO, 2001:table II.3) Japanese trade in the same period became more Asian–oriented (WTO 2001: table II.5)

Among the fifteen old EU Member States, trade regionalization took place mainly in the 1960s, with the generalization of European prosperity and stimulated by the Common Market of six countries starting in 1958, when intra–European trade was about a fourth of their foreign trade. Intra–bloc trade peaked, to date, in the early nineties, around the time of the inauguration of the Single Market in 1992, then sliding slightly in the second half of the decade (OECD, 2000: Annex table 64; WTO, 2000:table II.4).

However globalized, some parts of the globe are much closer to each other than others. In the case of trade flows, that tendency of spatial distance dependency has been strengthened recently, rather than weakened.

## Global Governance and the World of Law

Global governance operates without government, through relations of power and force, certainly, but also by way of norms, standards, and institutions, by nesting nation–states in trans–national webs of actors, institutions, and norms.

On one, quasi–global side of trans–national entanglements, European countries take a modest part. They pay their dues to the IMF and the World Bank and toe the line, the so–called Washington Consensus, which de facto includes the US Treasury as the strongest player, while adding some humanitarian and environmental aid aspects to the World Bank.

It is in the normative framework of the UN, and also in the WTO, that Europe is playing a key part in the global institutional entanglement of states. Europe is pushing the UN Human Rights Conventions, the *Kyoto Protocol* on the reduction of pollution and the International Crimes Tribunal. In all these respects, the USA is the main counter–player. The UN Convention of the Rights of the Child, for instance, has been ratified by all countries of the world, although some with escape clauses added, except the USA and Somalia. This Convention, one of the most successful of the attempts at global normativity because of its active implementation monitoring committee, was, by the way, a rare instance in the Cold War era of a successful Eastern European–Western European cooperation. The idea of a Convention on children's rights was launched by Poland in the late 1970s, and then launched a ten–year drafting course due to strong Western European support (see further Detrick, 1992).

The 1948 UN *Declaration of Human Rights* is arguably the most widely invoked normative standard of the contemporary world. Although legally non–binding, it has been a recurrent source of inspiration to lawyers as well as to citizens worldwide. Its drafting was an impressive, truly global process, which succeeded in spite of the incipient Cold War and carried over the outbreak of the first Palestine war. Its legal language, however, derived from the French jurist René Cassin, its conception of rights more from the European (and Latin American) "dignitarian" perspective than from Anglo–American individualism, and its extensive articles on social and economic rights from the strivings of the European labour movement (see further Glendon, 2001).

Europe became the world's lawyer in the 19$^{th}$ century. The newly independent Latin American states adopted Napoleonic legal codes, which still weighed upon the hemisphere, not least in family law. Imperialist expansion brought European extra–territoriality to the threatened and bullied pre–modern polities of Asia, from the Ottoman Empire to Japan. In 1865 the British set up in Shanghai "Her British Majesty's Supreme Court for China and Japan".

Colonial conquest introduced European law to Africa and Asia, and created a new dual legal system, with domestic customary law, a duality of law that persists till this day in family matters. Meiji Japan imported a legal system from Europe, from France and, above all, from Germany, a legal change then inspiring Chinese attempts at law reform. Post–Ottoman Turkey later adopted a derivative of the Swiss Code. The Paris-based Institute of International Law in 1874 graciously accorded the theoretical equality of all nations, non–Christian as well as Christian, thereby proclaiming a universality principle of international law. (See further, e.g., Mommsen and De Moor, 1992). In these various ways, European law spread through the world, to what Kipling, in his famous, somewhat elegiac, imperial poem Recessional, with imperialist arrogance so typical of his era, called, "the lesser breeds without the Law" (Untermeyer, n.d.:510).

The weakened power of Europe has diminished the current global significance of European law and regulation. The dynamic of US capitalism and business education has also meant that international business law is informally gravitating to American conceptions. A crucial area of contest will be the World Trade Organization, where, it may be argued (cf. Cass, 2001), a kind of "constitutionalization" of international trade is taking place in the Appellate Body of the WTO. Here the EU tends to stand up for its rights even against the USA, and too much is at stake economically in a world order of trade for the US to shrink away lightly from a global jurisdiction. The outcome of the 2002 conflict over US steel protection was therefore very important.

In the current world, however, the trans–nationality of European law mainly manifests itself regionally, as actual regional entanglement, and as a global source of inspiration for other regional and for world–wide arrangements intertwining national and trans–national concerns and rules. Europe is the world's highest–density area of trans–national entanglements, and the lodestar of global entanglement. In order to capture this position of Europe, some more attention should be paid to the interaction of law and trade in the making of Europe.

## The Normative Area and the Common Market

In 1950 the Council of Europe adopted the first international, legally binding convention on human rights, enforced by a Commission, a Committee of Ministers with a majority voting system, and a Court. It was concerned with civil and political rights only, and it took more than a decade for its supra–nationality to be fully recognized by all Member States, but it did take effect. In 1961 an extensive European Social Charter was adopted, formulated as obligations accepted by the Member States, with a supra–national monitoring and complaint system, in the last instance issuing recommendations of the Ministerial Committee with two thirds majority (Steiner ad Alston, 1996: ch.10.B; Bundeszentrale, 1999:382ff).

Post–war Western Europe was, then, a normative area before it became a Common Market, the goal of the Rome Treaty of 1957, and a Single Market, the achievement of 1992. It is noteworthy that of the various European integration projects after World War II, it was the one concerning trade which was the most successful and far–reaching. On the world arena, it is also first of all in trading contexts that EU actually operates as one body, in the WTO for example. But it is also to be noticed, that law and legal regulation has played a crucial part in this economic unification.

The European judiciary, the European Court of Justice with support from the national judiciaries of the EEC/EU Member States, has constituted a major supra–national force in the construction of a new Europe. In a couple of early landmark decisions (Van Gend & Loos—1963[1],

Flaminio Costa v. ENEL—1964[2], *Internationale Handelsgesellschaft*—1970[3]) the Court established the principles of *direct effect* of Community law, and of its *supremacy* over national law, including, within its area of jurisdiction, over national constitutional law. In the latter case the Court stated that "the validity of a Community measure ...cannot be affected by allegations that it runs counter to ... fundamental rights as formulated by the constitution of that state ..." (Wouters, 2000:46–7; cf. Bengoetxea et al., 2001).

In more personal statements, leading European judges called on these judicial rulings to "take Community law out of the hands of the politicians and bureaucrats and give it to the people" (Federico Mancini, here quoted from Schepel and Blankenburg, 2001:11). Furthermore, there soon developed the practice that national courts petitioned the European Court on how the founding Treaty and subsequent European legislation should be interpreted.

The European Court has established its powers gradually and cautiously (Schepel and Blankenburg, 2001), as well as with impressive trans–national firmness, effectiveness and legitimacy. The latter has recently been partly contested in some cases, true, but in a world of states, the regional entanglement of European and national law and jurisdiction, the possibility for individuals and organizations to bring their state governments to an international court in a broad range of civic cases is a historical change of national sovereignty not to be found anywhere else in the world, although in looser forms it inspires attempts at regional integration on all the other continents.

## Tradition into Modernity: Hugo Grotius

Trade and law, together with the Christian religion, have long been characteristic features of Europe. The Mediterranean, with its Black Sea extension, was for a millennium at the centre of leading city republics, from Athens to Venice and Genoa, for which *navigare necesse erat*, as well as of the continent's most powerful empire. Navigable rivers, the Rhine above all, also made trade prosper. Trade and salvationist religion pushed Europe onto the oceans, when the traditional Eastern trade routes were cut off by the rise of Islam.

Law was, of course, not unique to Europe and nor was trade, but European law was distinctive in its elaboration and complexity. A specific *corpus* of Roman law was a central cultural heritage, differentiated and elaborated into Canonical Church law and secular law (cf. Berman, 1983). Out of trans–political long–distance trade and out of the fragmentation of secular power and secular law, there developed in Medieval Europe a particular trans–political normativity, a *lex mercatoria* among traders, and a normativity among Christian princes.

The most eloquent political expression of this legal complexity was the "Holy Roman Empire of the German Nation", which survived the Peace of Westphalia, although this was usually supposed to have dissolved it into a system of sovereign states. Indeed today's EU has a good deal of the complexity of the old Empire, a certain idea of unity, which is distributed among a number of institutions and actors, an actual set of quasi–sovereign member states, and held together by a symbolic head— then the Emperor, now the Commission—and by a supra–state judiciary, then the *Reichskammergericht* (the Cameral Tribunal) and the *Reichshofrat* (the Aulic Council), while lacking a proper administration, and having only limited or conditional military means. (cf. Gagliardo, 1980: Part I; Duchardt, 1990)

In early European modernity, trade and law were brought together by the Dutch 17$^{th}$ century lawyer, politician, diplomat, and erudite intellectual Hugo Grotius, both in his person and in his oeuvre. In legal history, Grotius is perhaps primarily known as the founder of international law, but he was also a major theoretician of natural law. In a current global perspective Grotius acquires a particular significance as a social theorist starting from a world of peoples, rather than from individuals either within or on the threshold of a state–bound society. This inter–state theory of society and politics constituted a background to Hobbes' political theory (cf. Haakonsen, 1996:1.3–1.4; Tuck, 1999:ch.3)

His major legal works dealt with "*Freedom of the Seas*" (*Mare Liberum*, Grotius 1609/1839/1983) and with "*The Rights of War and Peace*" (*De iure belli ac pacis*, 1625/1925), topics of outstanding importance in an era of colonialist rivalry and incessant wars. The former tract had been commissioned by the Dutch East India Company, as a legal defence of its challenge of the Portuguese claim to a monopoly in trading with the Moluccas. As his clients' lawyer, Grotius was later to provide eloquent arguments also for restrictions on free access to the sea, as the EEC had to do in its fishing negotiations with Britain, Denmark, and Norway (Ehlermann, 1985).

Grotius put an ancient European idea of humanity as a community in political and national division—further developed by his somewhat older contemporary the Spanish Jesuit jurist Francis Suárez, who said that "mankind, though divided into numerous nations and states, constitutes a political and moral unity bound by charity and compassion" (quoted from Pinto, 1985:48)—onto a less idealistic, more hard-boiled footing. Mankind has a basic social impulse, an *appetitus societatis*, as Grotius put it, from which follows by the "dictate of right reason" certain minimalist rules of social coexistence. Second to this natural law, according to Grotius, there also develops a "law of peoples" (*ius gentium*), out of the interdependence of all states, even the most powerful, and by tacit or explicit consent (Grotius, 1625/1925/1985: 233ff).

The other important point about Grotius in this context is how he moves back and forth between relations among states and relations among individuals or, as we would anachronistically put it today, NGOs. This capacity originated in the close intertwining of private business and public politics in the Republic of the United Provinces, where Grotius started out as a lawyer of the East India Company, became destined for the nearest equivalent of a Premiership, from which he was then toppled in 1618. Nowhere is this better expressed than in his work on *"The Rights of War and Peace" (De iure belli ac pacis)*, in which a just war to protect rights that have been violated may be a *bellum privatum*, a private war, as well as a public, state one.

The importance of this trans-polity normativity is highlighted by its serving as a starting-point for early modern theorizing about individuals and individual rights in a state-bound society. In the beginning there were states (or princes), the relations between them, and the norms that should govern their relations. Then came the individuals and the social contract. The moral universalism of the Enlightenment *philosophes* included an awareness of the political divisions, also of "polite" society.

The long historical experience of being part of an inter-state system as well as of a normative area predisposes contemporary Europe to a trans-national normativity, rather than to the typical US duality of moral universalism and political unilateralism.

However, if I am more or less right so far, why has there been so little said and written in contemporary public discourse about the Europe of traders and lawyers? Let us first make a little theoretical excursion.

## Position, Role, and Identity

Above we have been dealing primarily with the position of Europe in the world. That is, with something objective, not necessarily intended or even fully noticed, following from resources and actions. "Position" in this sense may be distinguished from two related concepts, "role" and "identity".

"Role" is usually taken in sociology as normatively expected behaviour, as scripted action. On the whole this concept has served social science well. However, there is also a more subjective conception of role that stresses aspiration and performance rather than norms. A role, then, may be taken as the social part you want to play. It is this latter definition that seems to me most fruitful in dealing with supposedly sovereign actors, like states.

Your identity, thirdly, is your conception of your self, of who and what you are, the self that has a position, good or bad, just or unjust, and who wants to play a particular role in the world.

The positions of trader and lawyer do not seem to figure very prominently in the roles that European leaders strive for on the world stage, particularly not the most conspicuous global position of a trading centre. Nor do we find much of trade and law in formulations of European identity, which have tended to concentrate on cultural legacy, on ethnicity (in Nazi Europeanism), and on the pluralistic state system (cf. Delanty, 1995; Pocock, 1997). In the Laeken Declaration of December 2001 on *the Future of the European Union*, Europe was characteristically defined as "the continent of humane values" (EU, 2001:20), a formula which manages to be simultaneously self–congratulatory and vacuous.

The ex–Great Powers of Europe are longing for a role for Europe as a big power polity capable of military interventions and muscular diplomacy, and see the question of European identity in that perspective. In this view, a European identity is to be shaped by global power play. In the language of the 1992 *Treaty on the European Union*, the Member States have "resolved to implement a common foreign and security policy including the eventual framing of a common defence policy ... thereby reinforcing the European identity..." (Council of the European Communities, 1992:4)

## Social Embeddedness of Trade and Democratic Trans–Nationality of Law

However, there is also a more complex set of reasons for the contemporary European discretion on trade and law than the character of the current political class. Today's Europe is not a re–enactment of its traditions. Trade and law in Europe have both been transformed.

When looked at from a global vantage point, the unique position which trade and law occupy in Western Europe today does not mean that European society is composed to any particularly high extent of sales people and lawyers.

The specific characteristics of European trade are its inter–national character—the high proportion of what is traditionally called foreign trade—and its social embeddedness. The thinkers of the Scottish Enlightenment, Adam Smith, John Millar and others, saw the emerging post–agrarian society as a "commercial society". In fact, post–agrarian Europe became an industrial society, and the only industrial society in world history, in the sense of the predominance of industry among non–agricultural employment. This was something which never happened in USA nor in Japan, and something which will not happen in Brazil, China, or India. European industrial society was, for several reasons, a uniquely class–conscious and class–organized society. (See further Therborn, 1995.)

Through a welter of class struggles, this resulted in a socio–economic combination which should surprise conventional economic theory, *the successful exporter with generous social rights*. Public social expenditure is much higher in the EU than in USA and Japan, in the late 1990s, standing at 28, 16, and 14 per cent of GDP respectively (Eurostat, 2001:111; ILO, 2000: table 14). Among the OECD countries there is a significant positive correlation between world market export dependency on one hand, and social expenditure on the other which in the early 1990s had a coefficient of 0.34 (Therborn, 1999:249)

Throughout the EEC/EC/EU, the embeddedness of the Common Market, and more generally of free trade, is embodied, above all, in agricultural policy. About half of the European integration budget is devoted to preserving the way of life of European farmers.

In brief, the social role, and probably the identity, of the European is that of a citizen of the welfare state, not of a salesman.

The courts never had an importance in modern European polities comparable to what they had and still have in the US. The *Rechtsstaat*, a state of law, very much part of the European conception of a modern state, developed in pre–democratic Europe. The state of popular striving centred on democracy, not on law, on the suffrage and on executive accountability to parliament. Only in the post–war Federal Republic of Germany did a court, the Constitutional Court, acquire political prominence that was originally inspired by the US.

The location of law in Europe is not summed up in the role of lawyer or judge. Rather, it is law as part of a democratic, trans–national normativity, "democratic", then, in a popular, republican sense, with connotations of popular will and popular needs, more than of individual freedoms, and individual litigation. This is a conception deriving from the principled struggles in Europe for and against democracy (Therborn, 1992). Trans–national, or less anachronistically, trans–polity normative is an old tradition of Europe, which Hugo Grotius built upon. The Middle Ages combined a fragmented, but complicatedly interlinked set of polities with a common normative pattern, Christian religion, Roman law, and Canonical law. It was shunted aside in the wars for and against the French Revolution, and in the World Wars, but then re–emerged in a clearer light.

## The Relevance and the Limitations of Europe

Despite their ancient and special origin, the mutated European traditions of socially embedded trade and democratic trans–national normativity do respond, it may be argued, to widespread needs and demands of the world today. Openness to technological innovations and productivity challenges, while safeguarding unique socio–cultural and environmental milieus, and, further, worldwide norms of human rights, respecting different popular manifestations, would both constitute major contributions to a decent global society.

The politicians of the once big powers of Europe do not see it that way. In Paris and London, no less than in Berlin and Rome, they are still opting for the "Heroes" against the "Traders", as the nationalist great German economic historian Werner Sombart put it in 1915 (Sombart, 1915). Opening the Convention on the Future of Europe recently, French ex–President Giscard d'Estaing expressed in polished form the aspiration of leaders of ex–big states: "If we succeed, ... Europe's role will be changed ... It will be respected and listened to, not only as the economic power it already is, but as a political power which will talk on equal terms to the greatest power on our planet... (*Financial Times* 1.3.02, p.2)

An outside observer should add three things to such a tirade, which is quite legitimate in itself. First, it is part of a debilitating schizophrenia of European politicians, at the same time clearly resentful of their subordination to the Americans, and sycophantically servile: "The Americans are absolutely right...", Tony Blair never tires of repeating, while Gerhard Schroeder proclaims an "unconditional solidarity" with USA. Secondly, the European politicians' yearning to play level with the Pentagon is naïve. The latter absorbs more than a third of all military expenditure of the world, and the recent budgeted *increase* of US military expenditure is more than double the *total* military expenditure of Germany. (Kennedy, 2002 :146; Sommer, 2002:4). Thirdly, by ignoring their own actual position and by assuming a misplaced or anachronistic identity, European politicians are failing their most important global role. To British, French, and German politicians, in particular, it is understandably difficult to accept a role of Europe as the world's Scandinavia—a decent place with a wide radius of institutional and policy inspiration, but without power aspirations and without power. However, by identifying themselves with USA and with world politics as big power politics, European fail to notice or appreciate the actual position of Europe in the world, and fail to adopt a socio–political role adequate to defend Europe's specific, positive contributions to the world.

There is a basis, this chapter has argued, in Europe's centrality in current global economic flows and in its long and refreshed experience of trans–national normativity, for a European role as a "power seeking to set globalization within a moral framework", as the *Laeken Declaration* put it. To what extent that basis, which is economic, normative and institutional, rather than political and military, will actually be used, is an open question.

# Notes

1. Court of Justice of the European Communities (CJEC), "Judgment of 5 February 1963, N. V. Algemene Transport—en Expeditie Onderneming van Gend & Loos/Nederlandse administratie der belastingen (Netherlands

Inland Revenue Administration), Case 26/62", in *Reports of Cases before the Court.* 1963, p. 1.

2. Court of Justice of the European Communities (CJEC), "Judgment of 16 July 1964, Flaminio Costa v ENEL, Case 6/64", in *Reports of Cases before the Court.* 1964, p. 585.

3. Court of Justice of the European Communities (CJEC), "Judgment of 17 December 1970, Internationale Handelsgesellschaft mbH v Einfuhr—und Vorratstelle für Getreide und Futtermittel, Case 11/70", in *Reports of Cases before the Court.* 1970, p. 1125.

# References

Bengoetxea, J., MacCormick, N., Moral Soriano, L. "Integration and Integrity in the Legal Reasoning of the European Court of Justice". In: G. De Burca and J.H.H. Weiler (eds.), *The European Court of Justice.* Oxford: Oxford University Press, 2001, pp. 43–85.

Berman, H. *Law and Revolution. The Formation of the Western Legal Tradition.* Cambridge Mass.: Harvard University Press, 1983.

Bundeszentrale für politische Bildung. *Menschenrechte. Dokumente und Deklarationen.* Bonn: Bundeszentrale für politische Bildung, 1999.

Casanova, P. *La République mondiale des lettres.* Paris: Seuil, 1999.

Cass, D. "The 'Constitutionalization' of International Trade Law: Judicial Norm–Generation as the Engine of Constitutional Development in International Trade", *European Journal of International Law* 2001/12 (1), pp. 39–76.

Council of the European Communities. *Treaty on the European Union.* Brussels–Luxembourg: European Union,1992.

Davies, N. *Europe. A History.* Oxford: Oxford University Press, 1996.

Delanty, G. *Inventing Europe.* Basingstoke: Macmillan, 1995.

Detrick, S. (ed.) *The United Nations Convention on the Rights of the Child. A Guide to the "Travaux Préparatoires".* Dordrecht/Boston/London: Martinus Nijhoff, 1992.

Duchhardt, H. *Altes Reich und europäische Staatenwelt 1648–1806.* München: R. Oldenbourg, 1990.

Ehlermann, C.D. "Grotius and the European Community's Common Fisheries Policy". In: *International Law and the Grotian Heritage*, The Hague T.M.C. Asser Instituut, 1985, pp. 294–97.

EU. *Laeken Declaration on the Future of the European Union*, Annex 1 to the Presidency Conclusions, Laeken, 14 and 5 December 2001, Brussels, SN 300/1/01 Rev 1, 2001.

Eurostat. *The Social Situation in the European Union.* Luxemburg: Eurostat, 2001.

Ferro, F. *Colonization A Global History.* London: Routledge, 1994/1997.

Gagliardo, J. *Reich and Nation. The Holy Roman Empire as Idea and Reality, 1763–1806.* Bloomington and London: Indiana University Press, 1980.

Glendon, M. A. *A Word Made New.* New York: Random House, 2001.
Grotius, H. "Mare Liberum" (transl. F. van Deman Magoffin 1916). In: L.E. van Holk and C.G. Roelofsen (eds.) *Grotius Reader.* The Hague: T.M.C. Asser Instituut, (1609) 1983, pp. 59 –93.
Grotius, H. "De iure belli ac pacis" (Latin ed.1839, English translation: F Kelsey, 1925), bilingual extracts, in: L.E. van Holk and C.G. Roelofsen (eds.) *Grotius Reader.* The Hague: T.M.C. Asser Instituut (1625) 1983, pp. 223–38.
Haakonssen, K. *Natural Law and Moral Philosophy.* Cambridge: Cambridge University Press, 1996.
ILO *World Labour Report.* Geneva: ILO, 2000.
Kennedy, D. "Der 500–Pfund–Gorilla". In: *Der Spiegel* Nr 6 146–49, 2002.
Maddison, A. *Monitoring the World Economy 1820–1992.* Paris, OECD, 1995.
Mommsen, W., and De Moor, J.A. (eds.) *European Expansion and Law.* Oxford/New: York Berg,1992.
OECD. *Economic Outlook,* Paris, 2000.
O'Rourke, K. and Williamson, J. *Globalization and History.* Cambridge, Mass.: MIT Press, 1999.
Pinto, M.C.W. "The New Law of the Sea and the Grotian Heritage". In: *International Law and the Grotian Heritage.* The Hague T.M.C. Asser Instituut, 1985, pp. 54–93.
Pocock, J.G.A. "What Do We Mean by Europe?" In: *The Wilson Quarterly,* Winter 1997, pp. 1–20.
Schepel, H. and Blankenburg, E. "Mobilizing the European Court of Justice". In: G. De Burca and J.H.H. Weiler (eds.), *The European Court of Justice.* Oxford: Oxford University Press, 2001, pp. 9–42.
Sombart, W. *Händler und Helden.* München/Leipzig: Duncker & Humblot, 1915.
Sommer, T. "Die Achse der Betonköpfe". In: *Die Zeit,* 28.2: 4, 2002.
Spence, J. *The Quest for Modern China.* New York/London: Norton, 1990.
Steiner, H., and Alston, Ph. (eds.), *International Human Rights in Context.* Oxford: Clarendon Press, 1996.
Therborn, G. "The Right to Vote and the Four World Routes to/through Modernity". In: R. Torstendahl (ed.), *State Theory and State History.* London: Sage, 1992.
Therborn, G. *European Modernity and Beyond. The Trajectory of European Societies,* 1945–2000. London: Sage, 1995.
Therborn, G. "The Global Future of the European Welfare State". In: G. Therborn (ed.) *Globalizations and Modernities. Experiences and Perspectives of Europe and Latin America.* Stockholm FRN, 1999, pp. 242–62.
Tuck, R. *The Rights of War and Peace. Political Thought and International Order from Grotius to Kant.* Oxford: Clarendon Press, 1999.
UNCTAD. *World Investment Report.* Geneva: UNCTAD, 2001.
Untermeyer, L. *The Albatross Book of Living Verse.* London: Collins.

Wang, T. "China and International Law. A Historical Perspective". In: *International Law and the Grotian Heritage*. The Hague T.M.C. Asser Instituut, 1985, pp. 260–54.

Woodruff, W. "The Emergence of An International Economy". In: C.Cipolla (ed.) *The Fontana Economic History of Europe*. Vol. 4:2, London: Fontana/Collins, 1973, pp. 656–737.

Wouters. J. "National Consciousness and the European Union". In: *Legal Issues of European Integration*, 27(1): 2000, pp. 25–74.

World Trade Organization. *Annual Report 2000*. Geneva: WTO, 2001.

Zacchia, C. "International Trade and Capital Movements 1920–1970". In: C. Cipolla (ed.) *The Fontana Economic History of Europe*. Vol. 5:2, London: Collins/Fontana 1976, pp. 509–602.

• LILIANA VOICU •

# Is a "Learning Society" a Creadible Concept in Central and Eastern European Countries?
# A literature review

## Introduction

**Context of the Analysis and Countries Involved**

*The learning society* is a concept which has gained increasing importance over the last decade, when scholars or administrators discuss the way forward for society. *Learning* in its lifelong dimension seems to be the only means to cope with the high speed of change promoted by globalisation and technological innovation and to attain economic success (Borras and Lundvall 1999, Lundvall 2001). Even if such a view aroused considerable criticism, it led to the Lisbon summit and the establishment of a concrete goal for 2010 to develop the European Union into a *knowledge–based economy*. Ever since, concrete measures to build a learning society have been designed, implemented, monitored and assessed both at the level of the European Union and among its Member States.

And yet the concept is far from being clear and generally accepted. There are controversial aspects to both theoretical reasoning and empirical evidence, leading to lively debate. The debates rely on different understandings of learning, knowledge and education in different communities, which are culturally embedded and historically shaped, meaning that the semantic behind the notion varies widely. This becomes particularly interesting in the Central and Eastern European countries (CEECs), which, historically speaking, have only recently abandoned a very coherent discourse in the analysis of the society, i.e., Marxism. Eight countries from the area joined the EU in 2004 and two others should follow in January 2007. The process of integration to the EU involves adoption of the *acquis communautaire* and commitment to the common goal agreed in Lisbon in 2000.

This gives rise to a set of questions: is there a living concept of a learning society in these countries? How far is it affected by the process of European integration? What are the differences in the national discourses between countries with such widely differing economic development, social cohesion, historical and cultural backgrounds? What are the major controversies and debates?
In order to answer these questions literature reviews were especially prepared in all the CEECs that have already joined EU or will join soon: Bulgaria, Czech Republic[1], Estonia, Hungary, Latvia, Lithuania, Poland, Romania, Slovakia[1] and Slovenia. In order to better assess the impact of EU integration on the learning society discourse a similar analysis was also done for the Russian Federation[2]. This paper relies on the statements and findings of the national reviews (Balica and Voicu 2004, Benke 2004, Kalous 2003, Kaminskienė et al. 2003, Koke 2003, Loogma et al. 2003, Mirčeva and Beltram 2003, Muraveva 2004, Ślęzak 2003, Tsakova 2004)[3].

## The Arrival of a New Society: Labels and Concepts

The concept of a *learning society* is relatively new. It arose from the wording used by overall analyses of the evolution of society together with other comprehensive notions, especially the *knowledge* (or *knowledge–based*) *society* and *information society*, which were, in their turn, preceded by the "post" fashion: *post–industrial society*, *post–capitalist society*, *post–modern society* etc. In the analysis here, as well as in the ten national reviews, the difference between these terms was ignored, even if sometimes, for reasons of accuracy, they are used as such, either because they were present in the background statements, or because they match the analytical context. However, it is first necessary to look at their specific characteristics.

Soon after the Second World War, human existence seemed to enter new paths of evolution and it became more and more evident that fundamental features of society were changing and a new structure was emerging. The principle behind this perception is the theory of modernisation, "the most influential instrument of the analysis of the development of contemporary societies" (Kalous 2003, 1). The theory of modernisation states that human society has evolved from incoherent, simple and undifferentiated structures to coherent, complex and differentiated ones. The power of the idea is perfectly illustrated by the laconic definition in a sociology dictionary: "modernisation—synonym of development" (Zamfir and Vlăsceanu 1993, 368). It dates back to the beginnings of sociology, in the analysis of the structural modifications provoked by the industrial revolution: "technological progress, changes in the employment structure, urbanisation, increase in anonymous social relations, individualisation of social life, secularisation, increase in the number of large organisations, bureaucratic system of rational management... weakening of the traditional authoritative systems and, last but not least, the existence of national states" (Kalous 2003, 1). Ironically taken from "an injury addressed by patristic humanists to medieval scholastics that developed the new philosophy and logics" (McLuhan 1975/1962$^4$, 140) the word "modern" designate in this discourse a higher stage of historical development, which was called "industrial" by Auguste Comte or "capitalist" by Marx.

After the Second World War, a new wave of technological innovations again disturbed the pace of life in society, influencing economic growth, market evolution, individual welfare, social distribution, and the advance of civilization. The only other period of change that is comparable with this in both depth and breadth was the industrial revolution, and the process is recognised in the liberal world as a *second modernisation* (Bell 1976/1973), although some less enthusiastic analysts consider that we are only observing a *self–reflective radicalisation of modernity* (Giddens 1990). The limits of the former concepts become evident and a need for a new comprehensive notion is felt. Some focus on the chronological element, and the new stage of the society is simply defined in a "post"–position: "post–industrial" (Bell), "post–capitalist" (Drucker), "post–modern" (Baudrillard, Lyotard). Others try to use a logical order, by identifying the central feature of the new society. At the beginning, the language used is placed in a broad variety of semantics: McLuhan speaks about a very technical "marconian galaxy" (1962) and a very human "global village" (1969), Toffler about a threatening "future shock" (1970) and a very abstract "third wave" (1981), Marxists about "the scientific–technical revolution". In the 1980s and even more so in the 1990s, terminology revolves around the word "society" in different combinations: "open society" (Popper), "network society" (Castells), "entrepreneurial society" (Drucker), "risk society" (Beck), and the list goes on. In this diversity of labels, little by little, one term seems to be taking over: "information society", because the central feature in the new society is the impact of innovation and information is the strategic resource that feeds innovation. Adaptation to the changes in the market is crucial in the new economy and this is possible only by having/using the appropriate information. With the on–going impact of the intensive and extensive use of information and communication technologies, creating, processing and distributing information becomes an industry in itself. However, criticism claims that "information" is not sufficiently exact, as it relies on a mechanical image of the world and is overly neutral in itself: information needs a semantic in order to be meaningful. For this reasons "knowledge society" is also used, especially in its more humanistic form of the "knowledge based society". Knowledge is processed information, it places human potential in the central position and it is not related to an impersonal technology. The partisans of the modernisation theory consider that "the concept of modernisation as a primarily technical and economic development has thus been complemented with the concept of the "social modernisation". According to Machonin (2000)… this implies a radical shift in the focus of the modernisation theory, as a result of which [modernisation] is interpreted as a complex process whose individual components are mutually conditioned" (Kalous 2003, 2). When the process itself becomes the emphasis of the reflection, we arrive at the "learning society", the most recent term in this line, which is becoming more and more used by analysts and in policy papers. The new label implicitly stresses the high dynamic of the society and explicitly the solution to cope with this dynamic: learning. Learning encompasses the creation of new knowledge, the effective use of this, and adaptation to the changes that this new knowledge brings. Learning is a specifically human way of adapting to reality: understanding its nature, reacting accordingly by appropriate modification of behaviour or of reality itself, then assessing whether the modifications are appropriate and re-adjusting them in a continuous cycle. This is valid at all levels of society—individual, group, company, community, nation state or international—as any human entity is able to learn. The common factor in these equations remains the individual, addressed by the most respectful formula that can be imagined—*the learning citizen,* which integrates the resource, the instrument and the reason for the progress of the society.

We do not want to imply a certain inner hierarchy among the terms and concepts mentioned above or other similar ones that did not enter our brief list. Nor are these synonyms, as the differences are important enough to encourage authors to use them in parallel up to the present. A certain specialisation can be observed, up to a certain level: in debates about globalisation, especially when new technologies are in discussion, analysts tend to prefer "information society", while discussion of the economy tends to feature "knowledge based economy" (or society). "Learning society" itself is used when education/training/HRD is the focus of the analysis. This is valid at the international level as well as for the territory covered by our analysis, CEECs being quite up to date with these debates, as most of the ten national literature reviews reveal. Almost all highlight limited use of the term "learning society" as such, with the terms "information (or "IT") society" and "knowledge (based) society", or sometimes "post-industrial society" being much more frequently used, although with a similar meaning: "Different terms are being used for the same phenomenon from *information society*, through *global capitalism, post-industrial age,* to *knowledge-based economy* and *organized capitalism...*" (Benke 2004, 3). It is interesting to notice that a specific Marxist term which marked the participation of communist countries in the international discourse on the new age—"scientific-technical revolution"—is almost absent. The term cited by many well known modern authors (the future analysts Naisbitt and Toffler among others) does not in fact appear in the analysis in any of the national reviews, except the Romanian paper (Balica and Voicu 2004, 4–5) and a brief mention in a terminology list in the Polish review (Ślęzak 2003, 2). There may be various reasons for this: either the semantic was considered to vary too greatly in relation to the learning society; or due to the novelty of the learning society concept itself, authors did not look so far in the past; or simply that the period of denial has not come to an end in these countries, the injuries caused by communism are too fresh and the time of healing has not arrived yet. To take one instance, the Lithuanian review mentions a specific conceptual approach: "the restitution of the good experience from the past", but considers that "in the case of Lithuania the source of such restitutions is the period of the first Lithuanian Republic of the 1918–1940" (Kaminskienė et al. 2003, 6).

In most cases there is no clear preference about the use of the different formulae. In some cases combinations are mentioned or a certain sector–specific term: "post–industrial society based on knowledge…" (Mirčeva and Beltram 2003, 10); "the term *information society* was often used in debates [related to new technologies], being accompanied almost always by the synonym of *knowledge society*: *information society–knowledge society*" (Balica and Voicu 2004, 5); "the concept of the *information/post–industrial society* is generally accepted in Estonia" (Loogma et al. 2004, 11); "the terms more widespread in the current literature in Russia are *knowledge–based society* and *information society*. These terms are used by economists, politicians and sociologists and only very scarcely by educators (mostly in the context of universities), while the notion of a *learning society* can more typically be observed in the rhetoric of educators" (Muraveva 2004, 17). In a few cases, the concepts are given different meanings, sometimes very different. "Lithuanian scientists give preference to the concept of a knowledge society. They stress that the concept of "information society" is narrower and distinguishes the particular role of IT in all spheres of human life" (Kaminskienė et al. 2003, 1); on the contrary, in Hungary, "since information technology development represents a dominant role in the change of the technologies nowadays, therefore the society of the future is called most often, having no real rival as a term, as the *information society*" (Benke 2004, 1).

There is, however, one peculiarity. In a few cases, the notion *learning* is replaced by derivations from *education*: "educated society" (Koke 2003, 1), "educational society" (Balica and Voicu 2004, 1). It may be that the new wording is present more as a sectoral concept, used by education specialists. Nevertheless, it may indicate that the focus is more often on the system than on the individual, as a continuation of the Marxist–type of analysis, at macrostructure level. At the same time, it may be an implicit reflection of the power of the traditional educational model, where the individual remains fundamentally the object, the "raw material" of educational activity, which is often seen in industrial terms as well: a determined quantity of raw material (students) enters the factory (school) and a similar quantity of finite products (educated people) are obtained by means of quasi–automatic mechanisms, using tested tools (such as manuals and standardised educational material), the whole process being fully controlled by engineers (teachers), who hold the *knowledge* and transmit it to pupils in such an efficient way that the latter are supposed only to swallow it and adjust their inner structures to absorb as much of this wisdom as possible... Quite apart from this ironical image, it should be considered that the concept of the learning society is much more evident in policy papers, as we will see, and the system centred notions are natural in strategic planning language.

This motley linguistic diversity can lead us to the early assumption that the learning society as such is not a very strong concept in CEECs. One reason for this could be the general novelty of the term, which is not much used at the international level either. Another reason could be the complex situation in these countries, the fundamental changes that their analysts had to face in the last 15 years being extremely challenging. It is not easy to reflect on the defining features of the society when everything is changing around. Nor should we forget how short a time it is since the Marxist ideology was dominant and how very despotic this was in some cases—Romania was almost completely isolated from the scientific world in the West in the 1980s. This can however have the reverse effect, the will to demonstrate participation in a worldwide discourse influencing the use of wording without any consistent reflection to back this up: "the term *learning society* is mentioned mostly for the sake of fashion, and not in the context of an in–depth analysis..." (Muraveva 2004, 17). This is in fact another way of being "up–to–date", fashion being itself a phenomenon of modernism... Purely linguistic reasons also matter: "learning society" and other related terms are imported from "Euro–English" and it is questionable whether their meaning coincides with that given elsewhere in Europe and whether they are meaningful at all—indeed in any national language.

What it is important to take from this terminology overview however is the fact that the language of analysts in CEECs does not differ fundamentally from the international one. Our working hypothesis sees the learning society as an evolving concept, taking the common aspects behind the diversity of formulae as a background and trying to reveal the concrete flesh of the notional construct. It is not the difference between learning society as a phrase and others such as the "post–industrial age", "information era", "knowledge based economy" (or others) that counts, but how the new structure is apprehended, what are the consequences for the individual citizen and if it helps us to understand how society should be organized for a better life. For this, "learning society" is linguistically more appropriate, being centred on evolution and on human potential: "A learning society is a society which has, in all features, properties and dimensions of its operation, installed learning as a generating power of development (Jelenc, 1999). The initiative for learning comes from an individual implementing his own learning projects as well as from the society (community, city, organization, group…) that is organised so as to make it possible to learn and acquire knowledge, by its basic operation. It is nothing but a promotion of learning as a way of life" (Mirčeva and Beltram 2003, 2).

## Reasoning of the Learning Society

As described above, the evolution of the new concept of the society was far from linear and smooth. The reconstruction process after the damages of the Second World War, together with the transfer of know–how from military industries to civil ones led to rapid development and evidence of new features of the society appeared first in USA, then in other countries of the Western world. Application of innovation stimulated labour productivity, which reached previously unimagined levels and freed up increasing amounts of human energy that could be diverted to specialised and more creative work. Evolving technologies allowed the diversification of production and soon the focus changed from quantity to quality, with the human factor becoming the most important element for economic success. The new organisation of work shifted relationships from vertical to horizontal flows. Widening international trade (and competition) led to the spread of innovations and to an awareness of the interconnected global community. The development of the mass media transformed news into an industry and allowed sophisticated influences to cross borders between different sets of values, based on comparisons between lifestyles. International organisations offered the background for and induced the habit of transnational debates on issues affecting practically everybody on the planet: the impact of globalisation, environmental issues, the idea of sustainable development. No territory could remain outside this process, and the CEECs were no exception: the early arrival of related concepts is noted in some of the national reviews and translations from international authors of the field and debates in specific domains are flagged up (Loogma et al. 2004, 12, Benke 2004, 6, Ślęzak 2003, 1, Balica and Voicu 2004, 4, Muraveva 2004, 18).

Having said that, it is important to note that the participation of CEECs in the international discourse could not be extensive. This was firstly for very practical reasons as the cold war brought the Iron Curtain, limiting contacts between the two political blocks. Secondly, the cold war affected cultural changes by introducing ideology filters for social and political concepts, which were more emotionally than logically driven. Thirdly, the widespread use of the English language allowed a much broader debate in the Western world, fed by massive flows of ideas, streamed to a more coherent discourse than was possible in the CEECs, where it was fragmented into national currents by the use of very different languages. And last, but not least, the economic progress in these countries, with its very different pace and state of the art, was unlikely to assure (if not for the most successful ones) the critical factual element to drive the theoretical reflection on societal change. For these reasons, most of the authors of the literature reviews highlight the lack of consistency in the concept of a learning society, especially in the scientific field—just one example: "The international scientific discussion is present and reflected in work of the Polish scholars… but in some points diffused via imitation only" (Ślęzak 2003, 1).

These general assumptions must be adjusted for two specific domains: ICT and education. ICT was a domain where the impact of innovation was the strongest and had a geometrical progression. The extension of ICT applications modified production in many branches of the economy and developed new human needs, the evolution of personal computers changed the organisation of work and democratised social relationships in many aspects, spread of Internet made geographical distances obsolete and brought a new dimension in our life: that of "virtual space". A new economy emerged and McLuhan's *global village* became very concrete in this new dimension. The terms "information society" and "knowledge based economy" are closely linked with the explosive expansion of ICT use, and analysts sometimes understand the new society only as an IT society. One good example is Umberto Eco's social classification of "the new information society, which is based on the access to and the use of information and ICT (1995):

- the lowest class—IT illiterate, will passively absorb information via the media;
- the middle class—users of computer networks, incapable of programming;

- the upper class—people eligible for full communication with computers and using the full extent of possibilities they offer (that is programmers)" (Ślęzak 2003, 10).

Even if we do not share this view, which reduces the social complexity to a technical aspect that cannot be but partial, it remains, however, an important thread in the international discourse. CEECs were also touched by ICT development, even if at a much slower pace before 1990, that was, at the same time, very different between the countries involved. They were not however exempted and therefore, debates on the social impact of innovation came naturally in this domain, and the influence of the international discourse, implicit or explicit, could not be avoided: IT specialists were an intellectual elite, early linked up to the world wide web and English, the language of the main software, was largely used by this group. "Information society" and "knowledge–based economy" (with their variants) were familiar terms in these debates: "a defined scientific interest in the domain of the new information technology was noticeable in the 1970s and 1980s. Even if new information technologies did not represent an extended presence in the Romanian society of the time, the scientific community of engineers and researchers in informatics and automation… launched a series of debates on the impact of the new technologies in the design of the society of the future. The term *information society* was often used in these debates, being accompanied almost always by the synonym of *knowledge society*" (Balica and Voicu 2004, 5). Such debates ensured the background for the latest evolutions, which could not have been possible on an empty ground—the Hungarian review speaks about social innovation islands dating from the early 1960s. These influences became stronger after 1990, with the end of the cold war and the entrance of these countries in the free world, but also with the expansion of the PCs that speeded and deepened the whole phenomenon at the planetary scale. Moreover, the rhythm of innovation in this field and, especially, its subsequent application for mass consumption became faster and faster, making adaptation to a changing environment a day–to–day need. That brought learning to the centre of the debate, a move that advantaged the CEECs because this brought to the general debates a sectoral discourse that was much more familiar to them: the educational.

The first advantage in this rationale is that education and culture traditionally have a high prestige in all CEECs. This prestige, sometimes dating back for centuries, was enhanced during the communist period, as the development of education was an explicit objective of communist policies, from the very beginning, in Lenin's Russia. Educational systems that were efficient both in terms of the range of population covered and of the depth of the knowledge acquired were developed and their successes rapidly became a source of pride that was widely proclaimed in the ideological battles of the cold war. One significant example is that the right to education was established as a basic milestone in international law as a consequence of initiatives promoted by the socialist countries in the UN system. The idea of creating more accomplished human beings by means of better education was part of the image promoted by communist countries in political debates, and even if the results were not so comprehensive as the former communist leaders pretended, they were indeed high. This last aspect is poorly illustrated in all ten reviews, but the high value placed on education is always mentioned. Thus, the Bulgarian paper describes the high educational attainments at national level from the beginning (Tsakova 2004, 1). In Russia, wide–ranging educational success remains a basic assumption: "Traditionally education was considered as open to all in this country, its high quality was hardly ever questioned, and despite the changing situation the stereotype is still alive" (Muraveva 2004, 17). While the Polish author states briefly that "formal education is very important for Poles" (Ślęzak 2003, 7), the Hungarian one describes "the importance of knowledge and learning [that] cuts across all levels of society" (Benke 2004, 15) and the "wide–spread perception of the teacher as a lantern that brings light to the people" (Benke 2004, 1), citing as a symbol an old proverb "We live and learn". We can cite another proverb to show the importance that education had for Romanians from immemorial times: "You have education, you have your fate made" to which we add an old original fairy tale about "The–lad–who–was–born–with–the–book–in–his–hand", where the hero solves all problems with the support of the wisdom he discovers progressively in the pages of the given book. For Latvia, "education… is an indicator of national identity, growth and competitiveness" (Koke 2003, 1). Similarly, in Estonia "culture and education have been a national pursuit enjoying almost a religious tinge at least since the mid–19$^{th}$ century" (Loogma et al. 2004, 13). It is perhaps interesting to know in this context that the compulsory status of primary education, seconded by effective implementation measures, was proclaimed in Romania in 1864 and in Hungary in 1868; at the time, this was the case only in Sweden and Italy (in the latter it became effective only in 1877) and in two states of USA; similar measures were adopted in the UK in 1870, in Switzerland in 1874 and in France in 1882 (Iorga 1971, 25).

The second advantage is the importance of the concept of lifelong learning in the discourse on the learning society. Lifelong learning is in fact the centre of the learning society discourse, together with its variant of French origin "permanent education", which continues to be used. Implicated in international debates and analyses within organisations like UNESCO, ILO or OECD, specialists in education from the CEECs early integrated lifelong learning into the national discourse as a new educational model, better adapted to accelerated social changes, globalisation and information explosion following the rapid progress in science and technology. In Bulgaria, the development of the learning society concept is considered to have begun spreading immediately after the translation of Jaques Delors' UNESCO report in 1996 (see Tsakova 2004, 1). The Latvian National Commission for UNESCO is cited as a factor of active development of lifelong learning and the learning society within the national plan of action, *Education for All* (see Koke 2003, 4). In Russia, the promotion of lifelong learning is linked with the development of adult education, the measures adopted in that respect by the Russian Ministry of Education in 2001 being officially based on the decisions of the V International Conference on Adult Education in Hamburg, 1997 (see Muraveva 2004, 28).

In Romania, the influences are traced back to the early 1970s: "The UNESCO report of Edgar Faure *"Learning to Be"* was translated very soon after its publication in the original language, being subject to debates of Romanian specialists on the role of education in the contemporary world. All pedagogical textbooks included chapters on *permanent education* from then on" (Balica and Voicu 2004, 2). In this stimulating atmosphere, we find one of the earliest definition of a learning society, under the title of an "educational society", considered as "a project of a society where the principle of education functions at the level of all social structures and learning is included in any type of social activity of the individuals, formal, nonformal or informal" (Balica and Voicu 2004, 3). But we can also find contradictory effects. Romania has experienced a special situation, having adopted in 1971 a "Law on Continuing Training", the rationale of which was "explicitly based on the concept of the "scientific–technical revolution". It was announced as a response to the need for continuous improvement of initial education and training of human resources in Romanian economy. A pragmatic solution was considered given these needs by establishing the framework for lifelong education on a mass level. However, the artificial mechanisms and the compulsory nature of the continuing training, both for the individuals obliged to participate periodically in the continuing training system, and for the enterprises obliged to organise these courses, together with the lack of adequate material and methodological resources, with a superficial attitude on all parties involved and, moreover, with its embedded ideology, rapidly transformed this system into the opposite of the original intention, so that it was perceived as the height of boredom and a permanent source of many popular jokes" (Balica and Voicu 2004, 4–5).

In Slovenia, the concept of lifelong learning has distant origins, emerging not from international currents but from genuine national reflection on educational objectives and modes. Karel Ozvald is cited as one of the founders of the concept, as far back as 1927, when he stated "that education and training of children and youth of school age should not have been anything else but preparation for self–education and autonomous learning that begin only after completion of the school and normally last until the end of the life." (Mirčeva and Beltram 2003, 2).

If other national reviews do not overly stress the history of the lifelong learning concept, it can be deduced that for most of the CEECs lifelong learning was already present in the educational discourse far before 1990 and was extensively discussed after 1990, being identified as a pragmatic tool to cope with the pace of changes in the society. "Lifelong learning is a factor enabling people to master and gain skills in order to keep pace with technological changes which influence their private and professional lives" (Ślęzak 2003, 11), being meant to "extend the goal of education in an ongoing lifetime process, carrying out education and instruction in the conditions of uncertainty and a quickly changing global world" (Tsakova 2004, 7).In the review for the Czech Republic and Slovakia, lifelong learning represents one of the main streams in the cultivation of knowledge. "The objective of this stream [is] to create a society in which people have opportunities to learn, want to learn and are able to learn throughout their lives." (Kalous 2003, 5).

A specific influence of lifelong learning on the definition of the learning society intervenes in the context of EU integration. Affected by the process of accession to the EU, with the exception of Russia, most of these countries show a strong influence, if not a direct borrowing from the language of EU policy documents. The consultation process on the *Memorandum on Lifelong Learning* is briefly or largely described by different authors (Benke 2004, 12; Koke 2003, 11; Kaminskienė et al. 2003, 9; Balica and Voicu 2004, 13–14; Mirčeva and Beltram 2003, 1). For Latvia, the learning society itself "entered educationalists' terminology in 1998 when the European Commission's *White Paper on Education* was translated into Latvian" (Koke 2003, 2). In the Polish political arena "the debate is to a large extent driven by the European Union accession and general guidelines regarding policies to promote a knowledge based economy" (Ślęzak 2003, 1). In Lithuania "the learning society in the policy context is regarded mostly as a declarative concept and used mostly in the discourses of different strategic documents. Therefore this concept lacks the local context and practical meaning" (Kaminskienė et.al. 2003, 10). While other authors are not so explicit (and critical), they present different programmes meant to guide and support the emergence of the learning society, most of them adopted during the process of EU integration (Tsakova 2004, 6–7; Benke 2004, 12–13; Koke 2003, 3; Balica and Voicu 2004, 7–8; etc.).

It is interesting to notice that for Russia the situation is different: "elements of lifelong learning are present in Russian education. However the existing practices are not analysed and disseminated and are not officially recognized as elements of lifelong learning" (Muraveva 2004, 27). We do not know if this difference in approach is caused by the absence of EU policy driven discourse, as Russia is removed from the EU integration process, but nor do we know the opposite. What we know is only that "practically no references have been observed in the publications to the *Lisbon Declaration*" (Muraveva 2004, 17).

In considering all these aspects, the specific situation of CEECs in the process of transition to a market economy and a democratic organisation of society should not be forgotten. If in the West the evolution of learning society concept is linked to economic dynamics and to the pace of changes introduced by this, in CEECs the torment of changes affected all aspects of the society simultaneously, meaning that any attempt at analysis was out of date almost as it was carried out, since every day meant a new step away from communism in their economies, societies and systems of values. There was neither the stability nor the distance necessary for an objective reflection on the magnitude of social, economic and political developments. CEECs were taking decisions and implementing measures related to structural reforms aimed at an objective that was not yet completely grasped and agreed in the West itself. It was natural to seize on concepts that could direct this fundamental process, even if they were still under development. Hence the approach was more politically driven than reflective: CEECs were not in the situation of reflecting on the coming society, but of ensuring that it came about. This is why most of the literature reviews in CEECs describe the conceptualisation of the learning society mainly as a process of the move towards the society of the future, as defined in the liberal world under the name of the information, knowledge or learning society, and policy documents are much more often cited than scholars' papers. With the exception of Russia, this difficult process was combined with EU integration in a very early stage, embraced consensually by national populations, so that the EU–led discourse inevitably entered straight into the national debates, not for reflection or questioning its rationale, as was often the case in the old Member States, but with the aim of eagerly finding ways to implement it in an acceptable manner, so that these countries can attain their most important goal since the early 1990s: full EU membership.

But it was in this context that a particular path for the conceptualisation of the learning society became possible, in the special case of Estonia. This conceptualisation evolved in Estonia in a very atypical manner, in an open debate occasioned by an original social experiment, using the scenario method. Run within the Estonian Education Forum, an active NGO which was established in 1995, with the aim of introducing pressures on the educational policy, driven by scholars but benefiting from a large public support, the experiment led to the "development of the learning society ideology [through] creating future visions, [the year] 2015 [being] chosen for the time perspective… It was commonly decided that one of the four possible scenarios—Learning Estonia—was accepted as a point of departure for the Estonian education strategy" (Loogma et al. 2004, 2). Even if, as the authors appreciate, "it is difficult to say to what extent the ideology of the learning society has become rooted in the consciousness of politicians and the population" (Loogma et al. 2004, 12), the process is distinct and noticeable.

## Overall Characteristics and Objectives: What is a Learning Society?

### Learning Society as a Coherent Concept

As seen above, there are important differences in how the concept of a learning society is understood in the ten countries analysed, meaning that there is a lack of consistency and coherence. The exceptions are Slovenia and Estonia, where original elements in the reflection on learning society features are described—in Estonia from the explicitly driven experiment of the scenario, in Slovenia from the old tradition of lifelong learning concept. In both cases the concept has arisen out of the debate on education, but it extends far beyond the domain of education, covering a wide range of aspects of social life.

The strongest image is given in the Estonian paper, offering a reflective construct on learning society: "a coherent and open society with a high renewal capacity, where a constant dialogue between the people, their groups, organisations and the network of all of these and learning from one another is taking place; where they are eager for innovations and are trying to foresee problems; where questions are asked, disputing takes place and solutions are being sought; new knowledge and technologies are created on the foundation of what has been preserved in the culture and where people, organisations and society as a whole proceed from such fundamental common values as human rights, democracy, sustainable development, as well as solidarity between and caring for people… A learning society thus described is a modern–day Utopia, which it is impossible to reach to a full extent… A learning society can be considered as the ecological point of view for people and society, which enables their sustainable development to be guaranteed. Learning society has no reasonable alternative under the sustainable development criterion." (Loogma et al. 2004, 5–6).

To this quasi–emotional view, the Slovenian approach comes with complementary operational elements, learning society objectives being defined as following (Mirčeva and Beltram 2003, 3):

- learning required by an individual for developing and recognition of the numerous dimensions of his/her personality—physical, intellectual, emotional and spiritual; it is important that educational policy and practice pay equal attention to both—learning as a means for greater economic efficiency and mobility on the labour market, and learning as a value developing other roles and needs of an individual;
- learning for all people—from the youngest to the oldest, which means learning and education that are lifelong as an organized activity and content;

- recognition of the variety of channels, chances and circumstances in which all people can learn as well as the variety of sources of learning;
- increasing of the responsibilities of local communities for development of encouraging environment for learning of all people—in the Slovenian strategy of lifelong learning local communities represent an environment that, beside the family, is the best at eliminating barriers to the involvement of all in education;
- development of all the components of the strategy of lifelong learning; the multifaceted nature of learning, learning in all ages of life, learning in various environments as well as with various sources and contents.

We may note that the above objectives are not very far from the key messages of the EU *Memorandum on Lifelong Learning*, but influences cannot be suspected, since the Slovenian document was defined earlier. Perhaps it is not accidental that both countries showing the "success" of learning society concept are very small, with populations of less than two million. In such conditions social awareness and solidarity may be higher and the implementation of policies and concepts easier. The two small nations also had a tradition of educational discourse which could become a basis for a more coherent analytical discourse on learning society. Under such circumstances, a special reflective experiment became possible in Estonia and in Slovenia the arrival of a learning society is described in terms of "when", the analysis is very concrete and goals are operational.

## Partial Approaches to the Concept of Learning Society

Unfortunately, in most CEECs, the concept of a learning society is not very strong, and we can find open statements about the lack of consistency of learning society concept in a number of reviews:

> "There is no completely developed concept of the learning society in Bulgaria." (Tsakova 2004, 1)
> "There is no unified understanding of the concepts "lifelong learning" and "learning society" in Latvia." (Koke 2003, 11)
> "The concept of the learning society is a very new and insufficiently researched and elaborated concept in Lithuania… No original or specific concepts of the learning society have been developed, nor has any specific research taken place." (Kaminskienė et al. 2003, 5–6)

However, while a clear and integrated perspective is largely missing, the concept is used in different specific contexts, so we can find partial (or "sectoral") approaches, even if the degree of consistency varies.

*ICT Perspective.* ICT comes naturally as one of the first domains where the discourse on the emerging society flourished. The cycle of the change can be described as the production, application and distribution of information, and ICT is the source, the instrument and the engine of this running cycle. The revolutionary growth of ICT has made it indispensable in many aspects of our life, so that it can be perceived as an absolute master of the new age—"the age of information"—most of the time because it is run by means of ICT: it is the age of the e–mail, e–trade, e–learning, e–groups, e–governance, the age of the virtual products, virtual friends, virtual universities, virtual communities. In Russia, for instance, the identified prerequisites of the information society are almost all ICT related (see Muraveva 2004, 19).

From this angle, society is seen as a computerised world, where using ICT, coping with digital environment and navigating on the World Wide Web are core skills, often referred as the new literacy—in Romania, a show on ICT innovation was for a long period shown on prime time national TV under the title "The Second Literacy"; the term is also mentioned in other CEECs (e.g., Kalous 2003). The power of ICT in the development process is so important that chances for success and quality of life are often measured by the number of computer and Internet users / population ratio, by the turnover in the virtual economy and by the extension of broadband Internet connections. In CEECs, access to ICT is often seen as the key element to effective and sustainable development, the knowledge based economy being intimately linked with the extensive use of ICT. In Bulgaria, the domain was considered so important that a special *National Educational Strategy in Information and Communication Technologies* was adopted (Tsakova 2004, 2). A similar strategy was adopted in Romania: *The National Strategy for Promoting the New Economy and Implementing the Information Society* (Balica and Voicu 2004, 8).

It is not in fact possible to analyse the new features of the emerging society without looking at the impact of ICT, either as a means or a background of change, which is multiple, complex and profound and gives members of the society new powers but also new roles:

"The changes induced by the recent technological developments force members of society, both participants and witnesses of change, to adjust to new life conditions to a new type of digital / virtual environment. Technology... is still interfering and changing human environment, not only economic, but social and political, forcing individuals to adjust to the new world" (Ślęzak 2003, 9).

But ICT alone cannot push the whole society to a new level and the learning society, even when called an "information" society, is not an ICT society, even if ICT is an important factor in the economy, the civil society and the day–to–day life. We do not need only computers and connections to transform the world for the better. We need also "to guarantee a fair competitive environment, to cultivate macroeconomic conditions favourable to knowledge, to consolidate the enforceability of law, namely in the sphere of the protection of intellectual property" (Kalous 2003, 6). Information in itself is empty. Technology is able only to multiply information up to unthinkable amounts, to make it instantly available, potentially to all members of the society, to create purely democratic links with no regards to space limitations or social stereotypes. It is able to provide an impulse to development but it cannot *create* knowledge and information. We need know how, we need creativity, we need maturity—we need the H factor: the human.

***Education and Learning Society.*** By its very nature, the learning society belongs, of course, to the jargon of educationalists, as learning is the content–matter of the educational sciences. It is not surprising that many of the national reviews identify the use of the term only or mainly within education circles, especially in connection with the concepts of "education for all" and "lifelong learning" (Tsakova 2004, 2; Kaminskienė et al. 2003, 1; Koke 2003, 1; Balica and Voicu 2004 etc.). The Estonian experiment was also rooted in the area of education. As education is the organised path for learning, the social tool meant to assure the ground elements for the individual's integration into society, when the stability of the society becomes dynamic and the way of life is in continuous motion, it is normal to discuss the need to reshape education and empower the individual not with behavioural algorithms meant to assure an individual's success for their life span, but with the ability to adapt to permanent change.

Education, by its very fundamental definition, needs a goal, an image of a society to which the products of the educational process should fit in, thus drawing inferences about general features of the society is natural for educationalists. The only problem is that education usually needs a static image, a map, in order to know exactly "where to go". When the general picture is itself in motion, then the instrument of adaptation needs to follow this movie and so needs to be fundamentally different. The concept of lifelong learning first emerged in this context, and it is not by chance that *Learning to Be* appeared almost at the same time as Daniel Bell's *Arrival of the Post–industrial Society*. We have already seen a very early definition of the learning society in Romania, dating from this same period (1974), that was based on lifelong learning perspective, where the engine of the society is "the principle of education", seen in a lifelong perspective.

It was therefore normal that the changing context of the 1990s in the CEECs affected by the transition process should be reflected in a new organisation of education. Far–reaching reforms were introduced in almost all these countries, with education for all and a lifelong learning perspective always as basic principles. Most of the national reviews speak about these as a living illustration of the conceptualisation of the learning society, and it is sometimes more difficult to find elements to show in theoretical reflection and scientific analyses. Reviews provide rather normative answers to the question "How to move from the existing society towards learning society?" than to a more reflective one "What distinguishes a learning society from the existing society?" Sometimes, references to more in–depth analyses relating to a learning society are signalled in connection to policy measures, especially with respect to the role of universities. But most of the time we remain in the field of strategic actions, which use the learning society as an ideology to push through different reforms.

The influence of the process of EU integration could not be but very strong: not only was the adoption of the *acquis communautaire* compulsory, together with its embedded philosophy, but also the strategic goals of the EU had to be taken on board in national policies. Negotiations referred continuously to these two sides of the coin—see especially the cases of Bulgaria and Romania, the only countries analysed that are still on the way to the EU. Education was directly targeted in this process, but it was not the only field affected and for this we would need to widen the perspective to take in general policies.

***Learning Society as a Policy Driven Concept.*** The *transition* process itself implies that the political aspect is dominant, since the transformation of the society is profound and needs to be guided by political tools. This requires an image of the "destination" towards which society is supposed to be heading: the clarity and concreteness of this image determines the transparency and effectiveness of the political measures. No one is to be blamed for the fact that this image was not very clear immediately after the end of the communist regime: it was a raw land where the roads needed to be built together with the means of locomotion and the trajectory itself. It is significant that, as it was so difficult to define where the transition was/is meant to bring the national communities, the CEECs commonly began to use *transition* by itself, describing themselves as "transition countries". The new society to be built was defined generally as "capitalism", simply because this label was used in earlier slogans as the opposite of "communism", but in the West the concept was very different, old-fashioned hard-core capitalism was considered obsolete and was identified with the past rather than the future.

The scholarly world does not adapt so quickly, but needs a period of reflection and confusion is normal in such a major transformation process. The political arena cannot wait for so long and this is why the learning society label (under different names) was quickly adopted by politicians who needed a roadmap and milestones, even if the conceptualisation was weak. This situation is well described in almost all CEE reviews, as the following show:

"The discussion in Poland, albeit versatile, is still at the early phase. It still lacks a clear, shared, multidisciplinary definition for all participants of the debate, of what, factually, is understood by the concept. Various strands of research adapt their own working definitions, originating from the information and knowledge society concepts. Furthermore, the policy makers, eagerly catching on it, use the concept extensively in documents and speeches without going much into depth of the meaning of the concept." (Ślęzak 2003, 11)

"The discourse about a learning society is only beginning to take shape in Russia, dating back to late 1990s... At this point it can be described as a blend of public and scientific discourse, as, on the one hand, even semantically it has not yet acquired a consistent and coherent form, and on the other—some political decision-making towards implementing measures aimed at building a learning society have been taken and public and political forces have formed groups to foster the development of a post–industrial society." (Muraveva 2004, 17)

This parallel shows us a similar situation, irrespective of the EU integration process. We assume by this that it is the *transition* that generates it. This does not mean that the influence of the EU accession is less important, but rather that it is not necessarily the main cause. It is the political will for a fundamental change in these countries that is the cause, and it was natural for the political discourse to take over from the scholarly one.

The only difference is that in the countries that decided to join the EU soon after entering the path of *transition*, the political language of the EU intervened early and guided the wordings to a mainstream which is not only stronger but also more coherent. Lisbon 2000 brought the concept of the learning society to the foreground and this is why the use of the wording in many of CEECs is directly linked to the EU accession process, with the adoption of the *acquis communautaire*, with debates organised around the *Memorandum*, and with the development of different strategies under EU coordination—NAPEs, NDPs, etc. Sometimes the concept may seem purely declarative and empty, but even when it is more consistent, it remains rooted in EU policy discourse:

"Strategic schemes of these [programming] documents… are dealing with the concept of *knowledge–based society* which has roots in the European Commission's definition of the knowledge–based economy" (Mirčeva and Beltram 2003, 9).

Of course, the influence is not felt by all CEECs, and where it is, it is not linear and has a very different impact in the different national contexts. The deep theoretical reflection described in the review on the Czech Republic and Slovakia, the genuine evolution in Slovenia, the scientific and academic progress in Hungary and Poland, and, most of all, the special experimental development in Estonia cannot be measured by the same system of reference.

Moreover, this prevalence of the political factor is not bad in itself. Eventually, what really counts is not the driver, but the clarity and the concrete content of the driven concept. This means, after all, that we are dealing with a living concept. The discourse is fed by different mainstreams, but it is, nevertheless, very much alive.

## The Learning Citizen: an Individual in the Learning Society

One common element is evident in the different approaches towards the learning society: the individual is the centre of the new philosophy of social organisation and its functioning. Images of the learning citizen are described in many reviews. Features such as openness, flexibility, tolerance, trust, are among the most important elements and the most commonly described in the new profile; the focus on personal interest is combined with a wider perspective in terms of social consideration:

> "The citizens of the "learning society" are considered as more flexible and mobile as compared to the generation of their ancestors, but in the same time they are more focused on their personal interests in the highly individualised world". "A "modern personality" exhibits attitudes such as openness for innovation, tolerance, ability to wait for future benefits, interests in education, approval of a social change, trust, planning and ability to present opinions not directly related to one's interests etc." (Ślęzak 2003, 9, 6).

The learning citizen is often seen only in his/her working capacities, as a "specialist", and the ability to adapt to changing work conditions is fundamental in this respect:

> "A modern specialist has to be trained for working in new conditions both professionally and psychologically. The ability to adapt to continuously changing conditions of working, living and resting, becomes highly valuable." (Kaminskienė et al. 2003, 3)

But usually this angle is wider, with different aspects of life and society being considered. An increase of freedom of choice calls for increased knowledge capacities to help the individual recognise the best opportunity and to take responsibility for the consequences of the decisions taken, including the possibility to intervene to change the social conditions. The member of the new society is an active one:

> "Individual freedom and responsibility are increasing spectacular..., not only in the sector of consumption, but in the everyday work, in the economy and in the organization of social life as well... Individuals have to be able to tolerate changes, to adapt themselves to a new envi-

ronment, to recognize new opportunities, to create targets and ways to achieve them, to be able to choose, make selection, make proper decisions" (Benke 2004, 4).

A common word for this behavioural profile is autonomy, which implies being active and taking initiatives, but taking responsibility as well. This applies equally to both the active and the inactive population:

> "The active population is… expected to be more autonomous and dedicated to work, to manage more easily the unexpected cases at work as well as in performing other roles in society. It is connected with permanent learning. However the economically inactive population is equally expected to participate in the processes within civil society. This also relates to undertaking greater responsibilities and initiatives in community." (Mirčeva and Beltram 2003, 8).

This attitude applies not only with respect to the outside world, but also to the inner capacities of the individual, self–control based on self–cognition being the background and the precondition of appropriate social behaviour. In this perspective, far from being only a worker—a small unit in the big economical mechanism—the individual becomes "a personality":

> "The mission and nature of the learning society refers not so much to the scope, as to the preparation of the individual to be a personality. The person gains knowledge of him/herself—on the one hand, his/her inclinations, natural talents, abilities, limitations, and on the other hand—his/her spiritual image. Self–cognition has a key role and importance for knowing others." (Tsakova 2004, 3).

This image is not complete if we do not also consider the way this profile of the learning citizen can be reached. This is the role of education, which is supposed to prepare the individual to integrate appropriately into the society. In this rationale, the need for a new educational model is usually underlined, the act of learning having a new perspective, freedom and responsibility being features of the process itself, not only of the learning outcome:

> "The general scope of the education in Romania is defined in the *Education Law* (1995) as "the free, integral and harmonious development of

the human individuality and the training of autonomous and creative personality" (Balica and Voicu 2004, 10).

While not all pieces of this puzzle can be found in all the reviews, the different portraits of the learning citizen have similar features, so the concept can be considered quite cohesive from this point of view.

## Working and Living in a Learning Society

Working in a learning society is a natural aspect in our analysis, since the whole concept of learning society places so much stress on economic life, "knowledge based economy" being the fundamental wording in learning society discourse (and also in EU policy papers). At this high level of generalisation, there are some common features, with different degrees and nuances, in the image of the learning society reflected by the ten national reviews:

- the rapid pace of changes in the economy and in life patterns,
- information/knowledge becomes a production agent and/or capital, able to transform and improve other economic sectors,
- human capital is crucial for economic progress,
- changes in the organisation of work.

These features are intimately connected. The rapid pace of change is mainly linked with the impact of innovation that transforms knowledge into a production agent, reflecting the *quality* element of products, which is not only high–tech driven, but also client oriented, user friendly, sophisticatedly shaped, optional functions provided, time delivered, economically determined by the "manifest expression of the permanent need to raise the subjective feeling of the quality of life" (Balica and Voicu 2004, 10). However, if this complex image of the operation of the new agent/capital is present, most of the time it is linked to the singular technological aspect of ICT that appears as a factotum of the emerging society, "a panacea both for the economic growth and for the civil society consolidation" (Muraveva 2004, 20). Hence, not all branches of the economy are seen as innovative and knowledge based (see Koke 2003, 3), even if the influence of high–tech is expected to touch also traditional industries and domestic activities, such as gardening and handicrafts (see Loogma et al. 2004, 9).

Such an economy is dependent on the human factor, the only one able to create the highly qualified, creative, flexible and responsible worker who we can identify as the learning citizen, even if not always explicitly presented as such. Most of the analyses are concerned with the need of the worker to be competent, reliable, innovative and, at the same time, adaptable to rapid evolution not only of the market but also of the organisation of the work itself: new management rules, increasing flexibility of work, teleworking, temporary working teams, networking of companies. New forms of enterprises appear (see Benke 2004, 6–8), sometimes identified as an expression of the new concept of the *learning organisation*, depending on knowledge transfers not only from or to outside world but also within its inner structure:

> "The economy of the learning society also requires the learning organisation and efficient knowledge transfer as well as knowledge management, including the articulation of the tacit knowledge… The integration of work and learning and the orientation of the economy towards better servicing its customers will make the power relations within organisations less and less hierarchical." (Loogma et al. 2004, 8).

Under this perspective, the learning citizen is less individualized, more seen as an abstract–instrumental "human resource" (often under the older label of "workforce"), even when placed in the centre of the development policy, as in the Bulgarian governmental programme *People are the Wealth of Bulgaria*, where "people can be regarded as a significant factor in the development of investment in production" (Tsakova 2004, 3).

The concrete day–to–day life and interests of the individual seem to appear rarely and/or poorly in the sources analysed by the ten national reviews, the emphasis being put on the working life. The major challenges are related to changes in qualification requirements, most of them linked with the omnipotent IT skills (see Kaminskienė et al. 2003, 2–3), but also related to the ability to cope with "new and frequently changing tasks at work… to perform duties that are not confined to one occupational category, while teamwork has gained importance as well" (Benke 2004, 6). A lifelong profession is a concept that is on the path to extinction, careers are no longer linear and "people need their own life "policy" and the ability to find information and knowledge, which lie beyond their competences at the moment" (Tsakova 2004, 5).

At the same time, the same challenges also mean deregulation of the labour market and consequent social risks, the changes affecting not only the content but also the number and the quality of available jobs:

> "more flexible, less stable jobs, decreasing number of jobs in the traditional industry based on a less qualified work force... creation of new activities and jobs in the service sector... creation of new, small and medium sized enterprises demanding highly qualified employees." (Mirčeva and Beltram 2003, 4)

This deregulation may develop into division of the labour force into highly qualified and low skilled, which is sometimes considered as a path to social exclusion and, therefore, an implicit threat to the emerging society. The problem here is the underlying idea that the social contribution of people that are not involved in what is considered to be the knowledge–based economy is less valuable.

> "Not all individuals are agents of those changes as the majority of people are not active actors of changes, but rather passive witnesses and "takers" of changes, often incapable of managing them at a personal level" (Ślęzak 2003, 17).

However, innovation, change is not necessarily and not always positive *per se*. The human race has been so successful in mastering the planet over all the other species not because of its ability to innovate, but because of its capacity to share and preserve the positive changes previously acquired. When being an agent of change becomes a necessity, it is not a surprise that many individuals cannot cope with the new conditions and may find themselves suddenly in marginal positions. Far from blandly accepting this situation as a kind of redemption for their weaknesses, new ways of empowering these categories by means of lifelong learning can be expected to be designed, as a core element of the emerging learning society:

> "these developments should be regulated in favour of the disadvantaged sections of the population to preclude a further stratification of society and [ensure] consolidation of democracy and civil society" (Muraveva 2004, 21)

It may be that the new social risks are simply less perceived in the CEECs, possibly because they are newcomers to the market economy. Unemployment, social exclusion, regional disparities, ethnical and/or religious conflicts are threats for which these countries do not seem very well prepared, the short time that separates them from the egalitarian communist era being, probably, insufficient. Involvement in related programmes under the accession process may not be sufficient, as they address mainly administrative structures and the state is not the only entity that should act in this field. The role of the civil society is rarely mentioned and poorly analysed in the national reviews (see Tsakova 2004, 5; Loogma et al. 2004, 4; Benke 2004, 12; Ślęzak 2003, 9; Balica and Voicu 2004, 8), maybe because civil society is not always strongly enough present as a specific voice of the community, being damaged or simply destroyed by the former ideologically oppressive regimes.

The learning society image itself is built as an ideal, opposite to the previous society and the regime, therefore linked both with freedom and prosperity. Thus, the flaws and limitations of the idea of the learning society are barely examined:

> "a society based on knowledge brings new opportunities to reduce social exclusion through faster economic growth, a higher level of employment and the opening up of new modes of social inclusion." (Mirčeva and Beltram 2003, 12)

## Learning in a Learning Society

As the name suggests, learning in a learning society is supposed to be the central star around which the society is gravitating, the vector of the organisation of the society, in different aspects and at all levels: not only at the level of the learning citizen, who is the main actor of the new arrangements, but also for the learning organisation, the learning community, the learning region. This vision, encouraged and enhanced by the process of European integration as EU policy documents frequently use such language, was developed up to the "learning state", is popular in the Baltic States, with *learning Estonia* being the most illustrative. The two pillars of this notional construct are economic competitiveness and social solidarity, which become two interrelated goals of the development strategies. This twin rationale is very familiar, since the *Lisbon declaration* relies on both of them, but later EU documents stress less the reverse side of the coin, and concentrate almost entirely on economic aspects. In CEECs facing important economic difficulties in the restructuring process the emphasis was naturally directed towards the economy. In this approach, learning is the engine of the knowledge–based economy, because learning is a complex process. It is not only a passive apprehension of information/knowledge but, under a refined analysis, the "cultivation of knowledge", understood as a dynamic concept based on five key processes related to knowledge: knowledge production, knowledge accumulation, knowledge dissemination, knowledge application and knowledge management (Kalous 2003, 4).

Coming down to the level of the learning citizen, an associated notion to this approach is "literacy", because it is not related to the traditional approach to learning, where the learner is a passive receptor of the knowledge owned by the master, but describes a key ability, that under its classical understanding facilitates the access to active social and cultural life (see Ślęzak 2003, 4, Muraveva 2004, 8, Mirčeva and Beltram 2003, 4) and may be expanded to new meanings. We already mentioned the "second literacy", related to the importance of ICT skills, a popular term in Romania, well known also in other countries, under different wording: information literacy, computer literacy, digital literacy. In Romania, the proposed extension of the notion did not catch on—a series of articles in a specialised teachers' weekly mentioned the third and the fourth literacy (methodological and axiological), but only the "second" literacy became popular. In other countries[5], it was introduced to policy documents: *A Human Resources Development Strategy for the Czech Republic* (2003) describes four varieties of literacy: democratic literacy, economic literacy, methodological literacy, existential literacy (Kalous 2003, 3). And in Estonia it becomes the essential approach in education/learning design:

> "Instead of acquiring classical knowledge, literacy in the broadest meaning of the word becomes essential—scientific, social, economic, etc., literacy that would guarantee the ability to be oriented in different environments (nature, economy, society, and culture) reshaping them within the generally accepted boundaries of ethical norms when needed." (Loogma et al. 2004, 10).

These broad perspectives do not cover, however, an extended part of learning society discourse, more developed from the angle of educationalists. Here the discourse is wide and rich, based on diverse contributions, from policy developments (coming from the need to offer general perspectives to the change of the social system and more concrete conditions to the European accession process), to self–reflective analyses of the academic community and conclusions of educational research, stimulated by all these processes and separately integrated in the European streams by their own means and connections. Hence, the aspects treated, sometimes in detail, are very diverse and at different levels of analysis:

1. strategic developments of the education system, directed usually at:
    - ensuring education for all,
    - better quality of education,
    - diversified offer—private schools and universities, education for ethnic/religious minorities, alternative educational models, open and distance learning, virtual classes, etc.;
2. new curricular elements:
    - key competences,
    - focus on flexibility, creativity, responsibility, initiative, critical thinking,
    - widening and enhancing the general knowledge background,
    - special attention to civic education,
    - emphasis on languages and, especially, on ICT skills;
3. new educational approaches:
    - learner–centred model—teacher as facilitator and organiser of learning,
    - experiential learning,
    - reflective learning,
    - self–education: "learning to learn";
4. changing role of educational institutions, especially of universities:
    - from knowledge distribution to knowledge production,
    - transcendent borders between general and applied knowledge,
    - broader curricula, narrower specializations,
    - closer cooperation with employers and consumers,
    - openness to adult education and lifelong learning;
5. recognition/accreditation of non–formal and informal learning.

Some of these aspects seem directly borrowed from EU documents on lifelong learning (as sometimes they are). Certainly, the influence is strong, sometimes directly through the process of implementation of the *acquis communautaire* and the integration of the ten countries in most of the related European programmes. As an example, in all ten countries discussions around the *Memorandum* were organized with direct EU support. Even Russia, which remains outside of the EU integration process, is however connected to the $6^{th}$ Framework Programme and to international programmes that are influenced by European philosophy in the field (see Muraveva 2004, 3, 15, 22). For this reason, most of the analyses in the ten literature reviews remain focused on policy documents, general or sectoral—national programmes, development plans, official declarations. This does not leave much space for civil society, which appears rarely and vaguely in this discourse and offers, once again, a limited role to the learning citizen, even when they are in the central position.

## Major Controversies in the Debate

Strongly affected by the process of EU integration, the policy driven elements of the learning society notion also influence the general tone of the discourse. Controversies are rarely mentioned in the ten national reviews, which could lead us to the conclusion that there is a more coherent national conceptual approach, but could, at the same time, hide a less deep reflection. However, while critiques are not numerous, they are present, biased by the same wave of fundamental change and the need to understand the goal of this process.

One of controversies is related to the mighty power of information, especially when too much emphasis is put on the use of new information technologies and the Internet, as if access to ICT facilities would be enough on its own to create a learning society. Digital sources are considered in this perspective as the supreme means of informing and forming the individual, for "discovering the truth" (Balica and Voicu 2004, 12). Other voices against this image suggest analyses of paradoxes raised by the use of ICT, especially related to the difficulty to master the increasing flows of information, when knowledge becomes relative. Our ability to process information is limited, even when helped by powerful intelligent machines. When we know very many things, we know little about each. The concreteness and the quality vanish, leading to a "*misinformation* society", where "nobody can comprehend the problems totally" (Benke 2004, 16). The only solution is to develop the ability to identify the relevant/contextualised information that becomes crucial for the adaptation of the human being to the challenges of the flood of information electronically mediated.

Another controversy is related to the permanent stress derived from the stiff (global) competition and the constant change of the social environment, which may surpass human limits and disintegrate values and behavioural models too rapidly for society to reconstitute them efficiently. The "transition" is guilty of a hyper–accelerated pace, but the learning society means, actually, continuous change to which the learning citizen is supposed to adapt in a responsible way. This underlines barriers that appear from this point of view as imperative questions, pointing at "whether it is possible to live and be happy in a society where competition necessitates continuous and eager readiness of competitors for struggle... How long are people able to regulate the ideas, with the help of their biological qualities? How long can the global society be considered to be of human scale? Will evolution transcend human beings?" (Benke 2004, 16–17). A frightening fundamental question begins to emerge: is a learning society a desirable society after all?

Moreover, the approach itself to the new society, mainly normative and strongly dominated by economic reasoning, seems strange for countries that have recently abandoned the Marxist ideology and its fundamental assumption that the economic basis determines (eventually) social superstructure and conscience. It is true that the premises are not the same as in the communist discourse: they are built on democratic principles, and conclusions have a different meaning, with the market economy determining the rules of the game. But an implicit question may be derived: was it worth entering this painful process? Is there a good change in a mainstreaming discourse that seems to rely on human greed? Criticism coming from a cultural perspective attacks this mercantile reasoning, threatening to take over the human factor, and expressing the concern that humans are aborting their cultural and spiritual nature:

> "People today are the best fed, the most prosperous, the most free (with regard to space displacement) that humanity has ever known. At the same time, they are the weakest, the most addicted to comfort and consumption, the most enslaved to the mercy of arbitrary behaviour, the least autonomous in their judgement. [...] The recent human is the human that, once they cut off the past to better jump into the future, discovers that the present cannot shelter them any more and the future does not exist yet. The recent human is the human that, willing to sati-

ate themselves with all the world's phenomena—mastering them, changing them on their will and filling themselves with their whole substantiation—has awaken one day being only an epiphenomenon of their flowing, draining and trickling" (Balica and Voicu 2004, 13).

Such critiques are proof of deep original reflection and show that the march towards the learning society, even if generally desired (and accepted as the only solution for progress) is not a blind one, and voices are prepared to contribute to future conceptual developments, maybe new streams in the coming EU 27.

## Conclusions

Before drawing conclusions, it should be recalled that the picture we tried to design does not belong to the countries analysed, it was recomposed in the analysis, in an effort to understand the "how" and "why" of the conceptualisation of learning society in CEECs. In this process, elements of the ten national reviews were reinterpreted from the perspective of the overall image, which is why individual ideas, even strict quotations, may look different in their original context. At the same time, the description of the common features prevailed, and one should not forget the important differences between the countries in question: size, historical roots, transition paths, economic success, cultural background, ethnic composition, language, religion are very different. Even not counting the largest country, Russia, the ten remaining CEECs are still very diverse; therefore our image, sometimes too coherent in comparison to the actual situation, does not apply perfectly to all CEECs.

Coming back to our initial question "Is the learning society a credible concept in CEECs?" we realise that the answer is not easy and, maybe, not very clear. The analysis reveals a less coherent and more normative concept of learning society, which is policy driven and strongly influenced by EU accession. However, important elements of original reflection described are deeply rooted in the cultural traditions of the countries involved and correspond to their diverse situations and specific ways of action. This leads us to a general picture of a living concept of a learning society, defined by an increasing interest, ventilated from the policy field and educationalist jargon, through glamorous strategic reasoning and shadows of sharp criticism, to academia and civil society, finally making its way to the common language. It is there maybe too soon and too artificially, too abrupt and risky, but it is there. A few miles behind international discourse, but moving fast and growing.

With this certitude we may come to another question relying in the background of globalisation and in the EU strategic approach itself: "Is a learning society a credible goal for the CEECs?" or, in other words: "Is a learning society feasible in these countries?" Analyses are supposed to give answers and several of our background reviews have already answered "yes" and described the milestones of this itinerary and the wheels of the engines put in action to that purpose.

But sometimes, instead of finding answers, reflection raises new questions. "A well defined problem is half solved", says an old academic dictum. For good measurement we need a reference system, a Galilean point that may be considered fixed for the process. What is it on this road map? Broadening the perspective, the wording of the question shortens: *Is a learning society feasible?*

## Notes

1. As the principle of the literature reviews in the project was linguistic rather than geographical, Slovakia and the Czech Republic were covered in a joint analysis due to the similarity of their languages and to their long common history; in this case, therefore, we cannot speak of a "national" literature review.
2. The literature review in the Russian Federation, a country whose historical experience and transition processes in many respects resemble those in other CEECs but which is not involved in the process of EU integration, provided a comparison similar to a "control group" analysis.
3. The national literature reviews were prepared as background materials especially for this comparison. The copyright belongs to the project "Towards the European Society: challenges for education and training policies and research arising from the European integration and enlargement" (EURONE&T). Here we would like to acknowledge the work and to thank all authors of the reviews.
4. Due to the nature of the analysis and because time is an important element for the evolution of the concepts, we consider it important to indicate the year of the original publication.
5. Series of articles in "Tribuna învăţământului" (Education floor), 1991–1992, by Nicolae Radu.

# References

## National Literature Reviews

Balica, M. and Voicu, L. *Conceptualisation of the Learning Society in Romania—Literature Review.* EURONE&T, 2004.

Benke, M. *Conceptualisation of Learning Society in Hungary. Literature Review.* EURONE&T, 2004.

Kalous, J. *Conceptualisation of Learning Society in the Czech and Slovak Republics—Literature Review,* EURONE&T, 2003.

Kaminskienė, E, Kaminskienė, L., Laužackas, R., Palinauskaitė, A., Pundzienė, A., Tutlys, V. *Learning Society in Lithuania: Context, Features and Problems.* EURONE&T, 2003.

Koke, T. *Conceptualisation of the Learning Society and Outline of Literature Review in Latvia.* EURONE&T, 2003.

Loogma, K., Ruus, V., Vilu, R. *Towards the Learning Society: the Estonian Case.* EURONE&T, 2003.

Mirčeva, J., Beltram, P. *Conceptualisation of the Learning Society in Slovenia.* EURONE&T, 2003.

Muraveva, A. *Towards a Learning Society: Literature Review for Russia.* EURONE&T, 2004.

Ślęzak, E. *Literature Review about the Conceptualisation of the "Learning Society" in Poland.* EURONE&T, 2003.

Tsakova, Y. *Literature Review of the Conceptualisation of the Learning Society in Bulgaria.* EURONE&T, 2004.

## Other References

Aron, R. *Dix—huit leçons sur la société industrielle.* Paris, Gallimard, 1962.

Bell, D. *Vers la société postindustrielle.* Paris, Ed. Robert Laffont, 1976. Originally published in 1973.

Botkin, J.W., Elmanjra, M., Malița, M. *Universul fără limite al învățării. Dispariția decalajului uman.* Bucharest, Editura Politică, 1981. Original published in 1979.

Castells, M. *The Information Age: Economy, Society and Culture.* Vol. 1, The Rise of Network Society. Oxford, Blackwell, 1996.

Danvers, F. *700 mots—clefs pour l'éducation.* Lille, Presses Universitaires de Lille, 1991.

Drucker, P.F. *Post Capitalist Society.* Butterworth Heinemann, 1993.

Faure, E. *A învăța să fii.* UNESCO report. Bucharest, Editura Didactică și Pedagogică, 1974. Originally published in 1971.

Giddens, A. *The Consequences of Modernity.* Cambridge, Polity Press, 1990.

Iorga, N. *Istoria învățământului românesc.* Bucharest, Editura Didactică și Pedagogică, 1971.

Mc Luhan, M. *Galaxia Gutenberg—omul și era tiparului* (Gutenberg Galaxy—the man and the age of printing). Bucharest, Editura Politică, 1975. Originally published in 1962.

Mc Luhan, M. *War and Peace in the Global Village*. Bantam books, 1969.

Mullan, P. *Information Society: Frequently Un–Asked Questions*. December 2000. http://www.spiked-online.com/Printable/0000000053AA.htm. Cited 18.06.2005.

Naisbitt, J., *Megatendințe. Zece noi direcții care ne transformă viața*. Bucharest, Editura Politică, 1989. Originally published in 1984.

OECD. *Recurrent Education: A Strategy for Lifelong Learning*. Paris, OECD, 1973.

Patapievici, H.–R. *Omul recent. O critică a modernității din perspectiva întrebării: ce se pierde atunci când ceva se câștigă*. Second edition. Bucharest, Humanitas, 2001.

Toffler, A. *Al treilea val*. Bucharest, Editura Politică, 1983. Originally published in 1981.

Toffler, A. *Șocul viitorului*. Bucharest, Editura Politică, 1973. Originally published in 1970.

Zamfir, C. and Vlăsceanu, L. (coord.). *Dicționar de sociologie*. Bucharest, Editura Babel, 1993.

• MANFRED TESSARING •

# Human Capital and Benefits of Education and Training. European Challenges and Strategies towards a Learning Society

## Introduction

This chapter discusses the issue of human resources and the benefits of education and training for individuals, companies and the whole of society. These questions are currently the subject of intense discussion all over Europe, at national as well as at Community level—in particular in the context of the strategic goals and priorities for education and training systems set by the European Council in Lisbon (Presidency Conclusions, 2000), and the Ministers responsible for vocational education and training in Copenhagen (*Declaration of the European Ministers of Vocational Education and Training and the European Commission*, 2002) and Maastricht (*Maastricht Communiqué*, 2004). A number of steps have been agreed upon to transform the European Union by 2010 into a knowledge–based society while assuring economic performance, employment growth and social cohesion. However, currently there are increasing concerns that these goals might not be fully achieved due to slackening economic and employment performance and reforms of education and training systems. Europe has still a way to go to become a "learning society" where all people have access to learning throughout their life, where the provision, delivery and recognition of learning is based on principles of equity, and where environments conducive to learning facilitate the acquisition of skills, knowledge and competences.

However, European countries diverge somewhat in achieving the goals set in the Lisbon agenda. Three clusters of competitive countries can be identified (Leney et al., 2004): the "core countries", including Germany and France, with high labour productivity, social spending and well-developed social partnership; the "Nordic group", including Finland, Norway, Sweden and partly Denmark, with high economic performance and participation in the labour market and education and training, and a pronounced social partner approach; and the United Kingdom (together with the US) with high employment rates, reasonable economic performance, but lower social spending and a less developed social partnership.

The following chapters provide some evidence on the level of human capital and on the utilisation of human resources in European countries, with a special focus on the new Member States. Finally some main features of the European Union concerning the modernisation of education and training systems are discussed.

# Human Capital and Benefits of Education and Training Investments[1]

## Human Capital and Potential of Human Resources

There is widespread agreement that education and training, human capital and the development of human resources play a decisive role in achieving a number of economic and social goals. They are seen as important means to paving the way towards a knowledge-based and learning society and the formation of social capital. High-quality education and training contribute to the development of an individual's personality and enforce principles of citizenship. They are also expected to promote long-term individual employability and contribute to social and economic inclusion as well as equal opportunities. From an economic point of view, education and training and the knowledge and competences acquired—the human capital—are regarded as powerful levers for individuals, companies and the whole economy in terms of earnings and growth, productivity, employability, employment and competitiveness.

Over the past decades, countries in Europe and elsewhere have experienced a significant increase in the skills of their human resources. This increase has been the result of both individual preferences for higher qualifications and demand for highly skilled workers. And it has been supported by active policies with an emphasis on, for example, equal access to and delivery of education and training and the provision of appropriate education and training infrastructures.

**Table 1. Educational attainment of adults ([a]) in the EU–25 and selected OECD countries, 2002/03 ([b]), %**

|  | Low skilled | Upper/post–secondary | Tertiary |
|---|---|---|---|
| EU–25 | 32 | 47 | 21 |
| Australia | 39 | 30 | 31 |
| Canada | 18 | 40 | 43 |
| Japan | 16 | 48 | 36 |
| South Korea | 30 | 45 | 26 |
| USA | 13 | 49 | 38 |

(a) 25 to 64–year old population. Low skilled: ISCED 0–2; upper/post–secondary: ISCED 3–4; tertiary: ISCED 5–6
(b) EU–25: 2003; other countries: 2002
Slight differences by rounding numbers.
Sources: EU–25: Eurostat–NewCronos database (cit. 04.04.05); other countries: OECD: Education at a glance 2004, Table A1.1.

However, compared with other industrialised countries, skill levels in the EU are characterised by a relatively high share of people with intermediate skills, at upper and post–secondary level, whereas the proportion of low skilled is higher (except for Australia)[2], and that of people with completed tertiary education is lower than in the comparator countries (Table 1). The scale on which education and training and active labour market policies in the European Union have to operate becomes clear when we look at the absolute figures: almost 80 million people in the enlarged European Union are unskilled or low skilled (ISCED 0–2). This is roughly equivalent to the entire population of Europe's largest country, Germany.

## Figure 1. Educational attainment of European populations aged 25–64, 2003, %

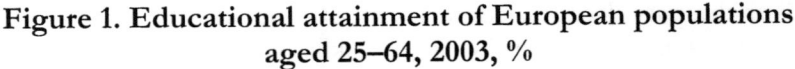

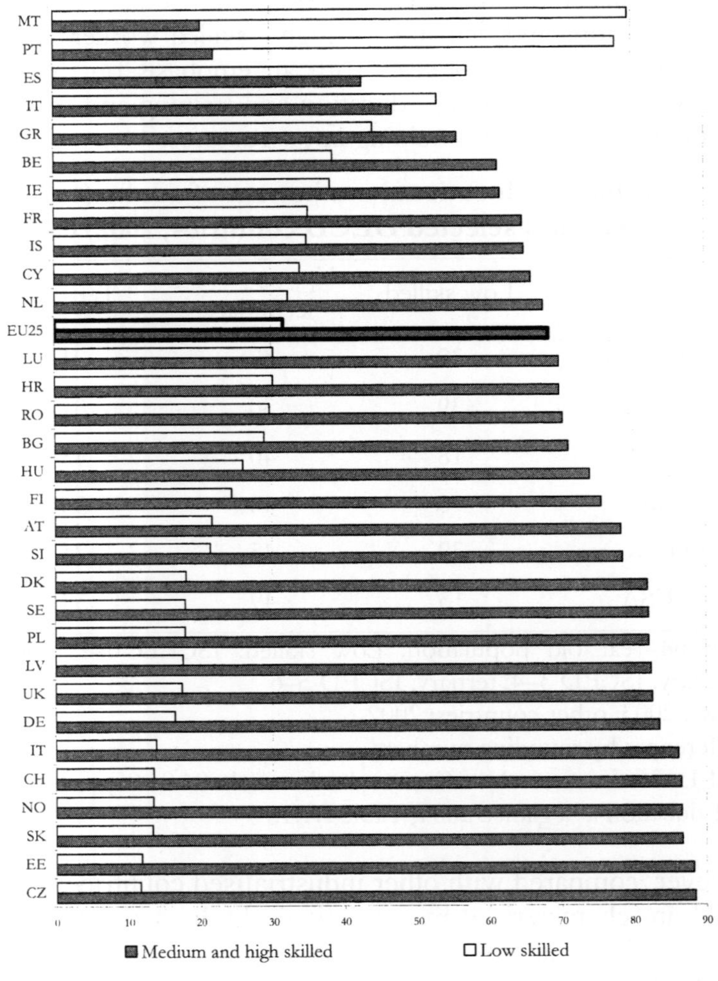

NB: The Netherlands and Iceland: 2002; countries sorted by low level of educational attainment. Low skilled: ISCED 0–2; upper/post–secondary/tertiary: ISCED 3 and higher; data calculated without non–respondents
Source: Eurostat—NewCronos database (cit. 04.04.05)

Within Europe, skill levels of working–age populations display a scattered pattern across countries. Figure 1 shows the skill structures in the EU–15 and the new Member States as well as in some other European countries, ranked by the proportion of lower skilled people.

Countries that have above the EU–15 average proportion of *lower* skilled people (35.4 %) include all Mediterranean countries including Malta, Belgium, Ireland and France.

On the other hand, the new Member States have high proportions of skilled people and correspondingly below average proportions of the lower skilled. This applies particularly to the Czech Republic, Slovakia, the three Baltic countries and Poland. Only a few old Member States are found in this advanced cluster, e.g., Germany, Sweden and the UK.

Increasingly, education and training at upper secondary level (ISCED 3) are regarded as the minimum entry level for skilled jobs. This conclusion can be drawn from results of the EU Labour Force Surveys (LFS) and the International Adult Literacy Survey (IALS): a literacy level of 3 or higher (which corresponds roughly to ISCED 3 and higher) is nowadays regarded as the minimum required to cope with the demands of everyday life and work in complex and developed societies.

The past increase in the skill levels of populations was due mainly to the higher skill levels of younger cohorts. This trend will, however, not continue in the future, at least in absolute terms. The number of younger—and more highly qualified—people will decline as a result of demographic change in most European countries. In the medium and longer term, the ageing of populations together with the declining potential of young people with updated skills will lead to increasing skill shortages in various professions and affect the renewal of the working age population. This renewal serves, amongst other things, to supply growing and prosperous sectors of the economy with updated skills and is considered to contribute to productivity, innovation and greater flexibility within labour markets.

This development calls for an appropriate design of education and training systems and for the coordination of all related policies, which should take into consideration long–term individual employability, and the demands of labour markets, as well as social cohesion. Furthermore, guidance and employment services and active labour–market measures should be mobilised in view of the considerable importance of education, training and skills. They should ensure a better transition of newcomers into the labour market and prevent labour–market imbalances. The falling skills potential could be offset by, among other things, continuing training of older workers within the framework of lifelong learning.

## Benefits of Education, Training and Skills

Investments in education and training at all levels, by individuals, enterprises and the State are increasingly being put to the test. They are evaluated in terms of returns and benefits, individual employment prospects and careers, the productivity and economic performance of companies and their contribution to economic growth, employment and social cohesion. This critical assessment of education and training is due to increasing cost pressure and competition for enterprises, persistent tight public budgets, and the expectations of individuals that the high outlay in time, effort and costs for education and training should pay off in terms of career, earnings and work status.

In general, the monetary costs of training—at least the direct ones—can be fairly unambiguously determined and attributed to investors; however, many major benefits are more difficult to grasp. This is particularly true for non–material or social benefits, such as impacts on health, criminality, parenting, social and political participation, trust, citizenship, etc. All these externalities influence directly or indirectly the economic performance of a country—and they are themselves influenced by education, training and people's skills.

***Human Capital and Growth.*** The contribution of education, training, skills and competences to economic growth, productivity and employment is not clearly measurable. Economic benefits are also generated by numerous factors other than skills and training. However, various analyses confirm the growing importance of knowledge, research and development, information and service functions (also within manufacturing industries) which have substantially changed the nature of work and of skill needs. Moreover, the abilities, skills and competences acquired through education and training are only partially visible and measurable: many occupational skills and competences are acquired through social interaction and through formal, non–formal and informal learning taking place in training institutions, at the workplace, at home and in the social environment. All these aspects make it difficult to attribute and measure the economic benefits of education, training and skills, and of human and social capital. They have generated a vast body of research work to examine these links.

The stimulation of economic growth and employment is one of the principal objectives of public education and training investments. Moreover, an increase in growth and employment is likely to facilitate the attainment of social objectives and the avoidance of social inequalities. Growth in gross domestic product (GDP) is a result of a combination of the production factors "real capital", "labour" and "human capital" and the investment made in them. While traditional neoclassical growth theories treated human capital, qualifications and technical progress as exogenous factors, new insight was provided by the theories of endogenous growth which explicitly take into account technical progress and its determinants, in particular knowledge, research and development, innovation and the skills level of the workforce, i.e., the "quality" of the human capital.

A number of empirical studies—but not all—on the sources of economic growth carried out in the past decade and based on the new theory of endogenous growth confirm the important role in GDP growth of research and development, and particularly of human capital, and the accumulation and dissemination of knowledge. Skills, and related investment in education and training, are identified as key determinants of economic prosperity, which is an important precondition for social cohesion and stability.

However, the extent of the contribution of human capital to growth differs considerably, depending on the country considered, time, the level of skills and, of course, the model applied. Wilson and Briscoe (2004, p.60), summarising research on the impact of skills and qualification on growth[3], point out:

> "Overall, these growth models demonstrate that higher educational investments have had a significant impact on levels of national income growth. Broadly, the weight of evidence suggests that a one percent increase in school enrolment rates has led to an increase in GDP per capita growth of between one and three percent. An additional year of secondary education, which increases the stock of human capital, rather than simply the flow into education, has led to a more than one percent increase in economic growth each year."

A recent study, based on the IALS, extends this focus by looking at the relationship between literacy and economic growth. Coulombe et al (2004) found out that the contribution of increasing literacy levels of populations contributes to growth in an even more pronounced way than merely education and training—although there are of course close links between literacy and education and training.

Research has shown, furthermore, that in less developed countries it is the increase in basic skills which impacts most on economic growth, whereas in the most advanced countries it is education and training at higher levels. Calculating the implications for growth of a successful achievement of the EU target for human resources and a "knowledge society" has, therefore, to take into account the different levels of advancement across European countries.

The OECD (2003, p.173) has calculated, in a decomposition approach, the contribution to growth (GDP per capita) from changes in (a) average hours worked; (c) the average years of formal education (used as a proxy for changes in the quality of labour, i.e., human capital; (c) hourly GDP per efficient unit of labour "which is equivalent to changes in GDP per worker once changes in working hours and changes in the average quality of labour are accounted for."

The analysis shows

> "that growth in output per employed person is partly attributable to increases in 'human capital' of those in employment. [...] OECD countries have invested heavily in education over past decades and this has resulted in a positive contribution of human capital enhancement in growth rates of GDP per person employed, on labour productivity. Over the past decade, skill upgrading amongst workers was particularly marked in Europe, although it was accompanied by sluggish employment growth because productivity gains were achieved partly by dismissals or not employing workers with low skills. [...] education plays an important role in this equation, not only as an input linking aggregate output to the stocks of inputs and technical efficiency, but as a key determinant of the rate of technological progress that affects the output per worker. [...] One of the factors behind the good growth record of some countries has been the availability of a large pool of qualified personnel, and skilled labour shortages are rightly considered as a constraint on the growth process." (ibid., p.173f.)

Figure 2 shows the contributions of these effects to GDP per capita growth for some OECD countries.

**Figure 2. The contribution of human capital enhancement to labour productivity growth, 1990–2000. Average annual percentage change**

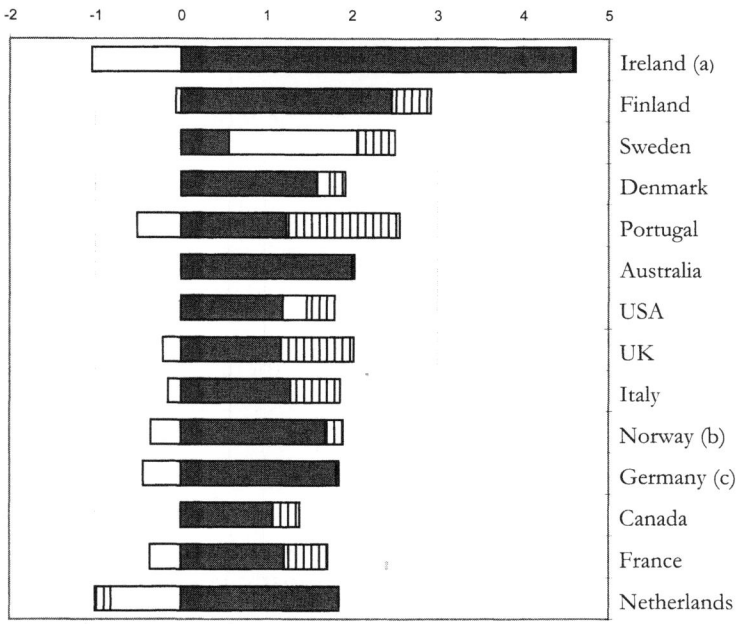

Contribution to growth in GDP per person employed from changes in (d):

■ Hourly GDP per efficient unit of labour
☐ Average hours worked
⫴ Changes in average years of formal education

(a) 1990–1999; (b) Mainland only; (c) 1991–2000; (d) based on the following decomposition: growth in GDP per person employed = (changes in hourly GDP per efficient unit of labour) + (changes in average hours worked) + (changed in average years of formal education as proxy for human capital)
*Source:* OECD 2003 (Education t a glance), Chart A15.3.

## Non-material Benefits of Education and Training.
Education, training and skills do not only yield material or monetary benefits but also social or non-material benefits both at individual and societal level. They include, for example, crime reduction, improved health, social cohesion, citizenship, and civic and political participation. Across European coun-

tries, some generalisations can be made concerning the macro–social benefits of education, training and skills (Green et al., 2004).

For some of these benefits there are common antecedents or indirect links, i.e., other influences which themselves are closely associated with education and skills. For example, violent crime and low tolerance are often associated with unemployment, poverty and alienation—which themselves are closely (negatively) correlated with education, training and skills of people.

Furthermore, the perception of social benefits such as trust, crime and tolerance depends to a considerable extent on the societal norms and inequalities in a given country, which are hard to change. In the longer term, this change could be fostered by education or training and other institutions involved in state formation. Thus, education and training have an important role to play on the formation of values and the removal of inequalities.

In a cross–country comparative view, there are specific historical conditions which influence the relationship between education and training on the one hand, and "outcomes" such as trust, tolerance and social cohesion on the other. Education and training will have important effects on many of these outcomes only if transmitting of values such as support for democracy and race tolerance are an important part of the school curricula. However, these outcomes are mostly conditioned by other—often more powerful—contextual determinants. Much of the work of explaining complex societal interactions will require more in–depth comparative analysis.

These conclusions not only suggest that the macro–social benefits of education and training

> "are rooted both in the distribution of educational outcomes and the values transmitted through education systems. They are also contingent on the relation between education and the labour market and other parts of the welfare state. Although there are cultural limits to the extent to which 'policy–borrowing' is appropriate with regard to education systems, there are clear lessons for policy–makers, in particular that raising educational, skills and training levels is neither a necessary nor sufficient condition of promoting macro–social benefits. However, improving the distribution of educational outcomes may be one way in which education and training can make some contribution to more general economic and social redistribution." (Green et al., 2004, p.163).

Green has correlated several indicators for education and income distribution with a number of macro–social indicators for social cohesion (Table 2)[4].

Table 2. Correlation of education and income distribution with social cohesion at aggregate level ([a])

|  | Macro–social indicators for social cohesion | | | | | | | |
|---|---|---|---|---|---|---|---|---|
|  | General trust | Civic participation | Trust in democracy | Cheating on taxes | Cheating on public transport | Violent crime | Tolerance | Risk of assault in local community |
| Mean level of upper secondary attainment in prose literacy | 0.354 | −0.120 | 0.244 | −0.376 | −0.487* | −0.55 | 0.491* | −0.505* |
| Educational inequality ([b]) | −0.592** | 0.333 | −0.283 | 0.265 | 0.171 | 0.398 | −0.060 | 0.404 |
| Income distribution ([c]) (Gini coefficient) | −0.562** | 0.595* | −0.032 | 0.125 | −0.004 | 0.660** | 0.270 | 0.628** |

(a) Pearson correlation coefficient.
(b) Ratio of prose literacy at tertiary educational level to prose literacy at lower than upper secondary educational level in the countries compared: Australia, Belgium, Canada, Switzerland, Germany, Denmark, Finland, Ireland, the Netherlands, Norway, Portugal, Poland, Sweden, United Kingdom, USA (high ratio: indicator of educational inequality)
(c) with control for GNP per capita.
* Correlation is significant at the 0.10 level (2–tailed).
** Correlation is significant at the 0.05 level (2–tailed).
Source: Green et al., 2004.

The results suggest that:

- there is only a weak direct correlation between education (proxied by literacy) and social cohesion indicators, e.g., tolerance, cheating and risk of assault;
- educational inequality displays a significant negative correlation with the general level of trust: the higher the level of educational inequality, the lower the level of general trust;

- income distribution (which itself is strongly correlated with literacy skills) correlates significantly with several indicators for social cohesion: higher income inequality is associated with a lower level of general trust, an increase in violent crime and an increase in the perception of risk of crime in a local community.

***Benefits of Education and Training for the Individual.*** Apart from monetary returns, education, training and skills yield considerable non–material benefits for the individual (and for society as a whole). Research has generally confirmed, for example, that higher skills significantly increase labour force participation and reduces unemployment risks over a lifetime. Moreover, education and training and skills are associated with better health and quality of life, career and social status, crime reduction, better parenting and avoidance of social exclusion. However, many of these non–material benefits are not a direct effect of education and training: higher skills increase earnings and reduce poverty, and reducing poverty is one of the most important conditions for crime reduction, citizenship and social inclusion.

All these benefits of education and training—monetary and non–monetary, material and non–material—are strong incentives for people to acquire higher skills and qualifications through formal, non–formal and informal learning. This has been confirmed, for example, by studies investigating subjective perceptions of individuals in the framework of life course and biographical research.[5] People increasingly perceive the benefits of learning and skill acquisition and are willing to continue learning beyond compulsory schooling. At aggregate level, this becomes apparent in ever higher enrolment rates in further training and higher education and, as a consequence, in higher skill levels of younger generations compared with older ones.

In this section we will focus on monetary benefits, measured by earnings and rates of return; benefits by avoiding costs and opportunities by fewer or shorter spells of unemployment, and benefits concerning participation in the world of work, proxied by employment rates.

***Monetary Benefits.*** Studies on the relationship between the accumulation of education, training and skills on the one hand and the increase in earnings on the other in general confirm the relevance of skills and qualifications acquired through education and training for individual earnings and the (internal) rates of return on education and training[6].

Table 3 provides some figures on earnings differentials between levels of educational attainment. It confirms that higher levels of educational attainment in general yield considerably higher earnings. We should add, however, that such a descriptive statistic gives only an initial indication; for determining the contribution of education and training to earnings, other factors have to be controlled for, e.g., by econometric methods. The data illustrate, secondly, the considerable lag of the new Member States in terms of earnings levels—although, here again and at lower levels, there is a strong positive relationship between education and earnings.

The OECD has compiled private and social rates of return on education for several OECD countries. These rates calculate the benefits and costs of people with upper secondary and tertiary education, whereby the rates of return with upper secondary are compared with lower secondary, and those with tertiary education are compared with upper secondary education. Table 4 shows the comprehensive rates of return for men and women in 1999–2000. The results suggest that in all countries the private rates of return are higher than the real interest rate and that investing in human capital is "an attractive way for the average person to build up wealth." (OECD, 2003: 160). The rates of return for both levels of education range between 10 and 15 % in most countries. Gender differences are more marked at upper secondary level than at tertiary level, and most strongly in Germany and the US.

A number of studies also find a positive correlation between initial or continuing education/training and higher rates of monetary returns over a lifetime. However, from a life course point of view, educational benefits—and in particular the effects of training—seem to diminish after a few years and even turn negative if no additional investment in further training is made. This indicates that rates of return on education and training are not constant over the life cycle. While returns rise in the first years of a career, the rate of increase slows in mid–career, stagnates and finally declines in the second half until retirement.

## Table 3. Mean annual earnings by education level 2002; selected European countries

| | Annual earnings in EUR | | | | Annual earnings: Index—Low skilled = 100 | | | | |
|---|---|---|---|---|---|---|---|---|---|
| | Total | Low skilled | Upper secondary | Post secondary | Tertiary | Total | Low skilled | Upper secondary | Post secondary | Tertiary |
| EU–25 | 26596 | 20440 | 26397 | 32119 | 35576 | 130.1 | 100.0 | 129.1 | 157.1 | 174.1 |
| EU–15 | 30247 | 21644 | 31140 | 37341 | 41975 | 139.7 | 100.0 | 143.9 | 172.5 | 193.9 |
| EU–10 | 6712 | 4706 | 5825 | 5503 | 9908 | 142.6 | 100.0 | 123.8 | 116.9 | 210.5 |
| Czech Republic | 6543 | 4215 | 5878 | – | 10539 | 155.2 | 100.0 | 139.5 | – | 250.0 |
| Ireland | 37865 | 26391 | 33441 | 35937 | 46877 | 143.5 | 100.0 | 126.7 | 136.2 | 177.6 |
| Latvia | 5383 | 3299 | 3961 | 4003 | 7256 | 163.2 | 100.0 | 120.1 | 121.3 | 219.9 |
| Netherlands | 33249 | 25384 | 30917 | 35576 | 45616 | 131.0 | 100.0 | 121.8 | 140.2 | 179.7 |
| Poland | 7577 | 5414 | 7206 | 6489 | 8822 | 140.0 | 100.0 | 133.1 | 119.9 | 162.9 |
| Slovenia | 11755 | 7515 | 10101 | – | 20594 | 156.4 | 100.0 | 134.4 | – | 274.0 |
| Slovakia | 4731 | 2755 | 4124 | – | 7322 | 171.7 | 100.0 | 149.7 | – | 265.8 |
| Bulgaria | 2161 | 1574 | 1955 | 2274 | 2470 | 137.3 | 100.0 | 124.2 | 144.5 | 156.9 |
| Romania | 2716 | 1814 | 2257 | 2726 | 4279 | 149.7 | 100.0 | 124.4 | 150.3 | 235.9 |

NB: Low skilled: ISCED 0–2; Upper secondary: ISCED 3; Post secondary: ISCED 4; Tertiary: ISCED 5–6.
Data for other countries not available.
Source: Eurostat—NewCronos database (cit. 14.04.05).

Research studies on changes in educational returns over time suggest that economic returns on various types of skills are influenced by system–immanent structures of the educational and occupational system of a given country. This is particularly true for returns on vocational education and training compared with general education. Countries with a high degree of institutional standardisation in their training system and a clear differentiation between general and vocational education display higher rates of individual returns on vocational education and training than countries with relatively low standardisation and differentiation.

### Table 4. Private internal rates of return on education in selected OECD countries (1999–2000)

|  | Return on upper secondary compared to lower secondary education (a) | | Return on tertiary education compared to upper secondary education (a) | |
|---|---|---|---|---|
|  | Males | Females | Males | Females |
| Canada | 13.6 | 12.7 | 8.1 | 9.4 |
| Denmark | 11.3 | 10.5 | 13.9 | 10.1 |
| France | 14.8 | 19.2 | 12.2 | 11.7 |
| Germany | 10.8 | 6.9 | 9.0 | 8.3 |
| Italy (b) | 11.2 | n.a. | 6.5 | n.a. |
| Japan | 6.4 | 8.5 | 7.5 | 6.7 |
| Netherlands (c) | 7.9 | 8.4 | 12.0 | 12.3 |
| Sweden (d) | 6.4 | n.a. | 11.4 | 10.8 |
| United Kingdom | 15.1 | n.a. | 17.3 | 15.2 |
| United States | 16.4 | 11.8 | 14.9 | 14.7 |
| Country mean (e) | 11.4 | 11.1 | 11.8 | 11.3 |

(a) comprehensive rates of return; (b) data for males derive from 1998 after–tax earnings data; (c) 1994; (d) for women, earnings differential between upper secondary and lower secondary levels are not large enough to permit a positive rate of return calculation; (e) data for men exclude Italy, data for women in upper secondary exclude Sweden and the UK.
Source: OECD, 2003, Table A 14.3.

*Unemployment and Participation in Work.* Unemployment and "hidden unemployment" in Europe are persistent phenomena that give rise to concern. If we add together (a) the number of registered unemployed, (b) the number of jobseekers who are not registered unemployed and (c) the number of discouraged workers who have withdrawn from the labour market but are willing to work, we arrive at a total for the year 2002 of more than 37 million jobless people, or almost one quarter of the total labour force potential of the EU–25.

In the EU–15, more than 7 % of the total EU labour force potential is registered unemployed and almost 6 % is hidden unemployed—altogether 23.5 million people who are out of work but would like to take up a job. In the new Member States, unemployment and hidden unemployment are even more marked: open unemployment in 2002 totals 12 %, and hidden unemployment 21 %. Altogether, almost 33 % of the labour force potential of the new Member States is unused, representing roughly 14 million people.

When looking at the unemployment rates of people with different levels of qualification (Table 5), again the close—negative—correlation between educational levels and unemployment risks becomes obvious. The unemployment rates by educational level for the EU–25 show that the unemployment rate for people with tertiary education (5%) is half that of people with upper or post secondary (9.6%). People at lower skill levels have the highest unemployment risk (12.3).

This ranking holds for almost all European countries included in Table 5. Exceptions are Greece, Luxembourg, Portugal, Croatia and Romania, where in some cases people at higher educational levels display higher unemployment rates.

Table 5. Unemployment rates by highest level of education attained, 2003 (%)

|       | Total | Low skilled | Upper and post–secondary | Tertiary |
|-------|-------|-------------|--------------------------|----------|
| EU–25 | 9.0   | 12.3        | 9.6                      | 5.0      |
| BE    | 7.7   | 11.6        | 8.0                      | 3.8      |
| CZ    | 7.5   | 21.9        | 6.9                      | 2.1      |
| DK    | 5.4   | 8.9         | 4.4                      | 4.8      |
| DE    | 9.8   | 15.7        | 10.0                     | 5.0      |
| EE    | 10.7  | 17.6        | 12.2                     | 5.2      |
| GR    | 9.3   | 7.7         | 12.2                     | 6.8      |
| ES    | 11.1  | 12.7        | 11.5                     | 8.1      |
| FR    | 8.4   | 12.1        | 7.5                      | 5.7      |
| IE    | 4.5   | 7.0         | 3.8                      | 2.7      |
| IT    | 8.9   | 10.5        | 8.1                      | 5.6      |
| CY    | 4.1   | 4.8         | 4.0                      | 3.8      |
| LV    | 10.6  | 16.9        | 10.2                     | 6.2      |
| LT    | 12.9  | 21.4        | 13.7                     | 6.4      |
| LU    | 3.7   | 4.0         | 3.3                      | 4.4      |
| HU    | 5.8   | 12.3        | 5.4                      | 1.4      |
| MT    | 7.5   | 8.2         | 7.2                      | 3.7      |

continued

|    | Total | Low skilled | Upper and post-secondary | Tertiary |
|----|-------|-------------|--------------------------|----------|
| AT | 4.1   | 7.9         | 3.5                      | 1.9      |
| PL | 19.4  | 26.1        | 20.8                     | 7.1      |
| PT | 6.1   | 6.1         | 6.7                      | 5.3      |
| SI | 6.5   | 10.3        | 6.2                      | 3.7      |
| SK | 17.1  | 47.0        | 15.9                     | 4.4      |
| FI | 10.5  | 18.3        | 10.9                     | 4.2      |
| SE | 5.6   | 8.6         | 5.3                      | 3.5      |
| UK | 4.8   | 8.9         | 4.8                      | 2.5      |
| BG | 13.7  | 24.6        | 12.5                     | 6.8      |
| HR | 13.9  | 14.0        | 15.8                     | 7.4      |
| RO | 6.9   | 5.8         | 8.2                      | 3.3      |
| NO | 4.2   | 8.9         | 3.8                      | 3.0      |
| CH | 4.1   | 6.7         | 3.9                      | 3.0      |

Source: Eurostat—NewCronos database (cit. 14.04.05)

Looking at participation in work, Table 6 illustrates that in all European countries employment rates increase with higher levels of education and training. At EU–25 level, 84% of people with tertiary education and 73% of those with upper or postsecondary education and training are in employment, whereas just over half (54%) of the lower skilled are employed. This ranking holds for all countries included in Table 6. However, some countries have achieved relatively high employment rates also for lower skilled people, including Denmark, France, Luxembourg, Portugal, Sweden, Cyprus, Norway and Switzerland.

Table 6. Employment rates of 25–64–year–olds by highest level of education attained, 2003 (%)

|       | Total | Low skilled | Upper and post-secondary | Tertiary |
|-------|-------|-------------|--------------------------|----------|
| EU–25 | 69.0  | 54.2        | 72.6                     | 84.0     |
| BE    | 66.6  | 48.8        | 73.3                     | 82.9     |
| CZ    | 73.3  | 44.5        | 75.6                     | 86.6     |
| DK    | 78.2  | 61.6        | 79.8                     | 85.0     |
| DE    | 69.1  | 50.2        | 69.8                     | 83.0     |
| EE    | 72.2  | 51.2        | 72.4                     | 80.0     |

continued

|    | Total | Low skilled | Upper and post-secondary | Tertiary |
|----|-------|-------------|--------------------------|----------|
| GR | 66.4  | 58.6        | 67.8                     | 82.2     |
| ES | 65.7  | 56.6        | 72.3                     | 81.8     |
| FR | 71.3  | 58.6        | 76.0                     | 82.1     |
| IE | 71.2  | 56.8        | 75.6                     | 86.2     |
| IT | 62.2  | 51.2        | 72.6                     | 81.7     |
| CY | 76.5  | 63.1        | 78.9                     | 89.0     |
| LV | 69.9  | 50.4        | 72.1                     | 81.1     |
| LT | 73.9  | 49.5        | 75.0                     | 85.6     |
| LU | 70.1  | 61.1        | 71.7                     | 82.6     |
| HU | 64.4  | 37.6        | 71.5                     | 83.1     |
| MT | 56.1  | 49.5        | 79.0                     | 85.8     |
| AT | 72.8  | 55.3        | 75.8                     | 85.7     |
| PL | 60.5  | 37.6        | 62.0                     | 83.0     |
| PT | 75.2  | 72.5        | 81.6                     | 88.1     |
| SI | 71.0  | 53.4        | 73.1                     | 85.5     |
| SK | 67.6  | 28.9        | 71.4                     | 87.9     |
| FI | 74.2  | 58.5        | 74.8                     | 85.0     |
| SE | 80.3  | 67.9        | 81.5                     | 87.1     |
| UK | 75.6  | 55.3        | 81.2                     | 88.1     |
| BG | 61.0  | 37.2        | 67.7                     | 77.8     |
| HR | 60.5  | 43.0        | 64.3                     | 81.1     |
| RO | 67.7  | 57.3        | 70.5                     | 82.0     |
| NO | 79.7  | 61.5        | 79.5                     | 87.8     |
| CH | 80.9  | 66.3        | 80.3                     | 89.7     |

Source: NewCronos database (cit. 14.04.05)

***Benefits of Education and Training at Enterprise Level.*** Recent research findings suggest that investment in training and a firm's human capital generate substantial gains for firms (Hansson and Wagner, 2004), in terms of productivity gains, profitability, market share and stock market value, and competitiveness. Furthermore there is evidence that it is not a matter of whether the training provided by firms is general or specific in nature and thus whether it is useful only for that firm or also for other firms, but more a question of how to stay ahead of competitors. Increasingly firms are financing all types of training—general as well as specific.

However, it appears that companies and investors on capital markets tend to underestimate the effects of investments in training. The results of, for instance, Bassi et al. (2001) suggest that firms and investors are neither aware of these investments nor have noticed the positive effects of investments in training and particularly continuing vocational training. It is thus likely that the lack of information in company reports about training provided by the company and about its returns leads to under-investment in valuable training programmes.

Supporting employee development practices and analysing training needs are seen as important elements in explaining and ensuring the provision of training and training outcomes. Similarly, innovative human resource management practices are in most instances reflected in firm performance.

The literature on human resource management argues that the skills of individual workers are often a critical factor in an organisation's competitive advantage. Comparative international studies emphasise the key importance of training in raising productivity, but employers in many countries still have a rather negative attitude towards investment in skills and training. Unless the institutional and legal infrastructure encourages employers to invest in training there is a tendency to rely on others to make this investment. Therefore governments should provide incentives to companies, either through tax allowances or direct grants, as well as through reforms to institutional structures, to encourage them to increase their investment in training. Such training can also provide strong spill-over effects for the whole society.

# European Education and Training Strategies

## Milestones at the European Level

European strategies to achieve the knowledge–based society started mostly in 2000 with a number of follow–up activities:

- in 2000, the Lisbon European Council set a strategic goal for the EU to become, by the year 2010, "the most competitive and dynamic knowledge–based economy in the world, capable of sustainable economic growth with more and better jobs and greater social cohesion". (Presidency Conclusions, 2000, p. 2)
- *The Copenhagen Declaration* (European Ministers of Vocational Education and Training, and the European Commission, 2002)

called for enhanced cooperation in vocational education and training on the following priorities: European dimension; transparency, information and guidance; recognition of competences and qualifications; quality assurance.

- In May 2003, the Council of the European Union (2003) adopted five benchmarks for the improvement of education and training systems in Europe until 2010:
    1. an EU average rate of no more than 10 % of people leaving school early should be achieved;
    2. the total number of graduates in mathematics, science and technology should increase by at least 15 % while at the same time the gender imbalance should decrease;
    3. at least 85 % of 22–year–olds in the EU should have completed upper secondary education;
    4. the percentage of 15–year–old low–achievers in reading literacy should decrease by at least 20 % compared to the year 2000;
    5. the EU average level of participation in lifelong learning should be at least 12.5 % of the adult working age population (25–64 age group).
- Reviewing *the Copenhagen Declaration, the Maastricht Communiqué* (2004) on the future priorities of enhanced European cooperation in vocational education and training, launched by thirty–two Ministers responsible for vocational education and training, the European social partners and the European Commission set a number of priorities at national and European level.

In following up these processes, numerous activities have been, and are being, initiated by the European Commission, the European Social Partners and the Member States to concretise and specify this strategy within the "open method of coordination".

## Benchmarks for Education and Training Systems

The Commission staff working paper *Progress towards the Lisbon Objectives in Education and Training* (EC, 22.03.2005) illustrates how far the EU Member States are on their way to achieve the benchmarks set for 2010. The data clearly indicate the gaps to be filled by tailored measures over the coming years. Table 7 summarises the achievement of the EU–25 and of several new Member States—Czech Republic, Hungary, Poland and Slovenia—as an illustration of the situation in these countries; in some cases, where comparable data are available, comparisons are also made with Japan and the USA. The table also includes the three best European performers.

Table 7. Progress in achieving the 2010 benchmarks for education and training set by the European Council in 2003

| Benchmark for 2010 (at EU average) | Progress made so far | | Three best performers |
|---|---|---|---|
| Reduce ratio of early school leavers to no more than 10% (values in % 2004) | EU–25 | 15.9 | Poland (5.7%), Czech Republic (6.1%), Slovakia (7.1%) |
| | CZ | 6.1 | |
| | HU | 12.6 | |
| | PL | 5.7 | |
| | SI | 4.2* | |
| Percentage of low–achieving 15–year–olds in reading literacy should have decreased by at least 20% compared to the year 2000, i.e., to 15.5% (values as % of low achievers 2003). | EU–25 | 19.8 | Finland (5.7%), Ireland (11.0%), Netherlands (11.5%) |
| | CZ | 19.4 | |
| | HU | 20.5 | |
| | PL | 16.8 | |
| | SI | – | |
| | Japan | 19,0 | |
| | USA | 19,4 | |
| At least 85% of 22–year–olds should have completed at least upper secondary education (values as % of 22–24–year–olds 2004) | EU–25 | 76.4 | Slovakia (91.3%), Czech Republic (90.9%), Slovenia (89.7%) |
| | CZ | 90.9 | |
| | HU | 83.4 | |
| | PL | 89.5 | |
| | SI | 89.7 | |
| Total number of graduates in maths, science and technology should increase by at least 15% compared to the year 2000 (i.e., to 783 000), while at the same time the level of gender imbalance should decrease (values in 1000, 2003) | EU–25 | 740.0 | Average annual increase 2000 – 2010: EU–25 average (+ 4.6%), Slovakia (+22.6%), Poland (+12.7%), Spain (+10.4%) |
| | Japan | 229.7 | |
| | USA | 430.7 | |

continued

| Benchmark for 2010 (at EU average) | Progress made so far | | Three best performers |
|---|---|---|---|
| Participation rate in lifelong learning should be at least 12.5% of adult working age population (age 25–64, values in % 2004) | EU–25 | 9.4 | Sweden (35.8%), Denmark (27.6%), Finland (24.6%) |
| | CZ | 6.3 | |
| | HU | 4.6 | |
| | PL | 5.5 | |
| | SI | 17.9 | |
| Substantial annual increase in investment in human resources; data relate to total expenditure (in EUR PPS) on public and private educational institutions per student compared to GDP per capita at lower and upper secondary level of education and training (Values: expenditure per student / GDP per capita in % 2001) | EU–25 | 27 | Cyprus (37%), Portugal (35%), Italy (33%) |
| | CZ | 22 | |
| | HU | – | |
| | PL | – | |
| | SI | 28 | |
| | Japan | 27 | |
| | USA | 25 | |
| Substantial annual increase in investment in human resources; data relate to total expenditure (in EUR PPS) on public and private educational institutions per student compared to GDP per capita at tertiary education level (values: expenditure per student / GDP per capita in % 2001) | EU–25 | 39 | Sweden (59%), Slovenia (57%), Denmark (53%) |
| | CZ | 39 | |
| | HU | – | |
| | PL | – | |
| | SI | 57 | |
| | Japan | 45 | |
| | USA | 64 | |

\* data unreliable or uncertain.
Source: Eurostat data, if not indicated otherwise; Commission staff working paper: Progress towards the Lisbon objectives in education and training. 2005 report, Brussels, 22.03.2005; OECD: PISA—studies 2000 and 2003.

These figures show that the European Union still has rather a long way to go to achieve the goal of a learning society and to become a world quality reference by 2010.

On vocational education and training, the *Maastricht Communiqué* (2004) required that reforms and investment should focus on four major priorities:

1. improvement of the image and attractiveness of the vocational route for employers and individuals;
2. achieving high levels of quality and innovation in vocational education and training systems;
3. linking vocational education and training with labour market requirements of the knowledge economy;
4. taking account of the needs of low–skilled and disadvantaged persons to achieve social cohesion and increase labour market participation.

These priorities are further qualified by concrete measures which should be implemented at national and/or European level, such as increasing participation in lifelong learning; reducing the number of school dropouts; strengthening lifelong vocational guidance and counselling; validation of non–formal and informal learning; constructing a European Qualification Framework and credit transfer system; ensuring more learning–conducive environments in organisations and schools; increasing mobility and transparency, ensuring high quality and appropriately skilled vocational education and training teachers and trainers.

To implement all these measures, increased investments in vocational education and training and ensuring equity of distribution of funding—particularly in the new Member States with private investments in education and training—are crucial. Investment is still far from sufficient to ensure a highly skilled workforce, given the long time lag between reforms of education and training systems and effects on the labour market. If investment does not increase, substantial problems, e.g., skill shortages and skill gaps, can be expected in the medium and longer term, particularly in view of the demographic decline and the ageing of workforces.

One cross–cutting issue is the improvement of evidence–based policy. This requires a substantial improvement in the scope, precision and reliability of vocational education and training statistics to enable regular evaluation of progress and an understanding of which interventions and decisions are required by all parties involved.

# Future Challenges and a Possible Initiative

Institutional settings and reforms of education and training systems, the quality and design of curricula and training programmes and the cooperation of all actors involved play a crucial role in strengthening the links between education/training, labour markets and society and moving towards a European learning society. It depends decisively on the capability of the systems of education, training and science to produce, impart and translate new knowledge into the world of work, to develop human capital and thus to contribute to innovation, growth and social cohesion. A particular dilemma is to reconcile economic growth on the one hand and social cohesion on the other.

For long–term educational planning—at State, individual and enterprise level—information is necessary on future changes and alternative options for policy actions, as well as on their impact. Research on the impact and benefits of education/training and skills for individuals, enterprises and society confirms the outstanding importance of human (and social) capital in contributing to economic growth, social inclusion, citizenship and a number of further material and non–material benefits at all levels. To pre–empt frictions and skill–related imbalances on labour markets in good time, it is essential to anticipate the future skill needs of individuals, companies and the economy and to devise strategies to shape education and training systems in a future–oriented way.

It is widely acknowledged today that the various social, economic and individual objectives associated with education and training cannot be fulfilled solely by the State nor solely by the market. Rather, they require cooperation and consensus among all actors. In consequence, education and training are increasingly being steered at decentralised levels in most EU–countries. This is expected to improve identification of local labour–market needs and to more efficiently monitor the assignment of expenditure. The role of the State—and partly of the EU—is to define the framework conditions and to promote cooperation and coordination.

An important target for the European Union is to put more emphasis on human capital, to modernise education and training systems in terms of effectiveness, quality, mobility and social cohesion, and to stimulate the relevant investment. The setting of concrete goals, objectives and work programmes started with the Lisbon process in 2000 and has in the meantime generated a number of promising follow–up activities. In several respects the new Member States start from a good basis, e.g., with respect to the skill and qualification levels of their populations. In other cases, they have a considerable distance, particularly concerning participation in lifelong learning, or in levels of literacy. The same applies to cooperation between different actors, especially with social partners and for policies to decentralise power to regional and local levels.

The question of whether the goal of becoming a learning society and, as the Lisbon goals formulates it, the most competitive and dynamic knowledge–based economy in the world can be achieved, and whether European education and training systems will become a world quality reference by 2010 must remain open for the moment. To move closer to a learning society and a knowledge–based economy,

> "Europe needs an innovation strategy to foster investment in, and the quality of, human capital. More effective use of resources, a future–oriented design of vocational education and training and new approaches to learning in schools and at work are essential ingredients of such a strategy. [...] To move forward, governments should identify the key issues of such an innovation strategy, supported by public–private partnerships and agreements on innovation pacts with social partners and other stakeholders. Setting benchmarks and regular assessments of progress made should become a joint activity for all those concerned." (Tessaring and Wannan, 2004: 9)

## Notes

1. Parts of this section summarise some findings of Cedefop's second and third reports on vocational training research in Europe (Descy and Tessaring, 2001; Descy and Tessaring, eds, 2004).
2. The relatively high share of low skilled people in Australia may be due to the high number of aborigines with no or little participation in education and training.
3. The percentages indicated by Wilson and Briscoe refer to percentage points of the growth *rates*.
4. Most of the data stem from the World Values Survey and the International Adult Literacy Survey.
5. See for example Heise and Meyer, 2004.
6. Returns on education and training include the benefits of education and training in terms of after–tax lifetime earnings and both direct costs (e.g., tuition fees) and indirect costs of education (opportunity costs, i.e., earnings foregone due to additional schooling). These returns on the resources invested in education and training can be computed into one single indicator—the internal rate of return. The internal rate of return on schooling is defined as the discount rate that makes the net present value of the lifetime earnings stream, generated by a change in schooling, equal to the present value of the relevant stream of costs.

# References

Bassi, L., Harrison, P., Ludwig, J., and McMurrer, D. *Human Capital Investments and Firm Performance.* Atlanta, GA: Human Capital Dynamics, 2001.

Coulombe, S., Tremblay, J.–F. and Marchand, S. "Literacy Scores, Human Capital and Growth in Fourteen OECD countries". *International Adult Literacy Survey.* Statistics Canada, Ottawa, Ontario. Catalogue N. 89–552–MIE, 2004.

Council of the European Union. *Council Conclusions on Reference Levels of European Average Performance in Education and Training (Benchmarks).* 8981/03 EDUC 83, Brussels, May 2003.

Declaration of the European Ministers of Vocational Education and Training, and the European Commission, convened in Copenhagen on 29 and 30 November 2002, on enhanced European cooperation in vocational education and training. "The Copenhagen DCeclaration", Copenhagen, 2002.

Descy, P.; Tessaring, M. *Training and Learning for Competence.* Second report on vocational training research in Europe: synthesis report. Luxembourg: EUR–OP, 2001. (Cedefop Reference series).

Descy, P.; Tessaring, M. (eds) *Impact of Education and Training.* Third report on vocational training research in Europe: background report. Cedefop Reference series, 54. Luxembourg, 2004.

European Commission (EC). *Progress Towards the Lisbon Objectives in Education and Training.* Commission staff working paper, Brussels, 22.03.2004.

Green, A., Preston, J. and Malmberg, L.–E. "Non–Material Benefits of Education, Training and Skills at Macro Level". In: Descy, P.; Tessaring, M. (eds) *Impact of Education and Training.* Third report on vocational training research in Europe: background report. Cedefop Reference series, 54. Luxembourg, 2004, pp. 119–177.

Hansson, B.; Wagner, P. "Impact of Education, Training and Skills/Competences at Company Level". In: Descy, P.; Tessaring, M. (eds) *Impact of Education and Training.* Third report on vocational training research in Europe: background report. Cedefop Reference series, 54. Luxembourg, 2004, pp. 261–319.

Heise, M. and Meyer, W. "The Benefits of Education, Training and Skills from an Individual Life–Course Perspective with a Particular Focus on Life–Course and Biographical Research". In: Descy, P.; Tessaring, M. (eds) *Impact of Education and Training.* Third report on vocational training research in Europe: background report. Cedefop Reference series, 54. Luxembourg, 2004, pp. 321–381.

Maastricht Communiqué on the Future Priorities of Enhanced European Cooperation in Vocational Education and Training (VET) (Review of the

Copenhagen Declaration of 30 November 2002), Maastricht, December 2004.

OECD: *Education at a Glance*. Paris, 2003 and 2004.

Presidency Conclusions, Lisbon European Council, 23 and 24 March 2000 (http://ue.eu.int/ueDocs/cms_Data/docs/pressData/en/ec/00100-r1.en0.htm [cit. 27.06.05]).

Wilson, R.A. and Briscoe, G. "The Impact of Human Capital on Economic Growth: A Review". In: Descy, P.; Tessaring, M. (eds) *Impact of Education and Training*. Third report on vocational training research in Europe: background report. Cedefop Reference series, 54. Luxembourg, 2004.

Leney, T. et al. *Achieving the Lisbon goal: The contribution of vocational education and training*. 2004 (available at http://www.refernet.org.uk/documents/Achieving_the_Lisbon_goal.pdf. [Cit. 25.05. 2005]).

Tessaring, M.; Wannan, J. *Vocational education and training—key to the future. Lisbon–Copenhagen–Maastricht: mobilising for 2010*. Cedefop. Luxembourg, 2004.

• JURAJ VANTUCH •

# Lisbon Process and a Knowledge Europe: A Policy Perspective of Central and Eastern European Countries

## Lisbon: the New Goal

The conclusions of the Lisbon European Council represented a turning point in European policy not only by announcing "a new strategic goal for the next decade"[1] and by the expression of the urgency "to agree a challenging programme"[2], but also as an attempt to address education and training more comprehensively from an EU point of view. Under the heading "Education and training for living and working in the knowledge society" the Lisbon conclusions stressed the importance of adapting education and training systems "to the demands of the knowledge society", to meet six identified targets. The first of these was "a substantial annual increase in per capita investment in human resources" ; while "to undertake a general reflection on the concrete future objectives of education systems, focusing on common concerns and priorities while respecting national diversity" (§I.25–27) was the most significant for future strategy. Building knowledge infrastructures, enhancing innovation, modernising education systems; Lisbon indeed seems to be a crucial step in the effort to make education and training a real element of genuine European policy, despite the limitations set by the Treaty on European Union[3] and the principle of subsidiarity.

"Preparing the transition to a knowledge–based economy and society by better policies for the information society and research and development" (Lisbon 2002, §1.5) and understanding that "people are Europe's main asset and should be the focal point of the Union's policies" (Lisbon 2002, §1.24), all seem to be heavily influenced by Third Way political programmes. There is nothing wrong in recognising finance, knowledge and social capital as driving forces of modern economies and in the Third Way beliefs that result from correct criticism (Leadbeater 2000) of the New Right and Communitarianism. Nevertheless, the central point is the fruitfulness of such a change and the importance of this change in policy measures rather than the change in the rhetoric itself. So what needs to be stressed here is

- the gap between new ideas and the introduction of detailed policies about how such ideas can be implemented;
- the gap between two transitions: the transition to a knowledge–based economy of the EU old members and the "double transition" of post–communist countries simultaneously facing a) transition to democracy and a market economy after the collapse of communism, and b) transition to the knowledge–based economy; and
- the gap between the understanding of "an appropriate macro–economic policy mix" (Lisbon 2002, §1.5)[4] by diverse politicians and diverse countries' political representations.

## The Lisbon Strategy

The Lisbon conclusions addressed lifelong learning in harmony with the development of active employment policies. In this context the stress was on "giving higher priority to lifelong learning as a basic component of the European social model, including by encouraging agreements between the social partners on innovation and lifelong learning; by exploiting the complementarity between lifelong learning and adaptability through flexible management of working time and job rotation" (§1.29). The conclusions of the Santa Maria da Feira European Council confirmed the lifelong learning as "an essential policy for the development of citizenship, social cohesion and employment" and invited "the Member States, the Council and the Commission to identify coherent strategies and practical measures with a view to fostering lifelong learning for all..." (§ II.B 33).

This call for coherence in strategies is worth stressing here for two reasons: as evidence of an early recognition of the importance of achieving coherence; and, at the same time, as a signal of future inconsistency between economic and social reforms:

- preparing the transition to a competitive, dynamic and knowledge–based economy;
- modernising the European social model by investing in people and building an active welfare state.

One might think that investing in people is considered more important for people's quality of life and the sustainability of the traditional welfare state rather than for the competitiveness of the economy and its future adjustment to the challenge of technology and a knowledge–based economy.

This is interesting, predominantly in the light of subsequent developments. At present the failure of the EU to achieve the main goal of Lisbon is already clear, largely due to a lack of coherence in policies and to the difficulties in the new conceptualisation and maybe even the re-definition of the "welfare" state.

Of course, increasing competitiveness and building a knowledge economy must be accompanied by wide–ranging implementation of new information and communication technology and relevant activities in this field must also be highlighted. The *eEurope Action Plan*, a crucial part of the Lisbon strategy, was also adopted in Feira in 2000 with the aim of increasing business, school and household connections to the Internet within the next three years[5], followed by similar goals to be achieved by 2003 within the *eEurope+ Action Plan* launched by the then thirteen Candidate Countries at the Göteborg European Council in June 2001[6]. Insufficient utilisation of the ICT infrastructure resulted in the eEurope 2005 Action Plan endorsed by the Seville European Council in 2002 with the aim of creating modern online public services (eGovernment, eLearning, eHealth) and a dynamic e–business environment making use of a widespread broadband access at competitive prices by the end of 2005 (EC 2002, 3)[7]. However, as discussed later, the performance of new Member States remains significantly below the EU–15 average.

The Lisbon Council requirement to "undertake a general reflection on the concrete future objectives of education systems" (§1.27) was addressed by a report presented to the Stockholm European Council in March 2001 (Education Council 2001), which set out strategic objectives. The Barcelona European Council subsequently accepted the detailed Work Programme for 2010[8], reaffirming Stockholm's basic principles of improving quality, facilitating universal access and opening–up to the wider world; and explicitly stated the additional main goal for education and training systems by setting "the objective of making these educative and training systems a world quality reference by 2010" (Barcelona 2002, §43).

Furthermore, the Stockholm Council conclusions explicitly named "IT and digital skills"(§III.10) as a top priority with regard to the EU main Lisbon goal and called for the elimination of the shortfall in the recruitment of scientific and technical staff, the encouragement of more young people to take up scientific and technical studies, and for the recruitment of qualified teachers in these fields (§III.11).

Interestingly and significantly, further actions "to introduce ... closer co–operation ... in the context of the Sorbonne–Bologna–Prague process" and "similar action ... in the area of vocational training" were promoted by the Barcelona Conclusions (§41). This was undoubtedly a clear invitation to follow the concept of "the European area for..." It paved the way leading through the Bruges process, the *Copenhagen declaration* and the *Maastricht communiqué* expected in November 2004 to the creation of the European area for vocational education and training and further strengthened coherence in respective education and training segments under the umbrella of lifelong learning. Barcelona finally made the explicit link between the European area for lifelong learning and the European employment strategy making the Lisbon process transparently comparable in importance with the Cardiff and Luxembourg processes.

## Lisbon and the Concept of Lifelong Learning

The Lisbon conclusions view lifelong learning as a result or consequence of the functioning of the new economy, i.e., as a tool for improving employability, reducing skills gaps and enhancing adaptability (§I.29). However, in addition to this genuinely economic context of the interpretation of lifelong learning, the Lisbon Conclusions have outlined another perspective as well—that of society—by "giving higher priority to lifelong learning as a basic component of the European social model, including by encouraging agreements between the social partners on innovation and lifelong learning; by exploiting the complementarity between lifelong learning and adaptability through flexible management of working time and job rotation; and by introducing a European award for particularly progressive firms"(§I.29). Lifelong learning is believed to be an important instrument for modernising this model, for combating social exclusion, for reducing disparities and inequities amongst different social groups, i.e., for attaining social cohesion.

Furthermore, the Lisbon Council has noted, though in a more covert and indirect way, the humanistic value of lifelong learning for individuals by underlining that "people are Europe's main asset and should be the focal point of the Union's policies"(§I.24). Lifelong learning should provide individuals with ways and means for personal development and self–realisation, for an active and fruitful life.

Thus, as these three aspects—economic, social and personal—show, Lisbon might be seen as an attempt to promote a holistic interpretation of lifelong learning, stressing its importance for the transformation of Europe into a competitive and dynamic society that gives its members the opportunity to develop and realise their potential as individuals, as citizens and as economic agents.

Until this is successfully put into practice, however, there is a risk that the first two aspects will prevail, leaving the third as mere political rhetoric.

Alternatively, Lisbon may be seen as a strategic vision which must be "processed" further. Such processing usually includes both a detailed elaboration and clarification of the initial ideas as well as further operationalisation which "translates" documents into versions ready for use in practical policy. Paradoxically, yet typically, there is a subtle distinction between clarification/refinement of the original message and a modified guise suddenly seen as diverted from the original message at least by part of relevant players. This is where we want to highlight the issue of correct interpretation of policy documents. Which interpretation of a policy paper is the correct one depends on the verification criteria and on how explicit the document is.

If verification criteria are based on democratic procedures, which is hopefully our case, there is no risk of historically well–known conflicts of orthodox interpretation and a variety of heretical deviations. There is no centralised power to decide about the "orthodox" version within EU, but there is, of course, a need to reach an agreement on the core final interpretation. Not surprisingly, political positions are heavily projected into alternative interpretations, indeed it could even be said that political standpoints are imposed on the Lisbon process interpretation. Although the final interpretation is being simultaneously identified and co–

processed in confrontation with concurrent proposals of interpretation/elaboration, there are already some clearly describable concepts behind the on–going discussion. Based on underlying assumptions as to the driving force of the Lisbon process, these could be termed globalisation driven (given the prevailing economic rationale) or Europeanisation driven (given the attempt to conceptualise the specific European path for development), and with an emphasis on one of the above aspects: economic, social and personal.

## Selected Lisbon Targets for Analysis

The Lisbon and subsequent summits also initiated the operationalisation of the general strategic vision and particularly the vision of lifelong learning and its translation into specific benchmarks and guidelines. One could argue about the extent to which the "translation" has been successful, but here we would like to mention only four selected targets expected to be implemented by Member States[9]:

- a substantial annual increase in per capita investment in human resources;
- the number of 18 to 24–year–olds with only lower–secondary level education who are not in further education and training should be halved by 2010;
- schools and training centres, all linked to the Internet, should be developed into multi–purpose local learning centres accessible to all, using the most appropriate methods to address a wide range of target groups; learning partnerships should be established between schools, training centres, firms and research facilities for their mutual benefit;
- the Member States should ensure that all schools in the Union have access to the Internet and multimedia resources by the end of 2001, and that all the teachers needed are skilled in the use of the Internet and multimedia resources by the end of 2002 (Lisbon 2000, §I.6.11).

Further analysis will be limited to the success and failures of the policy response of CEECs—currently new Member States of the EU—to the four above targets seeking to find out whether and how the Lisbon policy agenda has been adopted by candidate countries. This will be done on the basis of selected policy documents[10] of CEECs.

## New Member States' Response to the Lisbon Target "Increasing Investment in Human Resources"

The following is an analysis of how CEECs[11] have responded to the first of the above policy challenges.

Not surprisingly, the richest post–communist state, Slovenia, shows the highest public expenditure on education as percentage of GDP, closely followed by the significantly less wealthy Baltic states—Lithuania, Latvia and Estonia respectively (Table 1). Remarkably, the highest expenditure among old Member States is demonstrated by Scandinavian countries—Denmark, Sweden and Finland (Table 2).

Table 1. Total public expenditure on education in selected CEECs in 2002 (as % of GDP)

| Country | eu25 | nms10 | CZ | EE | HU | LV | LT | PL | SI | SK | BG | RO |
|---|---|---|---|---|---|---|---|---|---|---|---|---|
| ISCED 0 | 0.52e | 0.57e | 0.55 | 0.44 | 0.93 | 0.67 | 0.79 | 0.45 | 0.60 | 0.56 | 0.63 | 0.80 |
| ISCED 1 | 1.18e | 1.40e | 0.71 | 1.59 | 0.98 | 1.09 | 1.02 | 1.89 | 2.62 | 0.60 | 0.72 | 1.27 |
| ISCED 2–4 | 2.40e | 2.25e | 2.28 | 2.54 | 2.34 | 3.17 | 2.67 | 2.18 | 1.48 | 2.31 | 1.68 | 0.76 |
| ISCED 5–6 | 1.14e | 1.08e | 0.88 | 1.12 | 1.26 | 0.89 | 1.41 | 1.09 | 1.33 | 0.88 | 0.54 | 0.70 |
| Total | 5.22e | 5.31e | 4.41 | 5.69 | 5.51 | 5.82 | 5.89 | 5.60 | 6.02 | 4.35 | 3.57 | 3.53 |

eEurostat estimate
Source: Eurostat NewCronos database

Table 2. Total public expenditure on education in old Member States in 2002 (as % of GDP)

| Country | eu15 | BE | DE | DK | GR | ES | FI | FR | IE | IT | NL | AT | PT | SE | UK |
|---|---|---|---|---|---|---|---|---|---|---|---|---|---|---|---|
| ISCED 0 | 0.51e | 0.72 | 0.50 | 0.95 | 0.19 | 0.44 | 0.34 | 0.72 | 0.07 | 0.41 | 0.37 | 0.63 | 0.56 | 0.52 | 0.45 |
| ISCED 1 | 1.16e | 1.40 | 0.68 | 1.92 | 1.09 | 1.15 | 1.38 | 1.17 | 1.40 | 1.23 | 1.44 | 1.12 | 1.81 | 2.15 | 1.24 |
| ISCED 2–4 | 2.41e | 2.79 | 2.42 | 2.92 | 1.39 | 1.84 | 2.59 | 2.89 | 1.65 | 2.24 | 2.00 | 2.63 | 2.46 | 2.83 | 2.48 |
| ISCED 5–6 | 1.15e | 1.36 | 1.18 | 2.72 | 1.28 | 1.01 | 2.08 | 1.03 | 1.19 | 0.88 | 1.28 | 1.28 | 1.00 | 2.17 | 1.08 |
| Total | 5.22e | 6.26 | 4.78 | 8.51 | 3.96 | 4.44 | 6.39 | 5.81 | 4.32 | 4.75 | 5.08 | 5.67 | 5.83 | 7.66 | 5.25 |

e Eurostat estimate
Source: Eurostat NewCronos database

CEECs are aware of the need to increase investment in education and training but they are confronted with difficulties in finding proper ways and resources to satisfy this need. With regard to public budget contributions, the policy documents tend rather to list the difficulties and the reasons for not being able to make these increased investments (Bulgaria, Hungary, Romania, Slovakia), than to commit to particular figures.

In many countries politicians avoid being made accountable in strictly measurable terms. In a typical example, coming from Slovakia, during the consultation process on the *Memorandum on lifelong learning* an increase in investment in human resources was advocated for two kinds of reasons: first, the lag behind the OECD and EU levels, and second, the *Millennium* project proposals. The *Millennium* project, which was a sort of *Green paper* on education, explicitly suggested increasing expenditure on education to 5% by 2006 and to 6% by 2010. Similarly, there were specific requirements concerning research and development (0.33% of GDP in 2002 compared to the 1% of GDP considered necessary). Nevertheless, the final version of the *Millennium* project which was adopted by the government and parliament almost without changes as the *National programme of training and education in the Slovak Republic for forthcoming 15–20 years* does not contain any measurable commitments concerning the increase in investment. All initial proposals to increase investment in terms of percentage of GDP were omitted. Quite typically, the Ministry of Finance fighting to achieve Maastricht criteria strictly opposed any kind of measurable commitments which might increase public expenditures.

Not surprisingly, it was Slovakia that called for international action on the analysis of needs in financing education/learning, referring to "unintentional and hidden process", and "a risk of negative impact in weak transforming economies" : "In post–communist countries, the already noted lack of investment in the modernisation of schools and decline in the status of teachers can ultimately reinforce concerns about the irreversible disintegration of the education system and future threats to one of these countries' few comparative advantages—a solid level of education. Despite this, in the negotiation process, candidate countries quickly close the "easy" (but full of hidden problems) chapter 18 on education. ...Under the pressure of the "difficult" chapters and financially demanding commitments which the candidate countries must take upon themselves if they want to reach the European standard, hard "conditions" for the candidate countries' accession to the EU are also indirectly specified for the area of education. ... And so in a certain parallel to the recognition of the necessity of protecting and creating the natural environment, we put forth the idea of protecting and creating the education environment on the national and international stage..."[12]

Furthermore, a similar "unintended negative pressure" can occur as a consequence of the Common Agricultural Policy: generous EU subsidies for agriculture create an indirect pressure for savings in the public sector in new Member States, i.e., very likely also in education.

The difficult fiscal situation of post–communist countries is understandable, given that the GDP of these countries was well below the average in the Member States and many were working hard just to exceed the results of the former command driven economy at the turn of millennium (Table 3). Only Poland and Slovenia managed to significantly exceed the 1989 level, with Hungary and Slovakia slightly improving on their 1989 results.

Table 3. Transition countries' economies—2000/1989 comparison (1989 = 100)

| Country | BG | CZ | EE | HU | LV | LT | PL | RO | SK | SI |
|---|---|---|---|---|---|---|---|---|---|---|
| 2000/1989 GDP Index | 70.9 | 97.8 | 83.0 | 104.2 | 64.1 | 64.9 | 126.6 | 76.9 | 102.6 | 114.3 |
| 2000/1989 Real Wage Index | 54.6 | 109.7 | 70.3 | 83.9 | 67.1 | 46.9 | 98.6 | 65.5 | 81.9 | 906 |
| 2000/1989 RPE* Index | −61 | +34 | +56 | −3 | +60 | +63 | +55 | n.a | −23 | n.a |

*Real Public Expenditure "on pre–school, basic and secondary education" per school age child, 2000 and 1989 (per cent change), 1999/1990 for Hungary, 1999/1992 for Estonia, 2000/1993 for Latvia and Lithuania, 2000/1991 for Bulgaria and 2000/1990 for Poland.
Source: Social Monitor 2002 (Monee project), UNICEF 2002

The second line indicates that the average income was below the 1989 level in all countries except the Czech Republic (however, even there this was due to delayed economic restructuring and lax fiscal policy rather than to a healthy and productive economy). The third line shows that an increase in investment in education is not in line with economic performance; this will be discussed in more detail later.

The position of political parties managing the transition was quite difficult, not just due to the lag behind the efficiency of EU economy but also to sharp falls in living standards in transition countries. From the real wage index in the table above, one can understand why there is a risk of the popularity of hard core left wing post–communist parties and why politicians are driven by the most acute economic problems and thus often reluctant to increase funding in education which is a future–oriented investment.

All these countries suffer from a lack of resources for public finance and rely heavily on the assistance they will receive from the ESF. Nevertheless, there are interesting differences between these countries in priorities in public policies (see Table 4 and Figure 1).

Table 4. Public expenditures on education related data in selected post–communist countries (2000)

|  | GDP per capita | | Per capita education expenditure | EΨ*** (Education Political Support Index) | | |
|---|---|---|---|---|---|---|
|  | (PPP in $)** | Rank | (PPP in $)* | Index | EΨLCRW**** | Rank |
| Bulgaria | 5 254 | 8 | 958 | 18.2 | 66 | 7 |
| Czech Republic | 13 874 | 1 | 2 804 | 20.2 | 74 | 5 |
| Estonia | 8 551 | 5 | 2 345 | 27.4 | 100 | 1 |
| Hungary | 12 275 | 2 | 2 568 | 20.9 | 76 | 4 |
| Latvia | 6 340 | 7 | 1 706 | 26.9 | 98 | 2 |
| Lithuania | 6 840 | 6 | 1 526 | 22.3 | 81 | 3 |
| Poland | 9 547 | 4 | 1 782 | 18.7 | 68 | 6 |
| Slovakia | 10 878 | 3 | 1 644 | 15.1 | 55 | 8 |
| Ukraine | 3 499 | 9 | 457 | 13.1 | 48 | 9 |

Source: Initial data from the Monee project, tabled and calculated by author; quoted from *Social monitor 2002*, UNICEF, Fig.1.13 and Table1.4
* Public expenditure on pre–primary to upper secondary education per 3–18–year–old in PPP in USD;
** GDP in PPP in USD;
*** Education Political Support Index (EPSI or EΨ) measuring importance of education within country public policy priorities calculated as column 3 and column 1 ratio, i.e., per capita public expenditure on education (3–18 year olds) and per capita GDP ratio;
**** EΨ Leading Country Related Wage, respective country EΨ index compared to Estonian (leading country in this sample) EΨ index (in %), indicating perception of importance of education compared to the perception of importance of education in Estonia

Although somewhat wealthier countries, such as the Czech Republic, Hungary, Slovakia and Poland, are ranked first in terms of GDP per capita, the Baltic countries are ranked first in the importance of primary and secondary education among the country's policies measured as the per capita public expenditure on education (pre–primary to upper secondary) and per capita GDP ratio (Figure 1).

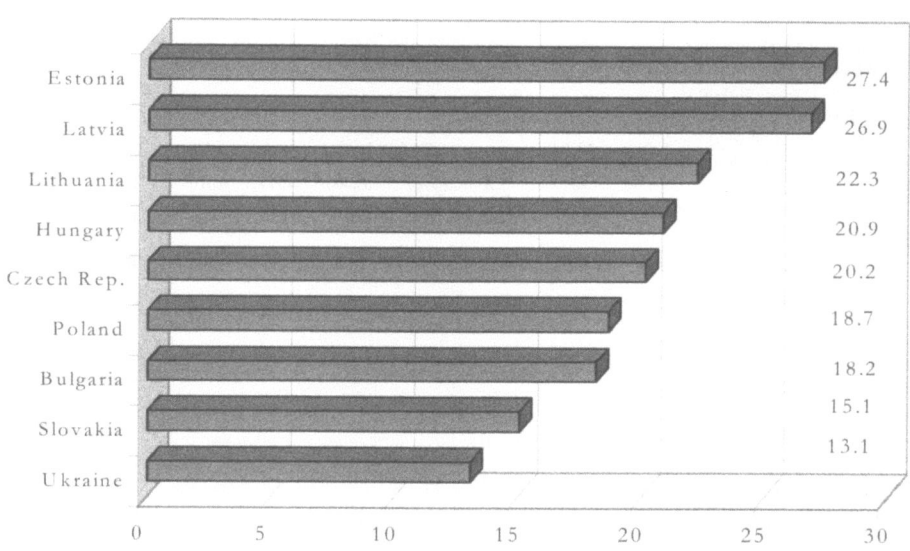

Figure 1. Education Political Support Index
(per capita public expenditure on education
in PPP / GDP per capita in PPP, 2000)

Source: Initial data from the Monee project

The EΨ index clearly shows Estonia as spending the highest share of GDP per capita on education and all the Baltic states significantly surpassing the wealthier countries in central Europe, whilst Slovakia is revealed to be severely under–investing in education. Analysing the ranking in more detail in relation to the EΨ Leading Country—Estonia (counted as 100%)—Related Wage, Slovakia is at only 55% of the value, behind Bulgaria (66%) and close to the level of the significantly poorer Ukraine (48%).

A very similar picture appears from the more recent data gathered jointly by UNESCO/OECD/Eurostat (UOE data) on per capita expenditures on primary, secondary and tertiary education public institutions. Total spending from diverse sources, including households, related to GDP and all adjusted to the purchasing power in relevant countries, can be considered an indicator of the investment in the future labour force (although private providers' contribution to the education and training is disregarded here).

**Table 5. Per capita expenditure on public educational institutions as compared to GDP per capita in 2002 (EUR in PPS)**

|  | CZ | EE | LV | LT | HU | SK | BG | RO | EU15 |
|---|---|---|---|---|---|---|---|---|---|
| P.c. public expenditure on education—all levels | 3052.3 | 2170.9 | 2107.3 | n.a. | 3441.8 | 2035.5 | 1328.3 | 1170.8 | 5763.6e |
| P.c. public expenditure on education ISCED 1 | 1790.2 | 1948.8 | 1927.0 | n.a. | 2604.2 | 1283.4 | 988.1 | 768.9 | 4596.1e |
| P.c. public expenditure on education ISCED 2–4 | 3187.1 | 2615.3 | 2114.6 | n.a. | 2849.8 | 1905.2 | 1138.8 | 1039.8 | 5930.9e |
| P.c. public expenditure on education ISCED 5–6 | 5533.0 | 4020.0 | n.a. | 3336.3 | 7083.8 | 4126.4 | 2421.4 | 2761.4 | 8207.9e |
| *GDP p.c. in PPS* | *14300* | *9800* | *8200* | *8900* | *12300* | *10800* | *6100* | *6000* | *23300* |
| Total p.c. expenditure/GDP p.c. | 21.3 | 22.9 | **25.3** | n.a. | **27.9** | 18.7 | 21.7 | 19.5 | 25.0e |
| Expenditure p.c. at ISCED 1/GDP p.c. | 12.5 | **20.6** | **23.1** | n.a. | 21.1 | 11.8 | 16.2 | 12.8 | 19.9e |
| Expenditure p.c. at ISCED 2–4/GDP p.c. | 22.3 | **27.6** | **25.4** | n.a. | 23.1 | 17.5 | 18.6 | 17.3 | 25.7e |
| Expenditure p.c. at ISCED 5–6/ GDP p.c. | 38.6 | **42.4** | n.a. | 36.5 | **57.5** | 37.9 | 39.6 | **45.9** | 36.1e |

e Eurostat estimate
p.c.—per capita
Data for Poland and Slovenia are not available
Source: Eurostat NewCronos database. Calculations are made by Eurostat from detailed data.

At a first glance it seems that CEECs with higher GDP per head also invest more in education (e.g., Czech Republic and Hungary, Table 5), but the relative measurement of spending to the GDP shows a somewhat different picture. Hungary and Latvia show a particularly high future labour force investment indicator. If, however, we look at the structure of per capita investments in public educational institutions by level of education as compared to GDP per head, we can see that public education investment in Hungary is concentrated on higher education and it is Estonia and Latvia[13]—with much lower GDP per capita—that invest heavily at *all* levels of education. At the primary education level, Latvia is leading, while at the secondary education level Estonia is in the lead. It is interesting however that, if measured in relation to GDP per head, at the tertiary education level all new Member States invested relatively more than the EU15 countries (average—36.1). This perhaps demonstrates the weight given to tertiary education in allocation of resources and in the policy under the pressure of reforms directed towards developing a learning society and knowledge–based economy in new Member States. Although the data on the third "Baltic tiger" are missing, one cannot ignore a public will to invest in education and thus readiness to build a knowledge–based economy in the economically developing but still less wealthy Baltic countries.

Of course despite the public will to invest in education in CEECs, one should remember that in absolute numbers these investments are still behind that of other EU countries—in line with the GDP per capita which is also radically lower in transition economies (in the Baltic countries over 3 times less!). This situation will persist at least for some years, and in such conditions private investment becomes invaluable. From the national policy perspective such investment may be supported by certain legal instruments and by support for a HR–investment–friendly climate.

In policy documents of CEECs a particular attention is given to measures to encourage employers to provide training for their workers. Plans include improvements in current incentives, both in terms of training grants from some specialised funds (Poland, Slovenia, Hungary) and a system of tax relief for training expenses (Romania, Poland, Latvia, Slovakia).

SMEs and large companies are often contrasted. Large restructured companies with foreign strategic investors and/or owners bring their own culture, experience and, as a rule, more means allocated for training. This is, of course, not applicable for low skilled and low value–added work and products. Special measures to assist SMEs' investment in human resources are advocated by several countries (e.g., Latvia explicitly called for state policy development aimed at preparing SMEs for future ESF activities).

Investment in initial vocational education and training is a special case worth mentioning. There are countries that still rely almost exclusively on state financing of initial vocational education and training (typical examples being the Czech Republic and Slovakia). These countries, however, face the challenge of reforming the financing initial vocational education and training. One option is based on levy–type funds, where a typical example with several years of positive experience is Hungary. In Hungary, employers already contribute 1.5% of their payroll costs to the Vocational Training Fund and can retain 0.5% of their contribution for training their own employees. However, Hungary also stresses the fact that more attention needs to be paid to identifying training needs, organising and funding human resources development for employees of SMEs. Levy–type funds are often criticised as having high transaction costs, and measures based on tax relief are promoted by political right wing oriented experts. Nevertheless, such ideas remain too general (offering proposals on vouchers, tax deduction, individual accounts, without relevant financial analyses) and hampered by governments' usual reluctance to reduce the tax burden.

Improvement of the system of individual tax allowances for education and advanced professional training and the creation of a system of cheap loans are anticipated to meet individuals' education and training costs (e.g., Poland). Slovakia suggests the introduction of personal accounts in education that could be used to encourage people to contribute to the cost of their education by means of special savings and deposits supplemented by scholarships granted by public or private organisations. Worth highlighting is an Estonian approach that allows for 26% of the cost of learning (or of the learning of taxpayer's children) to be claimed back from the State Tax Office. Another approach could consist of business systems that allow workers free time or provide funding to attend classes of their choice or related to their occupation. Again, an example of good practice comes from Estonia, which guarantees paid educational leave for fourteen days a year.

As we have seen, Estonia and other Baltic countries, in spite of economic hardship and scares financial means—in contrast to the wealthier Czech Republic and Slovakia—recognise the importance of investment in human resources and manage to demonstrate it in policy making and its implementation. If we go back to the data for Nordic countries in Table 2, this pro–educational stance could perhaps be partly explained by cultural similarities between Scandinavian countries and the Baltic enclave.

New Member States' response to the Lisbon target "Decreasing the number of school drop outs and youngsters with only lower–secondary level education"

The problem of school drop–outs and early school leavers and the follow–up actions aimed at those, not attending further education and training, is more urgent in the old Member States than in the new ones, as visible from the figures below.

Figure 2 ranks countries according to the percentage of the adult population (25–64 years old) that has completed at least upper secondary education (ISCED 3). There are two islands of success here: countries in the centre of the CEEC region, where education systems were historically influenced by Germany and Austria, and the Baltic/Nordic countries. However a comparison with the situation among the younger generation (20–24–year–olds) demonstrates that if Slovakia, Czech Republic, Poland and Hungary have managed to improve their situation, educational attainment in the Baltic countries has deteriorated—unlike in their Scandinavian counterparts Norway, Finland and Sweden. This raises the question of whether the high attainment among the adult population of the Baltic new Member States is not owing to the former Soviet education system where completion of secondary education was compulsory; with the introduction of more freedom of choice, and under the conditions of austere economic transition and perhaps uncertainty as to the future benefits of education, a younger generation is not always keen to pursue their education to higher levels.

**Figure 2. Percentage of the population aged 25 to 64 and 20 to 24 having completed at least upper secondary level of education\* (in %, 2004\*\*)**

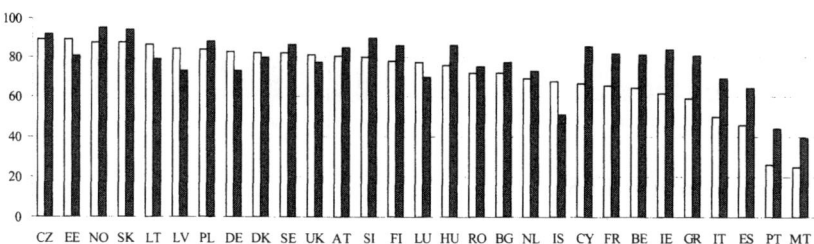

Source: Eurostat (LFS), calculation by the author
\* i.e., at least ISCED 3 level;
\*\* 2004 data on 25–64–year–olds were not available for all countries: 2002 data were used for Denmark and 2003 for the Netherlands.

Figure 3 ranks countries according to the percentage of young people aged 18 to 24 who quit education early (at ISCED 2 level, i.e., without completing upper secondary education). This confirms the above conclusions: here again the centre–north "alliance" is in the lead, with the Baltic new Members States in a noticeably worse position. Quite interestingly, Bulgaria and Romania, whose indicators are among the worst (markedly, along with other south European countries), managed to slightly improve the attainment situation among younger people as compared to the adult population (see Figure 2 above).

## Figure 3. Percentage of the population aged 18–24 with at most lower secondary education and not in further education or training (in %, 2004*)

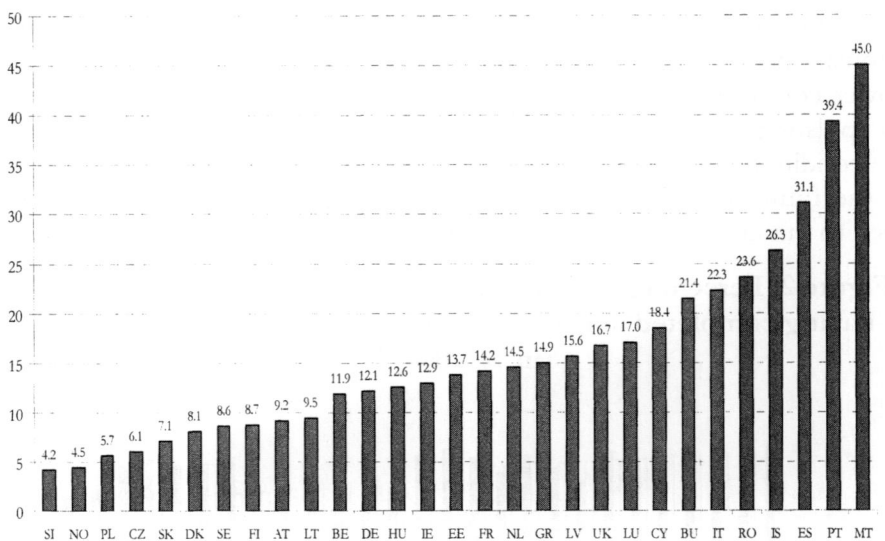

Source: Eurostat (LFS)
* data for Luxemburg are 2003; provisional data are used for Austria, Netherlands, Greece, UK, Luxemburg; data for Slovenia are not fully reliable.

This relative "advantage" of new Member States as regards early school leavers does not mean they are neglecting the issue. The policy documents analysed show, however, that there tends to be a rather one-sided approach to the issue–with an emphasis either on reducing school drop–out rates, or on "second chance" education and training where the issue is treated quite generally, without identifying young people between 18 and 24 years of age as a specific priority target group.

Poland is an example of the first approach and has set ambitious targets in its *National strategy for employment and human resource development 2000–2006 (Narodowa strategia*, p. 32) with regard to school–based education: raising the rate of participation in compulsory education from 98.1% in 1999 to 98.5%–99.5% in 2006; raising the rate of participation of young people aged 17–19 in secondary education from 82.0% in 1999 to 84%–86% in 2006; increasing the percentage 21–year–olds who have completed secondary school from 46% in 1999 to 65%–70% in 2006.

In contrast to this school centred approach Latvia has stressed the social aspect and the increased risks facing young people with a lower level of education: "...(if the problem of) young people with insufficient educational achievements (is) left unsolved, it directly transforms to a problem of social exclusion, or even marginalisation (drug addiction, alcoholism, delinquency)"[14].

Of course, decision–makers everywhere understand the close links between early school leaving and the risk of social exclusion. On the other hand, it is worth stressing that youngsters at risk of dropping out from school or who have already dropped out require a more complex approach than just repeated re–insertion into the environment which has already failed them.

Furthermore, there is a risk that in post–communist countries, traditionally low drop–out rates from schools mask a softening of formal qualification criteria required within school–leaving examinations. Schools are facing a dramatic decrease of population in different age cohorts and a high risk of lagging behind in the quality of educational infrastructure due to a lack of funding. Without functioning quality assurance systems there is a risk that the quality of educational and training output will be adjusted to new and harder conditions: schools prefer to keep their drop–out ratio low rather than maintaining their high standard of output. Moreover, there is a question whether post–communist countries' schools, traditionally oriented towards "teaching" and "transmitting" the knowledge to students and heavily supervised by the previous regime, would be able to cope with a new environment and the increase of social pathology which accompanies the process of social liberalisation in these countries.

Additionally, there is a risk that in post–communist countries the proportion of early school leavers with ISCED 3C (i.e., education which does not provide access to the tertiary level) or lower levels of education may increase as a consequence of rising "new poverty" and demotivation of youngsters to study without a clear perspective of real higher earnings after graduation. Post–communist countries fail to recognise the value of achievement. The sudden transformation from wage–levelling under the previous regime to the possibility of profiting from the opportunities thrown up by the changes could lead to a decrease of the quality of education and training of the population and the labour force as a whole. Furthermore, lacking strategic planning by individuals in their newly gained freedom, e.g., the low absorption of regional labour markets and the attraction of new opportunities offering "earning without sweat", might lead to a fall in the value placed on education/learning in the sensitive period of initial education.

Post–communist countries have to pay special attention to the reprofiling of secondary education with a refined system of certification based on a modular approach and a wider variety of post–secondary non–tertiary education that is both better adjusted to the needs of the labour market and offers alternative opportunities for personal development to the narrowly academic education within traditional tertiary education. Diversification in the provision of the post–secondary education, including non–university tertiary education is an urgent challenge, which is in practice linked with a slightly less urgent reduction in the numbers of drop–outs and/or early school leavers.

New Member States' response to the Lisbon target "ICT in schools" and to the "eGovernment" objective

The first progress report on meeting eEurope+ objectives (Ljubljana 2002) proved that Bulgaria, Romania and Slovakia are lagging behind other CEECs. The final progress report (Budapest 2004) included a large number of comparative data on CEECs and revealed that Bulgaria, Romania and the Slovak Republic, the latter alone among the current EU Member States, showed an extraordinary anomaly in the extent of access to the Internet: the number of access points from Internet cafés exceeded the number in schools (Table 6). There is no stronger evidence that the IT infrastructure of education has lagged behind the potential and needs of the population. It may be possible even to claim that the level of computer literacy level of the population is higher and does not match the level of ICT education in these countries.

**Table 6. Interviewees having used the Internet in last three month by place of access (%)**

|  | BG | CZ | EE | HU | LT | LV | PL | RO | SK | SI |
|---|---|---|---|---|---|---|---|---|---|---|
| Place of education | 9 | 18 | 15 | 26 | 35 | 21 | 43 | 13 | 23 | 15 |
| Internet café | 42 | 10 | 4 | 3 | 14 | 20 | 32 | 26 | 28 | 3 |

Source: *eEurope+ household survey*, June 2003 (*eEurope+ progress report* 2004)

Furthermore, the report has shown that the highest increase of the Internet users was in the Czech Republic, Estonia and Slovenia. In these three countries 50% of respondents from the household survey had been connected to the Internet three months preceding the survey. This is, to a large extent, due to relatively low costs of access to the Internet. It can be seen from the following table that twenty hours of telephone connection in peak time represented 15% of household income in Slovakia and over 20% in Poland (Table 7). This far exceeds the average of former candidate countries (9.8%) and it cannot be compared to Slovenia (2.4%), the Czech Republic (5.5%) and Estonia (6.8%,), not to mention the economically much stronger new Member States of Cyprus and Malta.

**Table 7. 20 hours peak dial up cost as a % monthly household income**

|  | BG | CY | CZ | EE | HU | LT | LV | MT | PL | RO | SK | SI |
|---|---|---|---|---|---|---|---|---|---|---|---|---|
| Cost (%) | 20.7 | 0.8 | 5.5 | 6.8 | 10.8 | 13.2 | 13.8 | 2.4 | 20.5 | 14.4 | 15.0 | 2.4 |

Source: *eEurope+ telecommunication operator and NSO survey*, June2003 (*eEurope+ progress report* 2004)

The Lisbon conclusions see the Internet as becoming a major medium for the transmission of information, communication, transaction and media in Europe by 2010. Nevertheless, the most common way to access the Internet in post–communist countries, if any, is through dial-up connections. Although the provision of broadband for large corporations and even large schools is progressing steadily, the availability of broadband for households, SMEs and small, often rural, schools is hampered by the underdeveloped market in telecommunications. Broadband is necessary to stimulate the use of the Internet by enabling convenient access to information and usage of services. The "widespread availability" targeted by *eEurope 2005 Action Plan* (EC 2004) needs to be stimulated by targeted policies of central government or local authorities, but this is still far from being the general case. DSL and cable television, as well as microwave connections, are still too expensive in absolute terms and in comparison with gains from the Internet for mass clients in post–communist countries. National information policies are often rather declarative and free market powers are hampered by the old stakeholder—the State—as well as the strategic investor / new owner from taking advantage of the monopoly. The last mile problem is often not rectified due to inefficiency or even reluctance to do so on the part of the state and telecommunication regulator, leading to a vicious circle of low demand not stimulating supply and low and costly supply holding back demand.

## Table 8. New Member States and Candidate Countries' eGovernment rankings* (2004)

| | Overall score | Connectivity and infrastructure | | Business and legal environment | | Education and skills | | Government policy and vision | | eDemocracy | | On-line public services for citizens | | On-line public services for business | |
|---|---|---|---|---|---|---|---|---|---|---|---|---|---|---|---|
| Category weight | | 0,20 | | 0,10 | | 0,10 | | 0,15 | | 0,15 | | 0,15 | | 0,15 | |
| Estonia | **5.87** | 3.37 | 3 | 6.80 | 2 | 7.67 | 1 | 6.50 | 1 | 4.60 | 1 | 6.38 | 2 | 7.52 | 2 |
| Czech Republic | **5.67** | 3.98 | 1 | 6.95 | 1 | 7.33 | 2–3 | 6.10 | 2 | 3.60 | 3 | 5.68 | 5 | 7.57 | 1 |
| Slovenia | **5.33** | 3.68 | 2 | 6.60 | 4–5 | 7.33 | 2–3 | 5.00 | 5–6 | 2.90 | 5–7 | 6.73 | 1 | 6.68 | 4 |
| Poland | **4.74** | 2.43 | 7 | 6.60 | 4–5 | 6.67 | 5–7 | 5.30 | 4 | 2.90 | 5–7 | 5.98 | 3 | 5.33 | 9 |
| Hungary | **4.69** | 3.15 | 4 | 6.66 | 3 | 7.00 | 4 | 5.50 | 3 | 3.30 | 4 | 5.00 | 6–7 | 4.19 | 11 |
| Turkey | **4.64** | 2.67 | 6 | 4.23 | 11 | 5.67 | 9–10 | 4.90 | 7 | 4.20 | 2 | 5.70 | 4 | 6.00 | 8 |
| Lithuania | **4.62** | 2.21 | 9 | 6.36 | 6 | 6.33 | 8 | 4.70 | 8–9 | 2.60 | 8–11 | 5.00 | 6–7 | 7.08 | 3 |
| Latvia | **4.58** | 2.34 | 8 | 6.32 | 7 | 6.67 | 5–7 | 5.00 | 5–6 | 2.60 | 8–11 | 4.79 | 8 | 6.35 | 5 |
| Slovakia | **4.44** | 2.80 | 5 | 6.28 | 8 | 6.67 | 5–7 | 3.80 | 10 | 2.90 | 5–7 | 4.46 | 9 | 6.08 | 7 |
| Romania | **3.99** | 1.43 | 11 | 5.42 | 10 | 5.33 | 11 | 4.70 | 8–9 | 2.60 | 8–11 | 4.08 | 10 | 6.16 | 6 |
| Bulgaria | **3.71** | 1.92 | 10 | 5.50 | 9 | 5.67 | 9–10 | 3.10 | 11 | 2.60 | 8–11 | 3.95 | 11 | 5.08 | 10 |

Source: McCauley 2004
* Maximum score in each category: 10

Similarly, a lack of investment in eLearning is hampering the acquisition of new skills by teachers and trainers in weak economies, leading to low demand for eLearning solutions, which throws up questions about the need for investment without policy decisions. Estonia and Slovenia offered good practice examples in contrast to Poland and Slovakia, despite quality programmes. eGovernment and eLearning solutions are declared rather than made real to a full extent. Teachers and trainers in post–communist countries are at higher risk of sticking to traditional face–to–face instruction due to the lack of funding of inevitable ICT infrastructure. Universities face severe difficulties in offering on–line services, not to speak of the sustainability of virtual campuses which are unable to expand their services after funding from a given project expires.

The Lisbon strategy stresses the importance of support for raising the quality of digital services in public administration, commerce and education that should be available for all EU citizens. The EIU's White Paper (McCauley 2004) confirmed the results of previous reports; Estonia, Czech Republic and Slovenia led the table and Slovakia ranked last among the new Member States. The following table gives detailed information on this, with the partial score, ranking and weight in the overall score (Table 8).

An unsurprising addendum to this analysis comes from the ICT expenditure statistics. 2003 Eurostat data[15] on expenditure on IT hardware, equipment, software and other services as a percentage of GDP confirm the leadership of Estonia (3.4%) and the Czech Republic (3.8%) as the only new Member States above the EU–15 average (3%) and with the Czech Republic even exceeding the USA (3.8%).

# The Lisbon Process in the Framework of the Accession Process

Integration into the EU provided all accession countries with space for adjustment to the "club" rules, harmonisation of law and not lastly the financial commitments in terms of inevitable investment in order to meet EU standards, i.e., in protection of the environment, the reduction of air and water pollution, drinking water supply and sewage systems, waste water treatment, etc. It is a serious challenge for many weak economies that entered the EU in 2004 and or will enter in 2007. Furthermore, all new Member States have to follow the Common Agriculture Policy, which offers generous subsidies to farmers, however at the expense of other sectors.

Thus, there is stiff competition for any kind of investment over and above the accession driven commitments and there are also other fiscal pressures influenced by NATO and European Monetary Union memberships. New NATO members are expected to expand military budgets up to 2%, which cannot be disregarded in the world after 9/11. New EU Member States in addition face the European Monetary Union entry and the need to satisfy the Maastricht convergence criteria:

- inflation rate not higher than 1.5% of the average of the three best performing countries,
- long–term interest rate not higher than 2% above the average of the three countries
- with the lowest inflation rates,
- exchange rate within the 15% fluctuation margins of EUR for at least two years preceding the entry,
- government budget deficit not higher than 3% of its GDP,
- general government debt not higher than 60% of the GDP.

The table below however indicates that all CEECs, except for the Baltic countries and Bulgaria, have faced problems at least with regard to one criterion, Hungary being at risk in all criteria with significantly higher indebtedness in comparison to all others (Table 9). Moreover, CEECs stand to exceed their budget deficits and their Ministries of Finance will hardly be open to any substantial increase of investment in education. The convergence programmes of these countries can barely reflect the call of Lisbon process to invest more in human resources from the public budget.

### Table 9. Eight new EU Member States main convergence indicators (2003)

|  | Inflation rate | Deficit (% GDP) | Debt (% GDP) |
|---|---|---|---|
| Bulgaria | 2.3 | –0.1 | 46.2 |
| Czech Republic | –0.1 | –6.6 (–12.9) | 37.6 |
| Estonia | 1.4 | 2.6 | 5.8 |
| Hungary | 4.7 | –5.9 | 59.0 |
| Latvia | 2.9 | –1.8 | 15.6 |
| Lithuania | –1.1 | –1.7 | 21.9 |
| Poland | 0.7 | –4.1 | 45.4 |
| Romania | 15.3 | –2.0 | – |
| Slovakia | 8.5 | –3.6 | 42.8 |
| Slovenia | 5.7 | –1.8 | 27.1 |
| Criterion | 3.6* | –3.0 | 60.0 |

Source: Eurostat, European Central Bank
*estimated according to the criterion definition

On the contrary, the Baltic countries with Estonia in the lead (and Bulgaria!), although not the wealthiest, are the most successful in terms of healthy macro–economic situation, and thus may have a better opportunity to increase investment in human capital.

## About the Appropriate Policy Mix

Post–communist countries are very different from the old EU members where the functioning market economy has a more or less successful long history. Except Slovenia, which could capitalise from a less rigid communist experiment and is already catching up with two of the old EU low performing economies (Greece and Portugal), all the other new countries have to struggle with the heritage of the command economy and, in some cases, with certain failures in the initial phase of their transition.

Table 10. GDP per capita in Purchasing Power Standards (PPS, EU 25 =100)

| | 1995 | 2000 | 2005** | Index of relative change* | | |
|---|---|---|---|---|---|---|
| | | | | 00/95 | 05/00 | 05/95 |
| Czech Republic | n.a. | 65.3 | 71.1 | n.a. | 108.9 | n.a. |
| Estonia | 34.2 | 41.9 | 52.3 | 122.5 | 124.8 | 152.9 |
| Greece | 72.8 | 72.9 | 82.8 | 100.1 | 113.6 | 113.7 |
| Ireland | 100.2 | 127.1 | 132.2 | 126.8 | 104.0 | 131.9 |
| Latvia | 30.1 | 35.7 | 46.1 | 118.6 | 129.1 | 153.2 |
| Lithuania | 34.4 | 38.8 | 50.4 | 112.8 | 129.9 | 146.5 |
| Hungary | 50 | 53.8 | 63 | 107.6 | 117.1 | 126.0 |
| Poland | 41.1 | 46.1 | 48.1 | 112.2 | 104.3 | 117.0 |
| Portugal | 73.8 | 77.8 | 73.1 | 105.4 | 94.0 | 99.1 |
| Slovenia | 69 | 73.7 | 79.2 | 106.8 | 107.5 | 114.8 |
| Slovakia | 45 | 48.2 | 52 | 107.1 | 107.9 | 115.6 |
| Bulgaria | 31.4 | 27.1 | 33.4 | 86.3 | 123.2 | 106.4 |
| Romania | n.a. | 25.5 | 32.4 | n.a. | 127.1 | n.a. |
| EU–25 | 100 | 100 | 100 | 100 | 100 | 100 |
| EU–15 | 111.8 | 110.5 | 109.2 | 98.8 | 98.8 | 97.7 |
| United States | 155.7 | 157.6 | 154.6 | 101.2 | 98.1 | 99.3 |

Source: Eurostat NewCronos database
* index of indexes (calculated from respective PPS data, which are related to EU 25 countries average set equal 100);
** forecast

Currently two clubs are visible among the rest of new post–communist EU members. The Baltic club has a balanced policy mix allowing solid funding of education and at the same time featuring macroeconomic stability. In contrast to this, there is the Visegrad Four club in the centre of the CEEC region with comparably lower investment in education but differing in fiscal policies. While the Czech Republic, Hungary and Poland have loose fiscal policies that have earned a lot of justified criticism from economists and in particular from neoliberals, Slovakia is applauded for the strength of its fiscal policy in the 2000s and for its harsh reforms in the Washington consensus[16] style. Nevertheless, it is not clear whether this harsh and unpopular cost saving policy will be eventually successful (and accepted by the electorate for the next policy term). The price for fiscal prudence and a maybe almost iconic attitude to macroeconomic data based on the short–term strategic decision—to enter EMU as soon as possible—may be very high. The deteriorating learning environment in regional schooling and the lag in ICT introduction in schools and society, with no top quality universities and with an insufficiently developed R&D infrastructure indicate serious difficulties in the future and could ultimately lead to a failure to build a knowledge–based society. It would be unfair to blame economists, in particular those responsible for public budgeting and/or such international players as IMF and World Bank (WB) who advocate restrictive policies with regard to spending, for doing their job, but there is a serious discrepancy in policies that is visible almost worldwide. Not just the European Union in the Lisbon strategy but also advocates of a new consensus in the WB as well as opponents of the Washington consensus among former WB leaders, i.e., all those who stress investment in education and technology[17] as a new important policy in support of growth and fighting poverty, have to find a balance between the two extremes:

- calls in favour of investment in human resources, which without measurable outputs and agreed criteria to meet, tend to turn to plain rhetoric and
- sticking to fiscal prudence (a balanced budged is doubtless inevitable in the long run), which might however turn to fundamental iconic approach to arbitrarily set criteria.

How much room should be left for discretion and flexibility in decision making? This is a well known and again crucial question in the dispute between advocates of "sticking to rules and believing in best governance" and advocates of the "ability to decide, believing in capable and honest decision makers". Macro–economic stability alone does not assure high growth. Post–communist countries, in their aspiration to successfully integrate into the EU and driven by strict rules of EMU, might be at risk of forgetting the areas left up at their discretion. It is a strange mix to see: the loudly proclaimed importance of investment in people, linked with a generally correct subsidiarity principle regarding the education agenda, and with "what–is–left" practice in budgeting and financing education at the national level.

Europe is at a crossroads. It is impossible to keep both a traditional welfare state (and still even after the reform, a too generous common agricultural policy, the aim of which is "to provide farmers with a reasonable standard of living..." according to the European Commission[18]) and become a competitive economy with highly skilled and educated people permanently able to produce high value added. This is the lesson from old Member States affected by globalisation and deteriorating employment situation with unpopular decisions waiting for politicians and citizens.

It is impossible to maintain both fiscal prudence for the sake of good macroeconomic figures and to prevent a lagging behind in R&D, quality education and training funded by both public and private investment and the increasing indebtedness of individuals lured by everyday consumption with finally inferior economic performance in the long run. This is the lesson from post–communist countries, unless you are an Estonian.

I hope I am not mistaken and Estonia and the other Baltic "tigers" have really managed to find a balance being a free economy and at the same time the most pro–learning country among newcomers into the EU and possibly within the EU.

Estonia seems to have achieved the coherence in policies so much stressed by European Councils and to turn rhetoric into working measures. The study of good practice is strongly promoted in Europe and it is well worth studying the Estonian example. Estonia seems to manage to be on the right track in the transition to a learning society and a knowledge–based economy without strictly imposed rules and stringent criteria. But for others it might be an asset to try to agree upon measurable objectives and checkable indices recommended within a sort of stability pact to secure a healthy learning environment for individuals, the fight against social exclusion and finally for labour force for European economy. Otherwise any broad recommendations to invest in education, training and technology development might be sacrificed to other priorities directly enforced by concurrent policies.

# Notes

1. "...to become the most competitive and dynamic knowledge economy in the world, capable of sustainable economic growth with more and better

jobs and greater social cohesion" (Presidency Conclusions of the European Council in Lisbon, 23–24 March, 2000, §I.5)
2. "…a challenging programme for building knowledge infrastructures, enhancing innovation and economic reform, and modernising social welfare and education systems" (Presidency Conclusions of the European Council in Lisbon, 23–24 March, 2000, §I.2)
3. The Maastricht Treaty signed on 7 February 1992.
4. Interestingly this was mentioned in the document immediately after the aim "modernising the European social model, investing in people and combating social exclusion."
5. For the results see *eEurope 2002 final report*, COM(2003) 66 and *eEurope 2002: progress made in achieving the targets*, SEC(2003)407.
6. For the results see *eEurope+ progress report*, issued on the occasion of the European Ministerial Conference on the Information Society, Budapest, 26–27 February 2004.
7. For the results see evaluation *eEurope 2005 mid–term review*, COM(2004) 108 final.
8. Detailed work programme on the follow–up of the objectives of education and training systems in Europe. *Official journal of the European Communities*. C 142 of 14 June 2002.
9. Some other targets, such as European framework definition for basic skills, European CV and mobility of students, teachers and research staff, appear less relevant for this analysis, as their implementation is heavily depended on actions undertaken at the EU level (though in collaboration with Member States).
10. Predominantly on CEEC national reports on the consultation process on the *Memorandum on lifelong learning, Joint assessment papers on employment policies;* and other policy documents when explicitly indicated.
11. It is focused mainly on eight CEECs that entered the EU in 2004 and on Bulgaria and Romania expected to enter the EU three years later. The discussion is predominantly based on the consultation process which followed publishing *A memorandum on lifelong learning* (EC 2000).
12. National Report of the Slovak Republic on the consultation process on the *Memorandum on lifelong learning*, chapter 3.2b, proposal No. 6.
13. Unfortunately the data on public investment at the tertiary education level for Latvia are missing.
14. National report on the consultation process on the *Memorandum on lifelong learning*, p. 2.
15. Eurostat NewCronos database, structural indicators http://europa.eu.int/comm/eurostat/structuralindicators (cited 15 May 2005).

16. Term attributed to J. Williamson meaning ten principles consisting of fiscal prudence end macro–economic stability, opening markets, privatisation, deregulation and decentralisation, and some others considered a good policy for economic growth and consequently for a model of the transition and transformation of economies in post–communist countries; for more see Williamson, John. "What should the world think about the Washington Consensus?" In *The World Bank Observer*, August 2000.
17. E.g., Joseph Stiglitz.
18. See e.g., presentation of EU activities from December 2004 at http://europa.eu.int/pol/agr/overview_en.htm (cited 15 May 2005).

# References

Barcelona European Council. *Presidency Conclusions*. 15–16 March, 2002.
Education Council. *The Concrete Future Objectives of Education and Training Systems*. Report to the European Council: outcome of proceedings, 14 February 2001 (5980/01).
*eEurope+ progress report*. Issued on the occasion of the European Ministerial Conference on the Information Society, Ljubljana, 3–4 June 2002.
*eEurope+ progress report*. Issued on the occasion of the European Ministerial Conference on the Information Society, Budapest, 26–27 February 2004.
European Commission. *A Memorandum on Lifelong Learning*. Commission staff working paper. SEC(2000) 1832, Brussels, 2000.
European Commission. *eEurope 2005 Action Plan: An Update*. COM(2004) 380 final. Brussels, May 17, 2004.
European Commission. *eEurope 2005: An Information Society for All*, COM(2002)263, Brussels, 2002.
Leadbeater, Ch. (2000): *Living on Thin Air: The New Economy*. Penguin Books
Lisbon European Council. *Presidency Conclusions*. 23–24 March 2000.
McCauley, D. (ed.). *E-government in Central Europe. Rethinking Public Administration*. A White Paper from the Economist Intelligence Unit. London, NY, Hong Kong: 2004.
Ministry of Education of the Slovak republic. *Millennium: The National Programme of Training and Education in the Slovak Republic for Forthcoming 15–20 years*. Bratislava, IRIS, ISBN 80–89018–36–X.
*Narodowa strategia wzrostu zatrudnienia i rozwoju zasobów ludzkich w latach 2000–2006* http://www.mgip.gov.pl/Praca/RYNEK+PRACY/Strategie/.
National reports on the consultation process on the *Memorandum on lifelong learning*.
Santa Maria da Feira European Council. *Presidency Conclusions.*19–20 June 2000.
Stockholm European Council. *Presidency Conclusions*. 23–24 March 2001.

• ADELA–LUMINITA ROGOJINARU •

# Learning Challenges for Social Inclusion in Transition Economies

## Introduction

This contribution analyses the current state of social integration through learning in all forms of education and training (formal schooling, self–education, work experience, etc). One of the main hypotheses of political reports and research which focus on the benefits of lifelong learning is that by increasing the scope and duration of education societies increase individuals' chances for social inclusion and for better integration in the workplace.

However, the main challenge in transition countries is that those at risk are mostly affected by skill mismatch, and we are constantly talking about the vicious circle of human resources. Patterns of exclusion are linked not only to the labour market but also to public participation and individual involvement in public life.

One of the main questions raised is whether the status of different social groups in Central and Eastern European countries (CEECs) is being influenced by "double transformation" and globalization. Can any key success factors of the policies for inclusion be identified? Are these valid in countries in transition?[1]

In analysing the risk factors that occur in particular social groups, it is necessary to choose between common sense and measurement. Common sense will dictate a conclusion based on opinion. Measurement will be focused on empirical evidences. One of the most controversial exercises when the European Training Foundation (ETF) launched the project for cross Central and Eastern European studies of *Vocational Education and Training against Social Exclusion* some years ago was to identify risk factors.[2] We may question the factors and the way many sub–divided groups could be identified by those factors. Is gender a single factor, leading to social exclusion? Is age a factor of risk of exclusion from the labour market? The model of multiple factors or cumulative disadvantage was finally chosen. Key factors were identified that are invariable in the process of social exclusion, in all respects, namely economic, social and public issues.

For the authors of the report on *Vocational Education and Training against Social Exclusion* in the Slovak Republic it was clear that the concept of social exclusion is relatively new and it emerges from the globalisation process "where events and trends within society are demonstrating that economic development does not necessarily result in the equitable distribution of the sum of what is produced" (ETF 2001a). Thus, according to the Slovak report, social exclusion is a result of the unequal distribution of wealth. A typical ethical issue about the corporate contribution to social wealth that fully contradicts in the 20$^{th}$ and 21$^{st}$ centuries the classical theory of Adam the Smith on the Wealth of Nations!

Social exclusion resulting from globalisation is typical not only of CEECs, nor of a transition process, although transition is a process of de–regulation. It also occurs in advanced economies, in which corporate contribution results, as described, in unequal access to profits, since most profits are directed to a small number of investors and stockholders.

This leads to the question of how far social exclusion is a new phenomenon in post communist countries? In the CEECs, exclusion from the labour market and community started to be associated with "post communism", namely the emergence of free market and capitalist mechanisms, at the beginning of the 1990s. One aspect refers to the distribution of wealth, the second to the justice model.

So, the correlated concept to be taken into account is the unjust economic system. When speaking about free market and the "invisible hand", we always are implicitly referring to limited justice systems. Post–communist countries changed the system towards capitalism, and market economies, but liberal *laissez faire* capitalism is structurally unfair, with its class separation and the accumulation of wealth by a minority leading group. Post–communist countries had the opportunity to create effective wealth producing systems, but the wealthier the system is, the more unjust, since wealth is distributed unfairly. Firstly, we should define the terms just and justice. Justice will ensure that people get what ought to be given and done to them. Justice can be analysed as "procedural" (administration of norms and rules), "corrective" (compensation), "retributive" (punishments), and "distributive", which relates to fairness in sharing social benefits and to what we understand by the unequal distribution of wealth and income. Basically, since the distribution favours a tiny minority at the top, a majority will receive less than the mean average. Income distribution follows the same logic, since a lower income leads to insignificant or insufficient possession of wealth.

Additionally, concentration of wealth results in concentration of power, which allows the rich at the top to influence and control the distribution of work in a society, use of the media, public opinion, and participation in high–level decision making. Therefore, an unequal distribution of wealth leads to an unequal distribution of power in society.

Critics of socialism see it too as an unjust system, since the lack or limitation of individual property constrains individuals to consume the whole of their earned wages, without the possibility of increasing their wealth, which is under the control of the public administration of the state. So, limits on private property make the socialist solution artificial in terms of fair distribution, since public authorities exert control over the accumulation of wealth.

But what is an egalitarian society, and what is not? Last decade communism, at least in Romania, claimed that the ideal society would distribute wealth to everyone according to their needs, but that the society would claim a contribution from everyone according to their capacity. Distribution according to need is fair and egalitarian, and it represents the basic approach to anti–poverty in society. Nevertheless, distribution according to need can seem unfair when held up against the measurement of merit. Merit is anti–egalitarian. Since capitalism distributes income according to individual merits, it can be seen as a just distribution. However, distribution by merit is not evenly applied in all sectors of societies, thus a great deal of individual effort and commitment are still not rewarded in capitalist societies. Socialism did little to recognise merit, although more in the direction of needs, and the utopia mentioned above formulated explicit goals of meeting needs.

Social markets and welfare capitalism are inclined to support fair distribution at the bottom, preventing people from falling below an acceptable level defined as minimum. To a lesser extent, it also regulates accumulation at the top.

Therefore the distribution of wealth remains unjust both in market driven societies, such as capitalist markets, or state driven ones, such as socialism. The accumulation of risks derives from this distribution and is inevitable. Exclusion is seen as a risk of individual freedom, and most of those people in the Eastern Bloc who feel some nostalgia will see this as always possible. Nostalgia will lead some people to state that political freedom is identical with *laissez-faire* capitalism, and a free market is basically wild and non–restrictive in economic terms. Equality and liberty are to be reconciled in these terms, towards a consensual view as far as ownership and control are exerted and concerned in different types of society.

It is not my intention to continue a theoretical overview on the distribution of justice. It is however clear that the accumulation of wealth and the exercise of power and liberty cannot easily be reconciled. It is a basic fact that private ownership in any form and the freedom to exchange it guarantees the public participation of people.

What happens in terms of economic and wealth balance in the post–communist transition countries? It could be a process that artificially separates the ideology of wealth from the wealth itself. In post–communist societies the application of the patterns of a new capitalist system becomes an exercise. There are individuals that could not take back or regain any form of goods and transfer them into private property (by accumulating shares and stocks from sold public properties for instance). Voucher privatisation—one of the most applauded State interventions for the transformation of the collective property into distributive values—did not bring any capital that is indispensable to the further development of companies, or long term committed workers who could in turn put better management in place.

Most reports on poverty and exclusion outline the fact that the communist utopia encouraged not only "education for all" (a concept now rediscovered in Western countries), but also "work for all", even if the provision of work was an artificial exercise of central planning, and an austere regime of work for the benefit of all except the individual. In the long run, "work for all" and *the alteration of self–benefit* destroyed not only self–confidence, but even the sense of private ownership and initiative.

In the paper *Measuring Well–Being and Exclusion in Europe's Regions* (2002) Kitty Stewart follows five main factors of well–being versus social exclusion (and subsequent indictors) in measuring regional disparities across Europe: material well being (average living standards in the region, the level and severity of poverty, the degree of income inequality, the quality of housing), productive life, education, health, and social participation (Stewart 2002).

As indicators of regional disparities, these factors are equally relevant for CEECs. With respect to material well–being, in all these countries poverty has been identified as one of the main factors leading to marginalisation and social exclusion. Nationally defined as the share of individuals living in households with an income below 60% of the national median, the data on poverty in countries like Romania, for instance, is alarming, and governmental anti–poverty measures represent one of the main policies aiming at alleviating social exclusion in the transition period.

As regards productive life, long term unemployment was also identified as one of the factors in the risk of social exclusion in CEECs. It is neither unique to nor typical of these countries; at the end of the 1990s, western countries were hit by long–term unemployment, reaching levels of between 30 and 60% of unemployed people, with higher rates of over 70% in southern Italy and Lazio, for example.

Alongside long–term unemployment, informal employment is also a result of huge deficits in the distribution of income. Informal employment provides a considerable amount of income, precarious as it is, and a form of market acceptance, despite the fact that such activities are underground and illegal and this process is stigmatised. Informal employment results from poverty and the lack of social security arising from transition processes. These processes are associated with social and political instability and with the erosion of the capacity of the State to intervene in formalising the public contribution (caused by tax evasion, corruption, heavy bureaucracy). As part of the transition, *informal employment*, as defined by Sabine Bernabé, is considered one way of counteracting social exclusion. Some experts try to answer to the question of how people survive during transition. The answer is "survival strategies", and Johnson, Kaufmann, and Ustenko (cited in Bernabé 2002) identify six types of such strategies in Russia: a) having another job; b) using a dacha or other plot of land to grow food; c) working as a private taxi driver; d) renting out one's apartment; e) business trips abroad (purchase goods for resale); f) renting out one's garage (Bernabé 2002, 21).

If one tries to group these strategies in some larger categories, the first category represents strategies dealing with the emergent structures of the labour market (types of "services" that are not profitable or fully regulated by the formal market). In legal or official terms, these strategies give them an informal character and some grey/underground activities are not legal (bribery, tax evasion etc). The second category refers to strategies relating to financial speculation and power networks (normally at the political level). The third category uses the formality/informality of institutions: part time work, undeclared income, etc.

A World Bank report by Sue Berryman stresses that "informal user charges" (i.e., hidden or not explicit payments for educational services, like extra tutoring) represent a burden for parents, although such costs tend to compensate for low teacher salaries. The very existence of such mechanisms prevents poor children from reaching a level of education that meets public targets. As Berryman legitimately says,

> "to the extent that the incidence of informal payments for education is unfair, limits the education opportunities of the poor, or increases regional disparities, corrective measures may be needed." (Berryman 2000, 53).

The factor of public participation is less sustained in these studies. Access to information can be identified among the risk factors leading to marginalisation , but not necessarily to social exclusion. Nevertheless, deprived areas inside countries or regions in Europe are significant for illustrating how unemployment can be caused by a lack of computer literacy and information processing skills. Globalisation seems to be a process that has single–handedly made an impact on social exclusion. It is a fact that global capitalism and its inequity have created at least two global epidemics—hunger and functional illiteracy. All papers are clear in blaming global markets and international capitalism for these two epidemics.

Loss of social contact and a failure to cope with new life styles are an important aspect of marginalisation and isolation. The report on social exclusion in the Czech Republic refers to research on structural transformations of the lifestyle, and shows that the unemployed people tend to hold the same social values with those of work but they mostly stay in contact with people of the same status (Strietska–Ilina et al. 2000). This phenomenon may lead to social isolation and the formation of an underclass.

The battle against exclusion is not an individually assumed process. In most cases the State intervenes through public policies and measures such as like active measures for employment or community assistance to facilitate the re–entry of excluded people into the labour market. To what extent are the "transition" policies in education and training contributing to deepen or to alleviate social exclusion?

Transition is a complex term because it refers to both policies and economies. The concept of "transition" as applied to the economies of post–communist countries in Central and Eastern Europe is the most politically correct and the least relevant to many of the real economic and social processes in many of these countries. In fact, some of the countries faced deep crisis at all levels, and a change of paradigm was needed in order to re–establish the rule of law and the state of democracy. In some others, new regulatory frameworks were progressively implemented, and these societies arrived at new structures by consensus.

The relevance of "transition" is a key element in analysing those social processes affecting the use of human resources through the practice of new collective attitudes and life styles based on private property and free competition, wealth and mass consumption, civil rights or free access for all to the labour market. Moreover for the last decade we have been witnessing an intensified transformation of the social texture, in both transition countries and in the European Union Member States.

In CEECs, this refers to the transition towards democracy / capitalism/ free market/ private property, towards new ways of thinking (social and political representations). Up to 2004, the main theme of all transition processes was the transition towards "accession" in the European Union, in the sense that most transition measures were accession driven.

In the specialised literature such as Sue E. Berryman's report, the term is mostly used to describe the state of progress from stage A to stage B, the latter being necessarily an improved one: Europe and Central Asia countries are moving at different rates from centrally planned economies to market economies (Berryman 2000, 7).

Does the period of transition towards accession represent a process of transfer of policies and practices? Transition is thus seen as a learning process, proceeding step by step, gradually improved by means of transfer and adaptation to new political and economic practices.

Could transition be innovative by nature? Innovation is a radical process, but transition is not considered to be so. Innovation is a synonym for rapid reform:

> "The underlying assumption is that the details of the trajectory are of secondary importance: any disruption experienced by the economy is

likely to be short–lived and can be neglected (or assuaged by an inflow of foreign aid)." (UNDP, 1999, 33)

Could transition be imitative? The imitation process is passive, while transition should be seen as participatory and process–oriented. Transition is the equivalent of sequential process–oriented reform:

> "The sequential reform strategy, in contrast, focuses on the transition process itself.[...]The underlying assumption is that the details of the trajectory are of critical importance because they in fact determine the speed at which the economy travels and the ultimate destination towards which is moving." (UNDP, 1999, 33)

These characteristics of the process of transition are non–radical/sequential, non–innovative/by transfer, non–disruptive/ participatory. Are they creating new contexts for new/alternative social practices in transition countries?

As a consequence, policies prove to be effective in the long run, while short term interventions remain local and limited in impact. Major reforms are undertaken in social security, as social insurance payments become state regulated and there are minimum social standards for living costs and wage/pensions. Unemployment benefits represent one of the common measures to prevent poverty, yet may lead to marginalisation if no other active measures are associated with such payments. Alongside social assistance measures, active employment policies, such as job creation, retraining, and business start–up facilities are the most appropriate for risk groups.

As for education and training, major restructuring of qualifications, reforms of curricula and teacher training as well as enhanced social partnerships of schools within communities are seen as basic interventions to prevent the social exclusion of young people from the labour market. Yet, the transition from school to work is not easy, employers often use discretionary powers in recruiting their workforce, combined with a lack of human resource development policy and there is not always any real connection either to community needs, or to structural economic crises.

Distinctions are made between strategic, long–term and visionary solutions, and short–term, reactive and compensatory or remedial interventions. As central bodies such as ministries normally implement most measures, the level of ownership on the part of beneficiaries is low. Therefore, seen in a positive perspective, the role of civil society and non–governmental organisations in assuring community empowerment seems to be critical.

The role of the civil society with respect to education and training is not clearly defined. The reports on social exclusion referred to complementary measures of civil society agencies that aid the implementation of policies relating to these target groups. Most of these measures aimed to consolidate the learning environment of young people who are having difficulties in coping with the curriculum or who belong to social groups which tend to face multiple risks of social exclusion, such as Roma people. It seems that non–governmental agencies in CEECs in general implement most good practices, but the impact of all these measures remains limited in terms of coverage and long–term investment. Therefore the sustainability of the measures, i.e., the implementation of successful actions in mainstream schools, is still a challenge with all these reported practices.

Cultural resistance to transition is a fact in all CEECs and forms of anomic behaviour are elements of this cultural transition that lead to processes like the marginalisation of vulnerable groups. This raises a number of questions: What are the main causes for this perceived anomie? To what extent is human capital valued in these countries? What are the social costs and/or benefits of transition and accession? To what extent does solidarity exist and/or prevail among different social groups?

The desegregation and rupture of the social consistency can be seen in terms of classes/categories /groups. People lose their traditions, which leads to a break down of the fabric of the community. The phenomena of power shifts create new community links, more at regional and cross regional levels; and less at that of nations, by means of enhanced mobility and self–capitalisation of knowledge.

Economic insecurity is a second main factor. All reports on post 1990 phenomena note that:

> "Overall, apart from long lasting deteriorating employment prospects for the people in the region, there is uncertainty about the future shape of the economies in the countries of the region". (ETF, 1999, 2)

The phenomena of social exclusion emerged in all CEECs, as evidence of the total disruption. All social exclusion reports start with strong statements about the recentness of social exclusion, since former communist regimes ensured education and employment for all, and moreover rejected the very concept of exclusion as incompatible with the ethical ideal of just distribution.

According to the report on social exclusion in Romania

> "human resources capital was affected by a process of dramatic erosion. The phenomenon of "human de–capitalisation" showed up during the transition period as a result of multiple factors, even though transition is usually considered to be a learning–by–shock process in itself." (Gheorghe et al. 2001, 13)

Human capital represents a new concept in contrast to the earlier one of a centrally planned workforce. Investment in education, quality of life, health and democratic participation are meant to accumulate and increase human capital. Knowledge is valued in theory. In practice, the phenomenon of a brain drain is widespread throughout Southern and Eastern European countries, as most transition processes illustrate the inability to absorb knowledge as long as massive (ineffective) industrial infrastructure is in place. This is why most effective projects and measures addressing social exclusion aim at reaching the grassroots, by means of micro–community networks, or enhanced entrepreneurship.

At the same time, most reports on social exclusion point at a skills mismatch. Investment in knowledge development is a controversial issue: on the one hand, new occupations are emerging and higher order skills are required, but on the other hand, rebuilding infrastructure still requires manual and low level skills in construction, physical labour and agriculture. Therefore, training courses such as pottery, bricklaying and basic manual work remain the main educational instruments for immediate employment.

The question to be asked is whether providing courses in low–level skills for young people is sufficient to achieve a knowledge society. Does such training raise motivation and self–esteem, even if some immediate employment benefit may be generated? Solutions for structural unemployment are not easy to find, unless liberal markets are encouraged and the state acts with its "invisible hand".

As the report on social exclusion in Estonia states,

> "low economic performance of a family puts a child at a risk of perceived social isolation, e.g., lack of positive contact with teachers and classmates and the increased perception of their lack of support. Children identifying their family's economic performance as poor, tend to experience relative psychological deprivation." (Annus et al. 2000, 25)

Going through studies and reports on social exclusion, the ideological and cultural side is missing. Groups at risk can generally be identified by analysing employment/unemployment forms and level of schooling and skills. Although young people are the first group to be dealt with, there is little evidence about the cultural process that normally happens in post–crisis and anomic societies, namely the emergence of youth subcultures.

The model of subcultures as generated by a class phenomenon is reminiscent of the analysis of Phil Cohen in the 1970s (Hall and Jefferson (eds), 1976), who illustrated the erosion of working class culture in post–war Britain, following the impact on family structure and the reconstruction of the local economy from family businesses into larger industries. It is a process that had a considerable effect on the development of new skills, splitting the working class into those with high–tech skills and those with routine labour intensive ones. According to Cohen, the young generation suffered the impact of the changes on their parents' culture, and tried to resolve the tension by means of a new ideological solution: "the latent function of subculture is this—to express and resolve, albeit "magically", the contradictions which remain hidden or unresolved in the parent culture." (Hall and Jefferson (eds), 1976, 32). Cohen's analysis of 1970s subcultures, looking at such groups as Mods, Parkers, Crombies or Skinheads, can be easily extrapolated to the Eastern Bloc in the 1990s. Subcultures could not be manifest under socialist regime. The very fact of being deviant was unacceptable to the regime, which aimed at the highest possible degree of homogeneity in the name of ideal fairness and justice for all.

Nevertheless, by the end of the 1990s in Romania, a phenomenon that was largely mediated but not extensively researched unfortunately became clear with the emergence of various gangs in the district of the capital, Bucharest, that were defined by the general public as "district boys", or "the boys of the neighbourhood".

Studies of gangs and juvenile criminality point to simplistic reasons, such as unemployment in families, dropout from school or poverty. Cultural resistance to new social developments is rarely explained, due to the lack of common understanding on what deviance means. The identification of criminal behaviour among young people is normally seen as procedural deviance, as challenging norms and rules, rather than as cultural resistance. Nevertheless, many cultural aspects identified in reports on social exclusion, such as ruptures of extended families and isolation, as well as the appearance of the "underclass phenomenon" lead to marginalisation and exclusion (Strietska–Ilina et al. 2000).

Is social exclusion a result of the transition process? As stated above, social exclusion in post–communist countries arises out of the accentuation of poverty and of social disorder. Most of the authors of the reports on social exclusion in CEECs refer to these processes as caused by the economic transition. The transition period to a market economy has had a significant impact on employment—affecting labour market volume, structure, efficiency, behaviour, institutions and policies (Strietska–Ilina et al. 2000).

The education system is inefficient and creates imbalances, and the market driven transition puts new pressure on education. Education is chronically underfinanced; there is still insufficient investment in infrastructure, teachers' wages, etc. Some of the state investment seems unproductive, such as reducing the institutionalisation of children in Romania, where the legal incentives to encourage direct support for families in order to avoid institutionalisation have not been as successful as envisaged, and the number of children in institutions remains high.

The shift in governance and the political transition represent general causes of exclusion, in terms of the depreciation of public services and shifts in the role of the State. On the one hand, more responsibility has been transferred to individuals who are not yet capable of responding to the unplanned and uncontrolled economic and social environment. On the other hand, new measures of structural transformations undertaken by the State itself seem to have provoked profound social disequilibria.

In the report from Poland, the new role of the State is identified as one of the causes of social disorder:

> "The role of the state has declined in importance. [...] The reforms, though in principle judged positively, have proved expensive and have affected the general condition of state and society. Other reforms, in social insurance—introducing a three tier system, in education and more local responsibility in health services—narrowed the scope of state responsibility." (ETF 2001, 11)

Such a statement on the negative impact of the reforms that deteriorated the credibility of the State and eroded the social texture reinforces the severe public judgment on the actual role of governments in transition. It also illustrates how the variety and the superposition of governmental measures affected the pace of change and its public ownership.

A similar conclusion was drawn in Romania where a new administration was elected in late 1996 against the background of growing economic and social imbalances. It gave a commitment to implement a wide–ranging structural reform, under a "shock therapy" programme (Gheorghe et al. 2001). The implementation of the reform package (closing down of companies, lay–offs, disruption of the previous economic networks, etc.) caused unavoidable pressures and social tensions. People faced high levels of insecurity—in employment and income, in personal safety, in family relations, in health and education, in pensions and in general social protection. These factors account for a large proportion of the worsening demographic trends.

This has not, however, undermined the role of the State. The State continues to be the main social stabiliser, at least by sustaining social security and the public order. The "social contract" should be respected, to allow the rationale governance and the rule of law. "… increasing reliance on NGOs should not imply that the state can be allowed to abdicate its central role and responsibility in providing social protection and maintaining human security." (UNDP, 1999, 64)

As for the social texture, its erosion is not caused only by chronic unemployment. The accentuation of problems related to human rights and minorities expands. The EU Member States are still facing the problems of settled immigration: how far the groups are assimilated vs. how autonomous they should be. There are two aspects: one, dealing with immigrants coming to work and their assimilation into the labour market, where the question is to what extent job integration creates civic awareness and full participation in public issues. The second aspect relates to settled minority groups that reject integration due to their cultural differences to majority groups. The problems that Ireland or France, for instance, face in the integration of travellers show how difficult the process of cultural inclusion is. In the transition countries the status of minorities is part of the social readjustment: is their inclusion in education and training having a large impact on their public participation? Do they thus contribute to the consolidation of the sphere of public power?

Social texture is also affected by social disparities between rural and urban areas: "a detailed analysis of value orientations showed a deep societal divide between the more educated urban part of the population and the less educated, rural part of the population."(Gheorghe et al. 2001). People tend to maintain living and working rituals and to manifest different types of social cohesion in these areas. In rural communities, where cohesion is more organic, participation in education and training as well as in employment is more linked to family and clan culture and is influenced by intergenerational transfers. In urban communities, on the other hand, which are more abstract in terms of human relations, participation in education and training, and employment is contractual, led by market relations of demand and supply, and influenced by career development models.

Moreover, far–reaching restructuring of industrial sectors causes regional disparities. As long as large state–owned industries benefited from discretionary use of the distribution of investment in CEECs, the fluctuation favoured the cities and the intensive industrial concentration. The decline of central planning and the introduction of capitalist mechanisms led to major restructuring of large industries and to large numbers of redundant workers, especially in areas reliant on a single industry. The redundant urban workers, who received large redundancy payments, then took advantage of self–employment in agriculture. This fluctuation between the rural and urban population is well explained in the Romanian report on social exclusion:

"... from 1992, the internal migration preserved its general direction from rural to urban, but the retrocession of agricultural land and unemployment of urban populations originating from rural areas facilitated an increase in the flows from towns and cities to villages and communes. In 1997, migration has modified its main traditional direction, reacting promptly to the changes operated at the economic level. A process of ruralisation of Romanian society occurred as a result of de–industrialisation of economy and a spontaneous orientation towards agriculture of those made redundant in the industry sector. Such an orientation was also facilitated by the lack of support measures for other sectors which could have otherwise been able to absorb redundant labour." (Gheorghe et al. 2001, 11)

How far this mobility contributes to the restoration of the cultural heritage in rural areas is however uncertain. Agriculture is underdeveloped in most Southern and Eastern European countries, where individual farming traditions have been lost because of the intensive state and cooperative ownership of the communist decades. In addition, the role of the family is less evident in maintaining rural cohesion, and the ownership of land has become an administrative issue more than a cultural one. The return to rural areas may have an impact on creating new lifestyles in the long term.

Vulnerable Roma groups are a sad reality in all transition countries. The report on *Current Practices across Europe to Assist in the Inclusion of Roma/Gypsy Populations through Education and Training and Employment Opportunities* shows that until recently there was no stress on training to make Roma people more employable and no real urge to create jobs for them. Key message 4 of the study urges the creation of a "flexible framework for employment for all", so as to provide a flexible approach between traditional and modern skills, as well as adequate schemes for the transition from school to work for young Roma. Key message 7 of the same report stresses promoting "unbiased public information and encourage more tolerance", with the aim of preventing the phenomenon of "info–exclusion". (ETF 2001b)

As for changes in education and training, enrolment rates declined after transition, as Berryman's report shows. Declining attendance rates at the upper secondary level are especially significant. Also, education costs represent a burden to families in a period of transition, since the resources of the State are limited and are concentrated on certain priorities, such as modernising State institutions, large scale privatisation of industry, ensuring the continuous increase of GDP, reducing regional disparities, etc. (Berryman, 2000). From this point of view, the report stresses that education finance remains a major lever for ensuring fairness, with a recommendation for the central administration of revenues, which can be channelled to local authorities through earmarking.

In terms of the content, all country reports on social exclusion stress the major restructuring of secondary education, especially vocational and technical tracks, to make it more attractive and more suited to the new labour market. Moreover, barriers between levels, programmes and tracks should be removed, by means of flexible transfers.

The conclusions stressed again that education is costly in all transition countries and one of the main instruments to counteract this is by rationalising administration costs in favour of quality and efficiency. Energy losses, teacher–student ratios and payment for non–educational inputs are some of the main factors that obstruct the efficient use of the resources in the educational system.

The next issue to be considered is whether lifelong learning is a tool for preventing unemployment and providing opportunities for lifelong work. Does a secure employment status protect individuals against exclusion? What are the prevailing aspects of employment patterns in transition countries concerning social exclusion?

A major shift from employment opportunities per se to learning opportunities is currently noticeable, much of it within the framework of the Lisbon process. *The Memorandum on Lifelong Learning,* launched in 2000 and extensively debated and adopted by all Member States, created a new perspective on education. The concept is not a new one in CEECs. In Romania, for instance, one of the most memorable processes of the late 1970s was "permanent education". However, as the concept was also embedded in the general rhetoric about the enriched "multilateral human being" of the ideal communist society, the humanistic aims of permanent education passed unobserved by many people.

In a country like Estonia in which education is allocated a higher share of GDP, the principle of lifelong learning represents one of a number of intervention strategies to combat social exclusion. The report states clearly that a rise in the professional education of the head of the household by one level (e.g., secondary vocational or higher education) reduces the risk of poverty by almost 20% (Annus et al. 2000).

Nowadays it is a truism that the higher the level of schooling, the better the integration into the labour market, but in 2000 there were no clear mechanisms in place. To better serve the aims of lifelong learning, governments are investing in information and communication technology (ICT) in schools and in modernising vocational education and training systems to facilitate a better match between supply and demand. In spite of formal efforts, the aspirations of individuals are lost somewhere between the institutional supply and the labour market demand. Some conclusions of the study *The Social Impact of the Continuous Vocational Training* in Romania show that most training programs are job driven, and despite their positive impact on the general professional attitude of the graduates, few courses are seen as developmental in nature (Birzea (ed.) 2001).

Creating learning opportunities for all people throughout their lives remains the European ideal and was put forward by the Lisbon European Council. On the one hand, there is still no room for individual aspiration in the process of matching supply and demand, unless it is included in demand. On the other hand, it is not immediately clear whether the new instrumentalisation of learning is more beneficial for reducing the gap between those people who are socially included and those who are excluded

The new "digital gap" that was created in the last decade represents the uneven investment and distribution of new technologies and e–learning and has created a "learning gap". Is the on–line learner the new model for lifelong learning, and if so, how relevant will off–line learning?

There is no evidence of the impact of new forms of learning on alleviating the participation of the disadvantaged. Recognition of informal and non–formal learning remains the big promise of lifelong learning, to make it an instrument to alleviate social exclusion.

It is a central principle that educational fairness alleviates social exclusion, but this does not always operate in isolation. Other factors are equally important in defining fairness, like the structure and income of households. The lower the family income, the lower the enrolment, and the weaker the interest in learning tends to be: "We already see a relationship linking educational attainment, employment status, wage levels, and poverty in the region" states Berryman's report. (Berryman 2000, 23)

Matching supply and demand seems to be the main problem in ensuring quality. Investment in upper secondary schools is intensive and politically desirable in order to encourage larger numbers of young people to reach level ISCED 3. According to the Lisbon European Council, by 2010, Member States should ensure that the average percentage of 25–59 year olds in the EU with at least upper secondary education reaches 80% or more. Nevertheless secondary and university graduates are seen as threatened by long–term unemployment in many CEECs, such as the Slovak Republic.

Within the whole restructuring, vocational education and training still looks marginal: Does it represent individual failure or a second chance for some vulnerable groups? Moreover, what level of vocational education becomes more attractive?

The two alternatives are contradictory. On the one hand, secondary education seems to offer the chance of employment: for several years there has been a shift from basic vocational to full secondary education, either general or vocational, and some basic vocational schools "produced" unemployed people (Noncheva et al. 2000). On the other hand, secondary education does not guarantee a job and a stable income, as the percentage of low–income people with secondary education is also relatively high (Noncheva et al. 2000).

One major recommendation points to the easiness of the progress in learning provided that quality is assured: "Easier" does not have to, and indeed should not, mean lowering standards (Berryman 2001). Fairness can be achieved either through mainstreaming, in which case a suspicion of integration/assimilation remains, or by creating alternative/individual pathways, in which case minority groups are likely to denounce the segregation.

Some definitions of the various strategies to be adopted are offered in the report of the European Training Foundation's (ETF) Advisory Forum, as follows:

> "Equal opportunities strategies" = assisting in overcoming "exogenous" handicap.
> "Equal treatment strategies" = elimination of discriminatory strategies.
> "Equal outcomes strategies" = *ex–post*, second–chance type provision.
> (Matheu 1999, 14–15)

Looking at the correlation of lifelong learning in employment terms, it is clear that lifelong learning does not necessarily lead to lifelong employment. Paradoxically, there is no change to a new employment paradigm to respond to innovation in learning. In the 21st century people can no longer devote their lives to basic limited occupations. Lifelong learning gives individuals more freedom and more responsibility for their own learning, skills and decision to work. Individuals should be free to find training, get trained, find employment or start a business, and eventually be successful in the market.

Ideologically, the lifelong learning paradigm is a liberal one, addressing a liberal market, but the same liberal market has been blamed for having created unjust distribution. To avoid this, the State should therefore intervene to create opportunities for learning for all, since, as we have seen, opportunities do not always match individual ideals and aspirations. The study of the social impact of continuous vocational training in Romania illustrates that most beneficiaries may consider themselves more highly trained but report no changes in their professional life, such as improved status or salary at their job place (Birzea (ed.) 2001). On the other hand, more learning does not always guarantee employment in a paralysed economy like some in Southern and Eastern Europe and the Western Balkan today.

The next question to be considered is whether States or/and societies are able to support the long–term costs of lifelong learning. Who is investing and for what? What are the costs of national education and training systems aimed at preventing discrimination against work and guaranteeing inclusion for all?

The willingness of governments remains the major instrument in combating social exclusion. In Romania, "education and vocational training, although declared national priorities by law, continue to confront serious difficulties with long–term negative impacts. The chronic underfinancing of the education system (less than 4% of GDP, which represents the minimum level established by the law on education) is an extremely difficult problem to overcome within a context of budgetary austerity." (Gheorghe et al. 2001)

The share of GDP spent on education varies between 3% in Romania and 6% in Estonia. In 2002, the EU–average percentage of GDP going to public expenditure on education was 5%, with the three best performing EU countries (Sweden, Finland and France) scoring an average of 7.4%.

It is obvious that the share of education depends on the general distribution of wealth. Moreover, the European Commission invites Member States to continue to contribute to the achievement of the Lisbon objective of substantial annual increases in per capita investment in human resources, and to set national benchmarks in relation to this. The Lisbon European Council with its aspiration to make Europe "the most competitive and dynamic knowledge based economy in the world" by 2010 clearly creates a paradigm shift in learning and education. But what new investment is needed to counteract the isolation, marginalisation or exclusion of some individuals and groups?

Some of the answers are provided by the key messages of the *Memorandum on Lifelong Learning*, such as key message 1 concerning "new basic skills for all", and key message 6 "bringing learning closer to home". As discussed above in speaking about the digital divide, both distance education and e–learning can be realistically achieved only by re–inventing the learning infrastructure based on new technologies.

The Memorandum provides an indirect answer by stating that people themselves constitute the leading actors of the knowledge societies, and that individuals should be able to follow open learning pathways of their own choice. One effect could be the increased mobility (geographical, professional, etc) of individuals, and self–administered education and training. In this respect the paradigmatic shift is from investment in formal learning to investment in non–formal and informal learning.

The foundation of education and training systems in all transition countries started with asking about the balance between national traditions and European and worldwide perspective. The changes have proceeded as different paces. Some of them affect large systems, as a whole. These are the large reforms undertaken in Europe to create a common educational space and the knowledge society. Meanwhile, some candidate countries like Romania and many other transition countries are investing continuously in modernising their education systems, introducing new technologies, creating qualification frameworks and flexible training structures. Some other countries, like those in the Western Balkans are facing major structural reforms aiming at both post–war reconstruction and the modernisation of vocational training.

Addressing young people as a vulnerable group has become more than an isolated phenomenon, since the European Commission launched the five European benchmarks in education and training, in order to reduce gaps in the school leaving age, achievements, gender, and young people's careers.

Increasingly, social partners have a say in all reforms in vocational education and training in Europe, and they stress the need to increase efforts to promote mobility within Europe. Addressing target groups is one of the results of this increased mobility.

But are individuals capable and responsible planners of their own learning? Are those affected by unemployment the first able to recreate themselves? Is European mobility the answer to the assumed limited ability of the workforce to absorb new labour?

Current political answers are not always the most adapted to long term reforms. Although most transition countries reported through the social exclusion studies that structural reforms are being undertaken and priority investment in allowing flexible education and training systems is a national *acquis*, most of these measures are critically reviewed in analyses by transnational donors. Here are some of the critical views of Berryman's report (2000), in the analysis of European and Central Asian transition countries.

***Allow Students Free Choice of Schools and Programmes.*** One main aspect of all major reforms of education in post–communist Europe was to grant schools the minimum autonomy to respond to students through a client–centred attitude. The importance of school choice however should not be exaggerated (Berryman 2000, 51). While choice is realistic in the case of urban schools, rural students have a more limited choice. The "consumer" value of the rural school is restricted, due to the lack of multiple offers. In the light of social exclusion statements, the location of schools relative to the possibility of students to travel is still a blockage for those countries in which exclusion derives from multiple deprivation factors, including the lack of public transport in rural and remote areas.

Therefore, free choice of schools and programmes continues to be restricted, and it cannot constitute an instrument to ease the individual decisions of young people.

*Major Investment in Vocational Education and Training.* All major reforms in the Eastern Bloc have given priority to secondary vocational education and training as the main tool to increase employability and prevent unemployment of the 15–25 year–old group. In spite of the slight decline caused by transition, more than half of all students still tend to enrol in non–general secondary schools, i.e., vocational education and training. There is, moreover, a strong European tradition of investing in specialised vocational education and training, including apprenticeships.

Berryman's report nevertheless states two negative consequences of investing in specialized vocational education and training in transition countries: first, the mismatch between the specialized skills provided by vocational education and training and the general foundation and meta–cognitive skills required by the new markets. Second, the costs of the training per student, which is 2 to 4 times higher in vocational education and training than in general education.

Individual pathways and broad–based vocational training are still to be defined and represent the challenge of vocational education and training for both transition countries and Member States.

*Increasing Public Expenditure on Education.* All studies of social exclusion show that the lower the public expenditure, the less the benefits for the educational system. Therefore, all governments tend to increase the percentage of GDP spent on education, training and school infrastructure. Berryman's report nevertheless illustrates deficits in learning outcomes at comparable input levels. It is therefore recommended that any public investment should be allocated on the basis of existing monitoring of its efficiency in terms of resources used relative to learning achieved.

*Large-Scale Teachers' and Trainers' Training Schemes.* The role of teacher and teacher training emerges from all descriptions of unequal treatment of students by schools. Phenomena like a hidden curriculum, abusive and discriminatory teaching, as well as non–standard discriminatory assessment of students are only some instances of unequal treatment of students in the classroom which may lead to exclusion. Most transition countries have created wide–ranging schemes of teachers and trainers training, mostly using the cascade model. Most of them use teachers for curriculum development and, all countries see teachers as change agents in the process of educational reforms.

It is nevertheless explicitly reported that all these new roles for teachers are not properly reimbursed in the transition countries. In the absence of proper incentives, most teachers let the quality of classroom teaching slip, and prefer to give extra lessons or start a small–scale business in order to survive. Berryman suggests that "governments need to consider gradually substituting a much smaller, better paid, full time teaching force for a larger, poorly paid, part–time teaching force". (Berryman 2000, 66)

Rationalisation of the school network, restructuring of the school offer to better respond to the labour market demand (in the case of vocational training), and concentrated investment in infrastructure and equipment are aims of current reforms at the expense of teacher–pupil ratios. Since all school reforms in the transition countries have benefited from wide–ranging support to teachers, any measures to make teachers redundant are extremely unpopular. The efficacy and the popularity of the reforms are difficult to reconcile.

***Curriculum and Quality Assurance.*** All structural reforms in the transition countries approached the curriculum with a clear view of both de–politicizing and updating the subject range and content. Berryman's report quite legitimately comments that all transition countries are confronted with the problem of reducing and simplifying a variety of subjects, which often present low importance in terms of acquisition of skills and knowledge. Her report stresses only a reduction in the number of specialised subjects, a process that has led to the adoption of large curricular areas, as in the Romanian curriculum for pre–university education.

Still, reaching the five European benchmarks in education and training will require further investment in curriculum restructuring in all Member States and transition countries.

What are the trends across Europe for increasing learning opportunities?

***The Ethical Base of Lifelong Learning.*** The *Memorandum on Lifelong Learning*, published by the European Commission in October 2000, should be considered one of the most humanistic and also encyclopaedic political documents. In its recommendations, the Memorandum harks back to the generous philosophy of the *Lumières,* to embrace all aspects of human emancipation through learning, guarantees for individual freedom and commitment to learning, as well as respect and encouragement of mutual responsibility of the individual and the community.

The background of the new lifelong learning model is much more ethical than technical, in the sense that lifelong learning is not a simple instrument to combat exclusion in shaping the Europe of tomorrow, but a deontological imperative. As stated in the Memorandum,

> "all those living in Europe, without exception, should have equal opportunities to adjust to the demands of social and economic change and to participate actively in the shape of Europe's future." (EC 2000, 3)

Moreover, civil governance in adopting the learning policy has been reached through the consultation, as the debate took place as close as possible to citizens themselves. Individuals decide and exert control over their life and careers, to freely achieve the two common aims of active citizenship and employability. It is therefore to be concluded that when speaking about two possible pillars of policies to counteract social exclusion in Europe, these should be active citizenship and employability.

The ethical basis of the lifelong learning exercise enriches the European dimension of education and training. In spite of all dissimilarities in Europe, the imperative of learning for all and throughout life will eventually lead to the acceptance of all in the European common space. "Overall, consensus can be surmised around the following four broad and mutually supporting objectives: personal fulfilment, active citizenship, social inclusion, and employability/adaptability." (EC 2001, 9)

***Economic and Social Cohesion is Aimed at Redefining Education and Training.*** Regional disparities are difficult to address, unless governments set national frameworks. The most valuable asset of recent years is multi-annual programming. This is helping to keep the goal setting process focused, and to provide incentives for regional and local planning of human resource development. In some candidate countries like Romania, most of the human resource development related investment is currently organised under the umbrella of economic and social cohesion programmes. The process is still accession and EU donor driven, but at the same time it constitutes a learning process for training providers, who should comply with the economic and social requirements of the regional and local markets.

Education and training gain new dimensions as regards management and accountability mechanisms. Centralisation versus decentralisation is no longer relevant in such a perspective. All reports on social exclusion showed that central initiatives did not ensure ownership, while local initiatives remained isolated. The loci of responsibility will therefore be different according to the responsibilities and power distribution. Central governance remains necessary to protect the aims of social cohesion, including ensuring educational fairness, as well as systematic use and monitoring of measures and instruments at regional and local levels. Regional governance is responsible for setting priorities, consolidating key institutions and allocating human and material resources. As for local governance, it can be responsible for ensuring feedback from beneficiaries, and making bottom up innovation possible in the system.

It is necessary to ensure that target groups are not left out of the entire process. Some answers to this are given by the European Commission (EC), some others by the European Union social partners. The EC answer, as discussed above, is the use of benchmarking, at both national and, if agreed, European level. The employers' answer is more oriented to grass roots actions. They strongly support innovation and best practices, with a special focus on the monitoring and diffusion of innovative actions. Pilot actions should be conceived much more in terms of learning processes, largely adopted by the whole range of players.

**Quality Rather than Quantity.** In order to become more accountable, education and training providers have therefore started to invest in setting indicators for quality, a process started under the Danish Presidency of the EU. *The Declaration of the European Ministers of Education and the European Commission, on Enhanced European Cooperation in Vocational Education and Training* was adopted in Copenhagen on 29 and 30 November 2002. Quality assurance is one of the main priorities of the enhanced cooperation in vocational education and training, based on three political objectives of the European Council, i.e., to promote employability, better matching between vocational education and training supply and demand, and better access to vocational education and training in particular for vulnerable groups on the labour market. According to the last political objective, quality management indicators draw attention to vulnerable groups, as they are defined at national level.

An initial focus on large structural reforms has now moved to an intensive redefinition of the very foundation of vocational education and training. Priorities are shifting from what kind of training and for what, to how the training is done and for whom. The focus on quality should ideally make educational systems more accountable to various stakeholders. At the same time, it will ensure that learning outcomes are part of the redesigned or revisited curriculum. It will be important therefore that quality indicators are adopted and used by the providers, in order to make systems flexible to innovation and the development of lifelong learning instruments.

***Lateral Self-Inclusion Processes are to be Revisited.*** Almost everything "informal", with the exception of informal learning, continues to be ambiguous. Is recognition of informal learning associated with the recognition of informal work? Should it be formalised?

As to the employment side, it is clear that hidden activities are caused by poverty and economic transition. Bernabé (2002) concludes that although hidden employment undermines government revenue, its authority and the respect for the rule of law, it may be considered an important source of economic growth, especially in contexts where heavy bureaucracy obstructs the development of private entrepreneurial activities. However, addressing informal activities is still ambiguous, and the most important issue is to what extent the hidden activities, especially the "underground" and the "illegal" ones, do contribute to the deskilling of human capital.

In any case, no matter what employment policies will be set in the future, the outcomes of the typologies set by Bernabé are important. What should be borne in mind is the distinction between small–scale income and employment–generating activities, which can genuinely be defined as "informal", and those that are genuinely illegal and underground, whose economic benefits are unclear and which lead to the social exclusion of those who undertake them.

As for the education side, informal payment in education illustrates how counterproductive informal user charges are for the educational system:

"Ideally, informal payments should be legitimized by law or regulations and special provisions introduced for poor regions or poor students." (Berryman 2000, 47)

Therefore, informal learning and employment should be revisited from the point of view of the possible benefits for individuals who are engaged in such activities at various stages of their life and career.

## *"All Different, All Equal": the Reinforcement of Ethnic and Cultural Tolerance in Europe.* The political declaration of the Council of Europe Ministers, adopted in Strasbourg in October 2000, reaffirms that Europe is pluralist and open, and "the fight against marginalisation and social exclusion must be continued" (EUROCONF 2000, 2). At the same time, the Declaration rather alarmingly states that certain media and politicians express hostility towards vulnerable groups.

As discussed above in speaking about Roma groups and the "info–exclusion" phenomenon, tolerance and public attention are not always awarded on equal basis. Education and training, as well as awareness raising practices, are strongly encouraged through the education and training measures formulated by the Declaration. Respect for human rights and cultural diversity is to be introduced in education, and teachers are also called to increase their responsiveness to these issues through teaching methodologies.

*The Memorandum on Lifelong Learning* does not refer explicitly to any vulnerable group, although the text is clear in stating that individuals must learn to live positively, with cultural, ethnic, and linguistic diversity. All transition countries increasingly adopt the orientation towards tolerance and intercultural education. Many interventions are however purely declarative and actual inclusion is not yet reached. The consistency of civil society varies in transition countries, and depends on cultural patterns. Collective societies are much more in favour of assimilating minorities, while individualistic societies lead to segregation of minority groups. A real balance of inclusion and acceptance may be only created by an open society, in Karl Popper's terms. That fact that Europe declares itself an open society is a constructive statement. Mechanisms to put open societies to work are nonetheless more complicated than political statements. It is widely known that the Open Society Institutes (OSI) created and financed by George Soros had the explicit aim of assisting civil society in post–communist countries, and consolidating civil governance. Paradoxically (or not), the OSI branch in Romania has been marked since the beginning with public connotations of "exclusive" and "elitist". Major non–governmental organisations operating in transition countries with issues related to gender, sex, or ethnicity, continue to struggle for credibility and for equal partnership with the State.

*To conclude*, I would reiterate that the purpose of this discussion is to explore some of the existing questions and dilemmas concerning social inclusion through increasing learning opportunities. The present analysis is not an exhaustive one. It was the aim here rather to review and report on all existing literature in the field. For methodological reasons, I limited the background to some of the existing studies in Romania, and across CEECs which aimed to identify causes and counteractions to social exclusion, with a special focus on young people. Some conclusions were provided in the two papers on informal employment and measuring well–being from the London Centre for the Analysis of Social Exclusion. Much more literature was used to back up the interpretation, as, for example, some works on ethics and democracy (Popper 1992) for the concept of the "open society" of Karl Popper. Last but not least, the Framework paper of the project's domain devoted to countries in transition represented an important intellectual tool, for both the arguments and the tone of this essay. (Strietska–Ilina and Freibergova 2002)

As for the corpus of studies on CEECs, I intentionally referred to European Training Foundation (ETF) publications, since I was one of the thematic coordinators of the issues on combating social exclusion through vocational education and training and employment during 1999 and 2000, and I continued to collaborate with the ETF on this issue.[3] Some of these reports, which were finalised in 2000–2001, may be well out–of–date in terms of statistical data. Therefore, I did not repeat information that I considered perishable, and I followed mostly the expert opinion on the social exclusion phenomena.

Although an essay cannot produce recommendations for immediate actions, some final remarks are necessary. We have seen here that there are many factors determining social inclusion, and the subsequent creation of opportunities for learning for all, and these factors are not all congruent. Both governments and civil society groups tried initially to adopt partial measures, and attack the phenomena locally, by means of concentrated interventions. At the same time, these practices created even more disparities, since the provision of learning opportunities for all is a subject of national policies and even cross–European ones. At the present moment, the process of social inclusion is being tackled in a reverse planning process: while in the first stage, the analysis concentrated on cause–effect mechanisms, now the cycle begins with expected outcomes and works back to prerequisites. All interventions that I listed as cross–European tendencies for increasing learning opportunities could be considered as such.

There is no perfect solution to learning opportunities for all. This is why the second shift in dealing with social inclusion through education and training was from intervention at the level of groups and communities to interventions at the individual level, and the concept of lifelong learning is a clear indication of this shift. As individuals are called on to reflect on and even create learning pathways, through all possible formal and non–/informal ways, a climate of self–inclusion will ideally be created.

But is this logic well founded or simply demagogical? To a large extent, the very concept of a knowledge–based society is not clear. Europe has been a cradle of knowledge par excellence, with rational roots in ancient philosophies. It seems that the new meaning of knowledge is more connected to a re–evaluation and reconciliation between culture and technology. Indeed, the two concepts have traditionally been separated, and derived concepts as "culture" versus "civilization" are still operational. The Europe of the future aims at a techno–knowledgeable society, with moral commandments. The fact that there has been such emphasis lately on enhanced European cooperation in vocational education and training is also a clear indication of the desired synergy between humanist aims of social cohesion and learning for all, and lucrative aims of stable employment and a strong economy.

Are individuals to have a role in the society of the future? Is this society structured around them, or is this a new utopia in Europe? The process of re–inventing contemporary society is ongoing. Definitions of post–modern, post–industrial, informational, post–capitalist or organisational (in Peter Drucker's terms) have emerged during recent decades (Drucker 1993). The very capacity of individuals has been questioned and they have come under a lot of pressure to change rapidly. It seems a bitter pill that new driving forces in contemporary society are creating both opportunities and strong barriers. At the beginning of the 1990s, all transition countries among the CEECs declared their willingness to adopt the model of capitalism to assist in the resurrection of their economies. In this way, as this paper illustrates, new injustices were added to old ones.

"Markets do not solve the fairness problem."(Berryman 2000, 33). As new ideologies emerged and tried to create alternative socially inclusive models (e.g., The third way of Anthony Giddens), elements of capitalism and socialism are no longer so distinct relative to inequality generation (Giddens 2001).

Although the pressure on the employment side is evident, learning opportunities and work opportunities are not synonymous. Moreover, besides transition countries, we are witnessing new processes of post–war reconstruction in the countries of the former Yugoslav Federation. Are the processes of transition and reconstruction similar? At the first glance, it appears that while transition is a smooth process, reconstruction is radical and much more traumatic. The recent phenomena of the reconstruction markets (recent examples in the Western Balkans, like Croatia or Montenegro) show the lack of willingness of young people to work in sectors like road construction. As a result, there is a shortage of labour in these domains, which are nevertheless key to economic reconstruction. Higher order and meta–cognitive skills are linked to a new meaning of working. Somehow, it is not very clear to what extent the new learning paradigm has absorbed latent processes like the conversion of attitudes to employment in countries that are not only in transition but also in economic reconstruction, as with the Western Balkans.

All these challenges will surely be addressed in the new European open space of learning for all and throughout life. These challenges should also be addressed through European mechanisms for youth learning and mobility, such as the Socrates, Leonardo and Youth programmes. Some other EU financing mechanisms, like the current Phare, TACIS and CARDS programmes in Southern and Eastern European countries will continue to adjust to these challenges. The Phare programming for Economic and Social Cohesion, which is creating a new framework to re–launch vocational education and training reform in Romania, is one example of this. Hopefully the "learning for all" paradigm will generate good practice across the recently enhanced post–accession Europe.

## Notes

1. By "countries in transition" we assume here those post–communist countries of CEEC which entered the EU in May 2004 and pre–accession countries expected to enter in the coming years (Romania and Bulgaria).
2. At the beginning of the year 2000, the European Training Foundation proposed to countries in Central and Eastern Europe still in accession process to European Union at that time, to survey the impact of the economic and

social transition on various social groups, to identify those at risk of social exclusion and to recommend way out strategies that could function in various contexts.
3. ETF has conducted a second round of studies on *Vocational Education and Training against Social Exclusion* of young people in the Western Balkans. The reports were finalised in 2003.

# References

Annus, T., Kutsar, D., Sõstra, K, Tiit, E.–M, Kliimask, J, *Vocational Education and Training against Social Exclusion: Estonia*. Report. European Training Foundation, Turin, 2000.

Bernabé, S. "Informal Employment in Countries in Transition: A Conceptual Framework." *CASE 56*, London Centre for Analysis of Social Exclusion, April 2002.

Berryman, S. E. *Hidden Challenges to Education Systems in Transition Economies*. The World Bank, Europe and Central Asia Region, Human Development Sector, September 2000.

Birzea, C. (ed.) *Social Impact of the Continuous Vocational Training*. European Training Foundation/National Observatory of Romania, Bucharest, 2001.

Drucker, P. *Post–Capitalist Society*. New York, HarperCollins Publishers, 1993.

EC. *A Memorandum on Lifelong Learning*. Commission staff working paper. Commission of the European Communities. SEC(2000) 1832. Brussels, 30.10.2000.

EC. *Making a European Area of Lifelong Learning a Reality*. Communication from the Commission. European Commission, Directorate–General for Education and Culture. COM(2001) 678 final. Brussels, 21.11.2001.

ETF Advisory Forum, Subgroup A. *Training against Social Exclusion*. "Part 1: Summary of the Discussions". European Training Foundation, Turin, 1999.

ETF. *Vocational Education and Training against Social Exclusion: Poland. Report*. European Training Foundation, Turin, 2001.

ETF. *Vocational Education and Training against Social Exclusion: Slovak Republic. Report*. European Training Foundation, Turin, 2001a.

ETF. *Current Practices across Europe to Assist in the Inclusion of Roma/ Gypsy Population through Education and Training and Employment Opportunities*. European Training Foundation, Turin, 2001b.

ETF. *European Report on Quality Indicators of Lifelong Learning: Fifteen Quality Indicators*. Brussels, European Commission. Report of the Working Group on Quality Indicators, June 2002.

ETF. *Thirteen Years of Cooperation and Reforms in Vocational Education and Training in the Acceding and Candidate Countries. What are the lessons to be learned from the perspective of the Lisbon objectives?* European Training Foundation, Torino, 2003.

EUROCONF. *All Different, All Equal: from Principle to Practice*. Political Declaration adopted by Ministers of Council of Europe Member States on Friday

13 October 2000 at the concluding session of the European Conference against racism. Strasbourg, 1 Final, 11–13 October, 2000.
Fukuyama, F. *The Great Disruption. Human Nature and the Reconstitution of Social Disorder.* The Free Press, New York, 1999.
Gheorghe, C., Serban, M., Platon, G., Simion, G., Peter, M., Nistorescu, D. *Vocational Education and Training against Social Exclusion: Romania.* Report, European Training Foundation, Turin, 2001.
Gheorghe, C., Rogojinaru, A. *Human Resource Development Strategy in Romania.* European Training Foundation/National Observatory of Romania, 2001.
Giddens, A. *The Third Way. The Renewal of Social Democracy.* 1998. Translated into Romanian: *A Treia Cale: renașterea social–democrației.* Iași, Editura Polirom, 2001.
Hall, S. and Jefferson, T. (eds.). *Resistance through Rituals: Youth Subcultures in Post–War Britain.* University of Birmingham, Centre for Contemporary Cultural Studies, 1976.
Held, D. *Models of Democracy.* Standford University Press, Standford, 1987.
Matheu, X. *Quality in Vocational Education and Training.* Report of the Technical Working Group. Copenhagen process, European Commission, DG for Education and Culture, Brussels, 2004.
Matheu, X. *Training against Social Exclusion. Final Report.* CIREM, Barcelona, Spain; Advisory Forum, Subgroup A, European Training Foundation, September 1999.
Medel–Afionuevo, C. (ed.). *Lifelong learning discourses in Europe.* Hamburg, UNESCO Institute for Education, 2003.
Medel–Afionuevo, C. (ed.) "Research Report 1997–2001". *CASE 17,* London, Centre for Analysis of Social Exclusion, September 2001.
Noncheva, T. (coord.), Beleva, I., Tzanov, V. *Vocational Education and Training against Social Exclusion: Bulgaria.* Report, European Training Foundation, Turin, 2000.
Popper, K.R. *The Open Society and its Enemies.* 1957. Translated into Romanian: *Societatea deschisă și dușmanii ei.* Vol.I–II, București, Humanitas, 1992.
Stewart, K. "Measuring Well–Being and Exclusion in Europe's Regions". *CASE 53,* London, Centre for Analysis of Social Exclusion, March 2002.
Strietska–Ilina, O. and Freibergova, Z. *Education and Training in Candidate Countries: Challenges and Opportunities of the EU Integration and Enlargement from the Perspective of Countries in Transition.* Conceptual framework paper. EURONE&T. National Observatory of Employment and Training, Prague, June 2002.
Strietska–Ilina, O., Czesaná, V., Havličová, V. *Education and Training against Social Exclusion. Report on the Situation in the Czech Republic.* Czech National Observatory of Employment and Training working paper. National Training Fund, Prague, 2000.
UNDP. *Human Development Report for Central and Eastern Europe and the CIS 1999.* United Nations Development Programme (UNDP), New York, 1999.

• RONALD G. SULTANA •

# Guiding Learners in the Learning Society: The Situation in Nine Central and Eastern European Countries

## Introduction

Up to a few decades ago, guidance was, in many countries, largely restricted to the provision of information and advice to individuals and groups as they reached stages in their lives where they had to make decisions as to which educational and career trajectories they wanted to follow (Madsen 1986; Collin and Watts 1996; Sultana and Sammut 1997; Budapest Conference Report 2000). Such decisions were often high–stake ones, in the sense that pathways were then conceived as linear and closed—once you embarked on a particular route, within specific curricular or occupational tracks, the likelihood was that you would remain within it, and that at best, mobility would be vertical and not horizontal. Indeed, traditional mainstream career development theories considered workers who changed jobs regularly as "immature".[1] The discourse about guidance has now shifted to accommodate a different view of both education and employment, as well as of the links between these two (Killeen 1996; Watts 1996a, 1996b).

Two main developments can in fact be identified as having had an impact on the definition and scope of guidance.[2] The first is the widespread legitimacy that the idea of lifelong learning has attained, whether among educators, policy–makers, or society at large. Lifelong learning is not a new idea, of course. Indeed, in classical Greece, a lifelong dedication to knowledge was considered the foundation and sign of a virtuous life (Lê Thành Khôi 1995). That notion and understanding, together with more economistic as well as humanistic and radical interpretations of the term (Ranson 1998; Jarvis 2001; Borg and Mayo 2002), started to become current in adult education in the west at the turn of the 20$^{th}$ century, culminating in what should perhaps still be hailed as the master text in the field, the 1972 Unesco report by Faure and his colleagues entitled *Learning to Be*.[3] What is new, as Gelpi (1985) has pointed out, is the favour and general popularity that the notion has attained at all levels of society. The idea of learning throughout life has been sustained by fresh perspectives on how individuals learn, by changing and more complex views on intelligence, and by advances in pedagogy, in assessment, and in information technology, all of which have led to the re–conceptualisation of educational pathways so that they provide young people and adults with flexible and multiple entry and exit routes (Sultana 2003a). Flexibility in provision, in certification, in entry and exit points will ensure that even those who have failed to profit from traditional education routes will now be successfully engaged in the education and training enterprise. Learning is much less bounded in time and space (Kress 2000; Young 1998), and as a result, many argue, young people and adults will need guidance throughout their lives in order to navigate complex opportunities into and out of specific education and training pathways, and into and out of employment routes.

A second development, which is both linked to and, in many ways, actually drives the first, is the notion of post–industrial, post–Fordist societies in "knowledge–based" economies. Internationally, it is claimed (*inter alia* Brown and Lauder 1991; Brown *et al.* 2001),[4] economies are restructuring—or need to restructure—themselves towards the high ability sector, demanding work profiles with a broad range of skills in the new technologies. This is the key strategy to gain and retain competitive advantage in a global market. Over and above competence in information technology, economies require workers to demonstrate a repertoire of "soft" skills, a personality package that includes such qualities as creativity, communication skills, linguistic competence, ability to work in teams, and so on. The key quality that anchors and permeates the profile of the worker/citizen in the learning economy is his/her flexibility. Given the vagaries of the open economy, and the accelerated developments in technology, workers/citizens need to be always open to new learning, capable of flexibly adapting to new environments, and of creatively re-structuring and re–inventing themselves so that they can retain their "use–value" in the labour market. It therefore becomes essential for what ultimately is an "unstable society" (Schön 1973) to provide multiple and flexible routes into learning and training, throughout a citizen's life. The learning society therefore becomes "a society in which learning is the whole of life and the whole of life is learning" (Van der Zee 1998, 75). It follows "naturally"—at least this is increasingly the view within mainstream policy discourse—that members of such a society require guidance in order to manage what has become an increasingly challenging life project.

This chapter sets out to critically consider the prevailing discourse about the learning society, and particularly the role of guidance within that society. The focus is on the way the discourse on "guiding learners and workers in the learning society" is produced within the European Union, and following that, more specifically on how such a discourse circulates in nine Central and Eastern European countries (CEECs). The goals of the contribution are therefore threefold. First, recent developments in lifelong guidance policies at EU level are presented. Second, a review is made of the state of the art in the provision of guidance in nine CEECs, with due attention given to the identification of trends, especially as these connect with policy developments in Europe. Third, mainstream notions of guidance within the learning society—as these are being articulated and promoted within the common European space,[5] and as they are being received by, and accommodated within, new Member States—are critically considered and challenged, with a view to considering more emancipative alternatives.

# Guiding European Citizens in the Learning Society

## The EU Policy Context for Lifelong Guidance

It is clear that the European Union has enthusiastically embraced—and indeed is equally enthusiastically promoting—the particular social and discursive construct captured by the phrase the "learning society", and the attendant notion of "lifelong guidance". From the point of view of the European Council, lifelong and life–wide learning has a key role to play in fulfilling the EU's aspiration to become "the most competitive and dynamic knowledge–based society in the world" (Lisbon European Council, March 23–24, 2000). Based on that premise, the Member States and the Commission were invited by the European Heads of Government/European Council "to identify, within their area of competence, coherent strategies and practical measures with a view to fostering lifelong learning for all". The Education Council/Council of Education Ministers was requested to "undertake a general reflection on the concrete future objectives of education and training systems, focusing on common concerns while respecting national diversity". As Gordon Clark (2002) has noted, "the European Commission's response to the invitation of the Lisbon Council was to develop, in cooperation with the Member States and Social Partners, a range of policy responses in the forms of Communications and Reports in education, training and employment and to undertake a number of interrelated initiatives in terms of follow–up work programmes."

One important *tranche* in the intensification of Commission and Member State activity in the field of education and training as a contribution to the strengthening of a knowledge–based Europe concerned lifelong learning, with the development of a *Memorandum on Lifelong Learning* and the launch of a wide consultation process in Member States, candidate countries, EEA countries, social partners and other civil society elements. On the basis of consultation input, the Commission issued a Communication entitled *Making a European Area of Lifelong Learning a Reality* (EC 2001a), while at the behest of the Ministers of Education of the EU, of pre–accession countries and EEA, following a meeting in Bucharest in June 2000 the Commission established a Working Group which produced a *European Report on Quality Indicators for Lifelong Learning* (2002a).

Guidance features in all of these documents,[6] and is defined as "a range of activities designed to assist people to make decisions about their lives (educational, vocational, personal) and to implement those decisions" (EC 2002b, 57). Guidance personnel are also considered to be "learning facilitators", inasmuch as they enable "the acquisition of knowledge and competences by establishing a learning environment" (EC 2002b, 58). Guidance is one of the six key messages proposed in the framework of the Memorandum with a view to structuring the open debate on lifelong learning, where the challenge of ensuring easy access to "good quality information and guidance about learning opportunities throughout Europe and throughout their lives" is considered to be central to the coming about of a competitive, knowledge–based economy, peopled by flexible and mobile workers constantly open to re–training. According to the Memorandum, *holistic* guidance, overcoming the traditional distinctions between educational, vocational and personal guidance, had to be continuously and locally *accessible* for all; it had to be *client–centred*, by reaching out to citizens and following up on their needs rather than waiting for them to come; it had to serve as a *brokerage* service on behalf of clients, and to be *networked* to related personal, social and educational services; it had to also be offered through such *non–formal and informal channels* as NGOs and community–based associations, so as to more effectively reach disadvantaged groups; it had to be a quality service, with agreed minimum *standards*, and improved initial and continuous *training* of guidance workers.[7]

These "policy leads" found a resonance in the Memorandum consultation process, as can be seen in the *Communication on Lifelong Learning* (2001), the strategy paper published subsequently by the Commission, which identified information, guidance and counselling as one of six "priorities for action".[8] This synthesised the various inputs and organised them around six strategic building blocks for policy development and implementation.[9] The implications for lifelong guidance are clearly articulated in several of these blocks. Thus, access to lifelong learning is facilitated if learning providers develop strong *partnerships* with those offering information, guidance and counselling services (EC 2002b, 21). Those involved in guidance can help develop *insights into the demand for learning* through the client surveys and consultations they are involved in (EC 2002b, 22). Guidance workers can promote lifelong learning if they "*raise awareness* of the individual/social/economic benefits of learning, and… encourage diversification of studies and non–traditional career/learning choices" (EC 2002b, 25). They can also facilitate access to learning opportunities by being a "key interface between learning needs and the learning on offer [and] in helping learners find their place in increasingly complex learning systems" (EC 2002b, 24).

Other concerns that arose from the consultation process, and from the Commission's own policy analysis of the field, included the allocation of European Social Fund resources to the training of guidance workers; the training of employees and managerial staff to act as guidance workers or mentors to others; the development of competencies among guidance personnel that would enable them to promote tolerance and democratic values, particularly given the challenges of living in multicultural societies;

and the promotion of a *European dimension of guidance*—through such actions as the European CV, the exchange of good practice Europe–wide, the launch of PLOTEUS (the Portal on Learning Opportunities throughout the European Space), and the mobilisation of the Euroguidance network as a source of information, responding to the needs of guidance workers to be familiar with other countries' education, training and guidance systems, labour market systems and programmes.[10]

Many of these guidance–related considerations have implications both for defining the field across Europe, and also for establishing quality standards—in other words, for benchmarking those aspects of the service that are promoted Europe–wide as worthy of emulation.[11] Indeed, two documents relate specifically to the latter dimension. The report on *Quality Indicators for Lifelong Learning* (EC 2002a) mentioned above,[12] for instance, notes that while common indicators had not yet been developed Europe–wide in this field, a number of areas ought to be focused upon, including (i) target group coverage, (ii) social, economic and learning benefits from counselling and guidance, (iii) qualifications of guidance and counselling practitioners, and (iv) frequency of in–service training of practitioners. Similarly, the document detailing the *Future Concrete Objectives for Education and Training Systems in Europe* (Council of the European Union 2001b) sets out three criteria for education and training systems, in the form of objectives that need to be reached in order to fulfil the aspirations for the EU as defined by the Lisbon Council. These include (i) the improvement of the quality and effectiveness of education and training systems, (ii) the facilitation of access to education and training for all, and (iii) opening up education and training systems to the wider world. Quality guidance provision is identified as one of the activities that operationalises these strategic goals by, for instance, assisting in broadening access to lifelong learning, increasing recruitment to scientific and technical studies,[13] and motivating young people and adults to participate and to continue in learning.

Many of these objectives, strategies, and policy leads in relation to guidance are also to be found in a parallel stream of documents linked directly to concerns regarding the European labour market and to the aspirations articulated by the Lisbon Council. In its *Action Plan for Skills and Mobility* (EC 2002c), for instance, the Commission identifies three main obstacles that the EU has to overcome if its labour markets are to be accessible to all. These are inadequate occupational mobility, low geographical mobility, and fragmentation of information and lack of transparency of job opportunities. Guidance is singled out as one of the measures by which all three inadequacies can be addressed, and the report notes that improved access to quality public and private information, guidance and counselling services is required, and especially so in the workplace, where such services are still largely absent. Member States are indeed encouraged to evaluate the existing services (with a view to ensuring transparency and coherence in provision), to widen access to guidance services (especially through the use of ICTs), to reallocate public funds to this area, and to set up a one-stop European Mobility Site as part of a wider European network to provide comprehensive and easily accessible information to citizens on key aspects of jobs, mobility, learning opportunities, and the transparency of qualifications in Europe. Guidance services are to facilitate the more effective matching of European human resources and the European labour market, through EU-wide mobility information campaigns, and through promoting an improved image of occupational sectors that are not attracting enough workers. In another document, *Increasing Labour Force Participation and Promoting Active Ageing* (EC 2002d) guidance is called upon to target the inactive and unemployed—and, by implication, older workers—in order to help create an adequate supportive environment in an effort to integrate them into the work force.

Other recent European Commission documents further feed into the overall effort to mobilise guidance services in support of attaining lifelong learning goals for Europe. The *Joint Employment Report* (EC 2001b)—which provides an overview of the employment situation and a political assessment of the progress made by Member States in the implementation of the agreed Employment Guidelines articulated with reference to the European Employment Strategy[14]—notes that only half of the Member States have achieved clear progress in developing comprehensive lifelong learning strategies, and these have remained at an early stage of implementation. Guidance is promoted as an effective manner for facilitating cross-sectoral learning pathways that help to improve the overall coherence of available learning. Similarly, and also in the context of the European Employment Strategy, the *Joint Statements of the European Public Employment Services on their Role in the Labour Market* (2002e) highlights the role of guidance in assisting jobseekers, employed and unemployed, and for processes in support of lifelong learning, including the responsibility of Public Employment Services (PESs) to assist individuals throughout their working lives in order to promote occupational mobility and flexibility. Those persons who are most difficult to place in employment are to be targeted for "more intensive counselling."

## An Evolving EU Agenda

The above review of recent developments in key policy documents leaves us with little doubt that, despite the sovereignty of Member States in educational matters, Europe has much to say in relation to guidance, and that the field has a broad appeal as a mechanism that facilitates the attainment of a number of central and inter–related EU goals. Indeed, going by the documents referred to above, the expectations from guidance are nothing short of enormous. Guidance, duly reconfigured to cater for new realities—including non–linear, multiple entry points into education, training and work across time (lifelong) and space (Europe–wide)—is called upon to:

- accompany the citizen throughout life, supporting transitions and promoting the attitudes, knowledge and skills needed to be active contributors to, and participants in, the learning society/economy;
- connect clients with local, regional, national and European educational and occupational opportunities;
- be impartial while at the same time fostering science and technology as an attractive educational and occupational pathway;
- enhance social inclusion, through re–engaging reluctant learners in educational and training tracks, and through acting as "job broker" on behalf of the unemployed;
- present up–to–date information that responds to client and employer needs, is transparent, user–friendly, and enables consolidation of knowledge across the educational and labour market sectors;
- cater for the individual and for targeted groups (e.g., women returnees, persons with disability, long term unemployed, unqualified school leavers, immigrants) in a way that responds to their particular needs;
- foster a personality package in clients that is functional to the labour market—including flexibility, mobility, entrepreneurship, and so on;
- establish itself more firmly within sites other than the school and the public employment service, including places of leisure and of work;
- network with NGOs, voluntary and community–based providers in order to more effectively respond to clients with specific needs, including minority groups, for instance;

- exploit more effectively the potential of ICTs in order to attain many of the objectives stated above—including transparency, accessibility, permeability, connectivity—and to encourage clients to engage more proactively in constructing educational and occupational life projects;
- mobilise itself more professionally, in terms of improved pre–service and in–service training, and in terms of developing sound quality indicators that are promoted and benchmarked across Europe.

This, therefore, is the EU's agenda in a nutshell. In view of arguments that will be made in the final section of this chapter, it is important to stress the point that this agenda is driven both by an *economistic* concern (how best to make Europe competitive in a knowledge–based global economy), and by a *social* one (how best to ensure access to productive and rewarding labour market involvement to as many European citizens as possible). It is an agenda that is increasingly taking shape and form, partly as the discourse around guidance intensifies and converges within formal documents, and partly as the Commission uses the instruments it has at its disposal to transform objectives signalled in such documents into action—whether through funding leads via EU programmes and initiatives, through promoting good practice, through open co-ordination, or other means.

Given the visibility and pull of the EU in the larger Europe, it is also an agenda that is increasingly having an impact on the candidate countries involved in the accession process as they try to "measure up".[15] In the section that follows, we will consider how nine Central and Eastern European countries, as candidate countries or as new Member States of the EU, are articulating goals for guidance, within a context that targets the upgrading of the knowledge and skills base of the population with a view to addressing unemployment, to meeting the demands of forward–looking knowledge–based economies, and to ensuring that the supply and demand of labour are in harmony.

# Guidance and Counselling in CEECs

## The Context for Comparative Analysis

Before launching into the presentation of the state of and developments in guidance in nine rather different CEECs—namely Bulgaria, Estonia,

Hungary, Latvia, Lithuania, Poland, Romania, Slovakia and Slovenia—it is important to justify why they are here being considered as a "unit" for the purpose of comparative analysis. There are, after all, important geo-political, economic and cultural differences both between—and sometimes even within—these nine countries. Some of the CEECs reviewed here—including Poland, Romania and Hungary—are quite large, while Estonia, Slovenia, Latvia and Lithuania are comparatively quite small.[16] Some of the CEECs have a relatively homogeneous ethnic composition (e.g., Poland, Slovenia), others are quite multi-ethnic (e.g., Estonia, Latvia). Some—such as Bulgaria, Romania, and Slovakia—have significant numbers of minority groups. There are also significant differences between the CEECs in the per capita income they can command (with Slovenia going beyond the 10,000 Euro threshold, with the rest ranging between 4,500 and 9,500 Euros per capita). In some countries, the political context encourages stakeholders to make important contributions to the policy-making process as well as to provision of services. Other states from among the CEECs appear to be more reluctant to adopt a social partnership model.

Different histories, traditions, ideologies, and policy regimes have had an impact on shaping the educational systems in the different CEECs, with some embarking only recently on questioning centralised systems that encourage early streaming and tracking, and that seriously limit the extent to which individuals can "choose" educational and occupational trajectories. Career guidance has deep roots in Latvia, Lithuania, and Poland, but in the other countries involved in this review it has developed only recently, without much of a heritage to build upon. Culturally too there are significant differences between the nine CEECs, with religion (mainly Christian—with its Catholic, Orthodox and Protestant varieties—but Muslim as well), and the family playing quite a significant role when it comes to shaping young people's futures, occupationally or otherwise. All these factors, together with the variable composition of the different countries' economies, have a significant impact on the way careers guidance is perceived, on how it is organised, on the challenges that have to be overcome, and on the issues that need to be addressed.

Over and above these differences, however, are a number of factors that make the attempt to consider the nine CEECs together a meaningful one. First of all, the countries in question are either one step away from accession in the EU (Bulgaria and Romania), or joined the EU in May 2004 (all other countries in question). As such, their own policy-making has been greatly influenced by EU policies, including *the EU Social Char-*

*ter, EU Employment Action Plans*, and structural indicators that focus on employment, innovation, social inclusion and economic reforms. Indeed, the very participation in joint thematic reviews such as the one concerning guidance, as well as in the "open method of co–ordination" in both the employment and social policy fields, tends to generate a concerted EU approach, even though legal competence and authority in such areas remain with the individual Member States.

Furthermore, the nine CEECs have only recently embarked on a transition from a centrally planned to a democratic market economy, which means that they have to deal with "radical changes in the role of the state, the individual and the economy", which have "an immense effect on the starting point, nature, and investment in, career development" (Fretwell and Plant 2001, 1). Indeed, most of these countries report an intensified interest in career guidance. This is understandable, given that labour demand and supply were previously an outcome of state planning, and as a result insecurity about employment and economic futures is a relatively new experience for many citizens in Central and Eastern Europe. As the Budapest Conference Report noted:

> After WWII the paths of East and West diverged sharply. In central and eastern Europe further development of career guidance and counselling services came to a grinding halt and remained in hibernation for almost half a century. Full employment under the command economy invalidated the need for guidance to be more than a referral service. [...] In general, the period of transition to a market economy, and the resulting turmoil in the labour market pushed the issue of career guidance into focus again. (2000, 7)

## Methodology

The premise therefore is that the underlying dynamics and processes connecting these nine CEECs facilitates comparative analysis, and certainly justifies the presentation of a cross–country state–of–the–art review of the guidance field. The review draws on a detailed database compiled by the European Training Foundation (ETF), generated on the basis of a questionnaire distributed to experts from CEECs during the summer of 2002. These experts completed their task by drawing on their own in–depth knowledge of career guidance in their country, and in some instances after an extensive consultation exercise with key decision–makers and providers in the field.

The questionnaire follows closely the survey instrument developed by the Organisation for Economic Cooperation and Development (OECD), as part of its recent thematic review of fourteen countries,[17] where the goal was to develop benchmarks—enabling participating countries to gauge how well they are doing in career guidance provision in relation to other comparable countries—and to facilitate the sharing of good practice, providing countries with an opportunity to promote their successes and to learn from practices elsewhere. On the basis of the proven usefulness of the OECD survey, the Commission, with the help of the European Centre for the Development of Vocational Training (Cedefop), extended the collection of information to the remaining EU Member States (France, Italy, Portugal, Greece, and Sweden) as well as one member of the EEA, namely Iceland, with the ETF overseeing the same exercise in relation to Bulgaria, Cyprus, Estonia, Hungary, Latvia, Lithuania, Malta, Poland, Romania, Slovakia and Slovenia. The World Bank, on its part, has launched a parallel review in seven middle–income countries (starting with Turkey, involving Poland and Romania again, and extending its purview to include Chile, the Philippines, Russia, and South Africa), again using the OECD questionnaire. The involvement of these key partners—all using the same survey tool—is expected to lead to the most extensive harmonised international database ever on guidance policy and practice. Each organisation has commissioned a synthesis report to be written on the basis of the outcomes of each cluster of completed national questionnaires (Sultana 2002; OECD 2004; Cedefop 2004; Watts and Fretwell, 2003). A "synthesis of syntheses" identifying the key points from all the reviews is also available (Watts and Sultana 2004).

## A State–of–the–Art Review

The information from the ETF database, presented in Sultana (2002), is here analytically organised around four main categories that are of most relevance to this essay, and namely in response to the questions:

- How is guidance defined and valued in the CEECs?
- Who is targeted for guidance in the CEECs, and in which contexts?
- What are the modalities for the provision of lifelong guidance in the CEECs?
- Who provides guidance in the CEECs?

These questions are addressed in turn, with an emphasis placed on developing critical insights on the construction of the field of guidance in relation to the knowledge–based, learning economy. Such critical perspectives are enhanced through the trawling through of the ETF, OECD and Cedefop databases in order to identify contrasting perspectives regarding guidance that exist in the CEECs and in those OECD and older EU Member States that took part in the survey.

## Defining and Valuing Guidance in the CEECs

The range of activities covered by guidance has been usefully summarised by Plant (2001) to include: informing, advising, assessing, teaching, enabling, advocating, networking, feeding back, managing, innovation/systems change, signposting, mentoring, sampling work experience or learning tasters, and following up. Generally speaking, guidance facilitates decisions that have to be made about trajectories through educational and occupational pathways, and in some OECD and older EU countries, boundary distinctions are drawn between more generic personal counselling types of activities—which address a range of developmental and inter–relationship issues—and educational and career guidance proper. These distinctions are rather loose, especially since, in some contexts, guidance personnel are also, if not primarily, counsellors, and that both "categories" of staff follow the same certification route, which often involves a specialisation in psychology.

It is clear that most of the CEECs covered by this review are engaged in several of the activities referred to by Plant, though such engagement obviously varies from country to country, and from sector to sector within each country. Despite the fact that guidance services have a rather long presence in some of the CEECs—in Poland, for instance, they started in 1918, while in Latvia and Lithuania guidance services were already being offered in 1929 and 1931 respectively—a history of central labour market planning generally militated against the notions of "individual choice" on which liberal guidance models are predicated—a point made earlier in this chapter. Occupational roles tended to be ascribed, in response to, and as a function of, the requirements of the economy, where the individual's aspirations were secondary to the perceived or projected needs of the labouring, producing community.

Such dynamics may partly explain why one gets the strong impression from the ETF database that guidance, as it is usually understood across in OECD and older EU countries, is more present in many of the CEECs discursively and in formal declarations than in actual practice. Many of the CEECs, for instance, have only recently promulgated legal instruments promoting career guidance and stipulating it as a citizen right (e.g., Bulgaria, Estonia, Hungary, Latvia, Lithuania, Poland, Slovakia). This "lag" is also partly due to the accession process itself, where specific policy models and strategies, not to mention policy discourse, circulates among the ruling elite both via formal channels associated with the *acquis communautaire*, but also through benchmarking and emulation of "good practices" promoted informally through, for instance, the "open method of co–ordination". All in all, however, there is a lack of determined strategic leadership in many of the CEECs when it comes to steering guidance, and most countries involved in this review note that several legal provisions have been adopted but have not been implemented. This is the case with Latvia and Poland, for instance, and Bulgaria has yet to establish the Career Information and Guidance Centres that its vocational education and training law refers to. Such implementation gaps are only partly due to the tight budgetary situation which prevails in most of the countries under review, where fiscal restraint translates into little funding accompanying the intentions expressed in legal instruments. The gap, together with a lack of strategic leadership, could also probably be attributed to the lack of expertise within Ministries—Estonia, for instance, is a case in point here—where bureaucratic inertia and a reluctance to give up old ways of doing things lead to policy torpor.

History and tradition could possibly also explain an approach to guidance in CEECs that to some extent contrasts with what can increasingly be referred to as "mainstream" definitions of the field. The ETF database suggests, for instance, that educational and career guidance is conceptualised rather more in terms of *provision* than as an activity that can be engaged in by the client in a self–service and self–directed mode. This is only partly due to the lack of resources, be they print or ICT–based. It reflects a view of guidance that is strongly marked by a psychological orientation, where it could be argued that, given the standing of that science/discipline in the academic and professional sectors in the CEECs, guidance ends up being defined as a psychological intervention where a more knowledgeable or expert provider comes to the assistance of a client or clients that are perceived to have a "deficit". This deficiency could be a lack of adequate information about educational or labour market opportunities, for instance, of job search and self–presentation skills, or even of the adequate personal qualities that make an individual more employable. Of course, as both the OECD and Cedefop syntheses suggest, this is not specific to CEECs—the difference is only one of degree.

The contrast between provision–led and self–service led approaches to guidance, and the balance struck between the two approaches, has important implications for the development of a service that is more routinely accessed and made use of throughout one's life, in response to specific needs linked to developmental, educational or occupational aspirations and opportunities. While in CEECs the balance is still clearly tilted towards a provision–led type of service, the ETF database does suggest that there is an identifiable effort, on the part of some of the countries under review, to develop strategies that enable clients to access guidance services proactively, and to engage in self–service mode. This is the case with the Vocational Information Counselling Centres (CIPS) in Slovenia, while the career guidance software developed in Poland (Counsellor 2000) also stimulates client input into the decision–making process. In some of the CEECs, therefore, we find an increase in the use of self–administered, self–scoring assessment instruments, with clients resorting to an individual guidance interview only after they have terminated the self–exploration process that has been guided by print– or ICT–based resources. Increasingly, therefore, one of the contexts for educational and occupational guidance will become the home and sites associated with leisure—though this of course will very much depend on the extent to which the personal computer and the Internet penetrate such sites.[18]

## Who is Targeted for Guidance in the CEECs, and in Which Contexts?

The repertoire of activities that Plant (2001)—and such professional bodies as the International Association for Educational and Vocational Guidance (IAEVG), for instance—associate with the field are addressed at a whole range of clients across most ages and identifiable by a broad range of social characteristics and ascriptions. Formal education for/about work can start as early as in primary schools, and educational and occupational guidance can accompany a citizen throughout life up to—and in some countries, beyond—retirement age. The rationale behind this is that in the learning economy "narrative", citizens are expected to be malleable and mobile, flexibly moving between jobs in response both to the needs of a rapidly changing labour market and, presumably, to their own aspirations. In such a context, guidance cannot be limited to key decision–making points at school, and at the moment of transition from school to work. Rather, guidance facilitates entry and exit routes into and out of specific educational and training options, as well as occupations. In addition, in some OECD and EU countries, guidance also entails "leisure management", especially when such leisure is experienced as an imposition (a paradox if ever there was one) through unemployment, redundancy, and retirement.

Despite these trends, however, much educational and career guidance remains focused on, or even limited to, the traditional clients, namely students who have to make choices between curricular and school options, young people who have to consider which occupational paths they will pursue, and the unemployed. This is to some extent also true of some of the OECD and EU countries, albeit to a lesser degree than in CEECs. Let us briefly give an overview of the key client targets, before we consider the significance of such trends for the construction of a learning society.

Educational and occupational guidance is, perhaps understandably, rare in primary education settings, though this will depend on the way the system is structured, the extent to which different curricular and "ability" streams exist, and the pervasiveness of high–stakes assessment measures that determine which tracks pupils will be placed into. Of the nine CEECs, only Slovenia and Slovakia report any forms of occupational guidance at this level. All CEECs, however, report that they offer a variety of guidance–related services at the secondary level, and increasingly at the post–secondary and higher education level. Interestingly enough, there is a divergence between countries in terms of whether vocational education and training establishments do offer guidance. Some, such as those in Hungary, do, while others, as in Slovakia, do not, arguing that students in vocational education and training have already made their educational and occupational choices, and are not in any pressing need for further guidance. The same can be said of university–level guidance, where the field tends to be quite underdeveloped compared to OECD and older EU countries, but where one can note an interest in developing services. Poland, Romania and to a lesser extent Estonia have made important strides in this direction, with guidance bureaux offering personal counselling, study skills, stress management, educational and occupational information, interview training, as well as job brokerage and graduate placement services.

Certainly, then, students are among the lead clients in the field, and as we shall see, the bulk of the resources carrying information and guidance–related functions that are created, imported or adapted are directed at them.

One category of student that has been specifically targeted by guidance services in many OECD and EU countries is the early leaver, or the "drop out". In the European context, this is quite understandable, given the emphasis on reducing unemployment and increasing labour market participation, particularly of those considered to be "at risk". It also connects with the "social inclusion" theme that sustains the social economy model adopted by the EU. CEECs, while generally demonstrating awareness of the special guidance needs of this group of young people, have not developed specific strategies or mobilised resources to effectively cater for them. OECD and EU country experience suggests that the best way to support the transitions of this group is to develop outreach services that are offered by community–based staff who are close to the realities of young disaffected people, and who can respond to their needs in a flexible manner. As the Slovenian report notes, it is very difficult for guidance personnel based in schools to connect with "drop–outs", because, despite good intentions, they are immediately associated with the setting which these young people are so keen to avoid.

Young people who have just left school, as well as a whole range of adults are, in all CEECs, a second main target group for guidance services, most often catered for within the context of public employment services. The main focus is on the unemployed, who are often classified according to specific categories associated with specific active employment measures, the goal of which is insertion—or re–insertion—in the labour market. Among the most common categories are young people without any experience of work, formal education, or certifiable skills; long–term unemployed; older workers who have been made redundant due to the impact of restructuring; women who wish to return to work after raising a family; and workers with disabilities. Another group that is of concern consists of young people and adults in the remoter regions of CEECs, with distance educational and career guidance increasingly on the agenda given the opportunities provided by ICTs in reaching clients who would otherwise not have access to a service. Poland, Romania, Estonia and Latvia all report efforts to create portals and Internet points in an effort to provide a flexible network of inter–linked services. Latvia, where Internet penetration is rather low even when compared to the other CEECs, has set up a peripatetic guidance service, with mobile teams meeting clients in the seven regions which do not have Professional Career Counselling Centres.

Information provided by the ETF database leads one to conclude that there are two main limitations with guidance services offered to adults. First is the fact that many of the activities organised within the context of public employment services in the CEECs do not carry much of a guidance function. Rather, the focus tends to be on supplying information, on getting clients into training or re–training, on helping them develop self–presentation and job–getting skills, and on acting as job brokers with a network of potential employers. This is, of course, understandable, given that the very *raison d'être* of the PES is to enhance employability, and to combat long–term unemployment. Indeed, the situation in the CEECs is quite similar to that reported for OECD and older EU states. It should be noted, however, that some countries have successfully integrated guidance functions into their active measures. Foremost among these have been Poland, Lithuania and Slovenia, where the unemployed receive support in drawing up an individual employment plan.

A second weakness or lacuna in the gamut of guidance services offered to adults is the lack of attention given to adults *in employment*. Much guidance remains remedial in nature, seemingly forgetting the needs of those adults who might require support in making progress in their careers, in switching tracks due to changing interests or changes in the skills provides required by the company they are employed in. None of the CEECs reported any incidence of leisure, third age, or retirement counselling. Such lacunae are serious, especially when contrasted with the rhetoric associated with the learning economy. The CEECs database suggests that this kind of adult guidance is only offered rarely, and then only in the largest of companies that have strong HRD departments or units. In contrast to the reports for some OECD and older EU countries, trade unions, even less than employers, fail to offer any formal guidance services through trained personnel—at best assistance is offered informally to members going through or facing the trauma of unemployment. Only Romania, and to a lesser extent Estonia, referred to a modest service that some trade unions are slowly building up.

It is important to point out in this context that some of the OECD and older EU countries compensate for the lack—or narrow range—of guidance services offered to adults via the development of *private* (e.g., Greece and Sweden) or *community–based* employment services (e.g., Luxembourg and Spain). Both are, however, largely underdeveloped in most of the CEECs, though increasingly the trend is for governments to outsource services to specialised foundations, NGOs, or even the private sector in order to make up for their own lack of capacity deficits (e.g., Bulgaria, Estonia). Changing legislation and increased acceptance of privatisation ideology, together with modernised lifestyles do suggest that private providers of guidance services might start to flourish, though at present, where they have been established (e.g., in Bulgaria, Latvia, Lithuania, Slovakia), they still currently tend to focus on job–brokering and job–matching functions, and to a lesser degree in the provision of print— or web—based information, including further study manuals. Community—based employment services, offered by NGOs in several of the OECD and EU countries, are still largely missing in CEECs, where the state is still the main or sole provider. It was only Bulgaria that reported a non—state, community—based initiative, in this case organised by the Open Society Fund.

## What are the Modalities for the Provision of Lifelong Guidance in the CEECs?

As has already been noted, educational and occupational guidance in the CEECs tends to give pride of place to the relaying of information, either via traditional methods or, increasingly through enlisting the potential of ICTs. CEECs report that educational institutions, public employment services, employers, and occasionally trade unions and private entities produce education— or occupation—related information in print format, usually as brochures, flyers, leaflets, posters, but also as manuals, adverts in the press, and so on. Much of the responsibility for the production and dissemination of such information remains with the state, with government agencies collecting data, organising it, and disseminating it free of charge. Information is often published at a national level in the CEECs, with data fed to a centre via a network of regional and local providers. Typically, such information includes classification of occupations, occupational descriptions, macroeconomic indicators and labour market trends.[19]

One of the problems that CEECs share with guidance services in OECD and older EU countries is that education and labour ministries and departments tend to collect different information, and not much effort is made to consolidate different data sets in such a way as to help clients make better sense of options and opportunities. As a result, connectivity between career information, educational information, and labour market data (such as vulnerability to unemployment, earnings compared to minimum salary, and so on) tends to be rare, though the situation is reportedly better in Bulgaria, Poland and Romania. Estonia and Slovakia are attempting to deal with the difficulty by organising joint seminars between the education and labour ministries and by establishing formal co—operation agreements, while Bulgaria has gone as far as to issue a law specifying the nature and extent of ministerial co—ordination in the delivery of guidance information and services.

There are signs that call—centre technology, with clients phoning in queries (as in Lithuania, for instance), is catching on, though such help lines tend to be used rather more to deal with crisis and personal counselling than with educational or occupational guidance.

Practically all the CEECs also report a keen interest in the use of ICTs, often to present the same information available in print formats, and less frequently to support guidance functions and to enable interactive education or career decision–making via CD–based software, career navigation systems, or the Internet. Much of the software used tends to be adopted from other countries, and adapted to the realities of the labour market in the CEECs. This is the case of Romania, for instance, which uses Canada's *Interoptions*. Slovakia and Slovenia use an adapted version of the British software *Adult Directions*. Others have successfully produced their own ICT–based systems, including *Counsellor 2000* in Poland, which permits a multi–dimension analysis of occupations, and stimulates clients' efforts and assists them in choosing an appropriate job. Similarly, Slovakia has produced a *Guide to the World of Occupations*, software developed under the Leonardo programme in co–operation with the Czech Republic, Greece, Cyprus and the UK. Funds for the development of new or adapted ICT–based guidance systems have also come from the World Bank (e.g., to Poland and Romania) though, as with most external funding, the challenge as to how to keep the system up and running and up–dated after the initial donor input has been used up still remains.

The "qualitative" or "formative" functions of guidance–related activities listed earlier—including advising, assessing, teaching, mentoring, sampling work experience—are less in evidence. Education for and/or about work does not feature centrally as a separate subject or as a cross–curricular theme in most of the school systems in CEECs, and it is only Romania, Poland and Latvia that report initiatives in this regard. Guidance certainly does not seem to permeate the ethos of schools as it does in a number of countries internationally, where the potential contribution of guidance to the evolution of a learning society has been carefully and strategically articulated, sometimes in school development plans. In CEECs, guidance staff typically broach the world of work with students via individual interviews and, less commonly, group seminars, often scheduled outside the regular school programme. Few schools have dedicated rooms for guidance–related activities. Stakeholder input is sporadic and minimal, with trade union officials, and more frequently employers, addressing students or providing information about their respective organisations and enterprises at career fairs and exhibitions.

Increasingly, schools in CEECs organise experiential and supervised exposure to the realities of the labour market and of employment via "work shadowing" or "work experience" schemes, and more rarely through in–school entrepreneurship projects. Most institutions organise these on their own initiative, though some countries—such as Estonia—have central policy leads that encourage the trend in this direction.

A key identifying aspect of educational and occupational guidance provision is the emphasis placed on giving a service rather than making resources available so that clients use them proactively to engage in a self–directed, decision–making process. Again, compared to OECD and EU contexts, and possibly due to the psychological orientation and centrally–led traditions referred to earlier, self–help, self–evaluation strategies where the client is in charge of his or her own development are still rare in CEECs, although Romania and Slovenia, for instance, have made a policy commitment shift practices to a self–service mode. This has important implications in ensuring access to the benefits imputed to guidance, particularly in contexts where supply of guidance personnel does not match demand.

## Who Provides Guidance in the CEECs?

As has already been noted, guidance is largely offered by graduates who have majored in psychology—or, less frequently, in a social science, such as economics or sociology, or in some cases (e.g., in Romania) even law or engineering. Very few CEECs offer specific degree or post–degree level training in guidance (e.g., Poland), though many do provide in–service specialised training which, in some cases, leads to formal certification (e.g., Latvia). Entry requirements into the profession differ both across CEECs, as well as between sectors within the CEECs, where there is no mutual recognition of guidance qualifications between education and labour services. This situation in fact prevails internationally, as McCarthy's (2001) review of the issue in 23 countries indicates. The training of guidance personnel has been boosted in many CEECs as a result of the process of accession, with staff benefiting from opportunities made available by Academia and Phare, and through the setting up of the Euroguidance network.

Despite the increasing opportunities for training, it is only in a few cases that CEECs have specialised staff providing guidance services in schools (e.g., Slovenia). It is more often the case that guidance is offered by regular and class teachers who have no specific training, other than through short in–service courses (e.g., Latvia, Bulgaria, Estonia, Romania). School staff involved in guidance also have a tendency to focus rather more on personal and educational counselling than on occupational guidance, partly because of the above mentioned predominance of psychology as the formative discipline in the preparation of professionals, but also because schools are increasingly the sites where young people act out their frustrations. Recourse is thus often made to specialised career guidance services outside of the school (e.g., Latvia and Lithuania), drawing on personnel from public employment services who have a better knowledge of labour markets.

Staff in the public employment services tend to have benefited more fully from funding resources in order to develop their professional capacities. This is in part due to the fact that tackling unemployment is top on the agenda for most CEEC governments, with the European Employment Strategy priorities framework also having an impact on developments in most PES setups.

Across both the labour market and education sector, and in contrast to the situation in many OECD and EU countries, CEEC staff involved in delivering guidance are, in most cases, not yet professionalized. Not only do they tend not to have specialised and regulated guidance qualifications, but there also are no clear entry, qualification or progression routes into and along clearly defined occupational roles, supported by an extensive network of professional associations[20] and research and training organisations. Only Poland and Lithuania report some developments in this regard, with Poland adding career guidance to the National Classification of Occupations and Trades, and with Latvia and Romania having associations that promote professional and ethical standards. In most cases, occupational roles and clear codes of practice and of conduct are not formally defined or regulated by legally–binding documents, and competence frameworks have not been formally established, except in Estonia, Slovakia and Poland. In addition to this, the practice of guidance in most of the CEECs has not been subjected to a degree of reflexivity, which is the hallmark of established professions. In other words, few of the CEECs report a capacity to evaluate their work, to measure the impact of educational and occupational guidance services on clients, to gauge the extent to which the services are being used, or to which clients are satisfied with the services they have received. There are exceptions of course—Latvia, for instance, regularly carries out surveys to establish the different guidance–related needs of school and students, and of the unemployed, while Estonia, Lithuania, Poland and Romania report that they do collect some quantitative data regarding outcomes of guidance in terms of client placement in employment.

One of the key features in the provision of guidance services in both OECD and older EU countries is use of para–professionals as well as stakeholders—a strategy which enhances effective delivery both because it makes up for the lack of availability of guidance personnel, and because clients can benefit from different perspectives brought to them. Few CEECs report the use of such para–professionals (e.g., Youth Information Officers in Romania and Estonia) or "linked professionals" (social workers) to support the work of guidance staff. It is more common for CEECs to make use of stakeholders—such as alumni, parents, business and community leaders, trade union staff, and so on—particularly in educational settings. Such attempts are often the result of personal initiatives on the part of institutions. Hungary, however, seems to have formalised such input through the activities of parent organisations that provide students and parents with information about educational and occupational pathways. Student organisations and associations are also increasingly active in providing information, particularly where, as in Estonia, there is a lack of government–funded provision. Even then, however, and as noted earlier, stakeholder involvement is underdeveloped when compared to OECD and older EU countries, possibly because the public is not necessarily fully aware of the benefits of a well–functioning career guidance service, and partly because some policy–makers have not yet embraced styles of leadership that involve social partnership.

# Guiding Citizens... Through the Traps of the Learning Society?

## Distilling Trends in Guidance

The overview presented above in answer to four structuring questions or categories provides us with quite a clear indication of the key trends that could be said to characterise the guidance field in the nine CEECs reviewed. The assumption is that, despite the differences between national contexts, a cross–country analysis distilling main flows in policy–making can be made. One way of presenting these trends is with reference to what I have occasionally referred to above as increasingly "mainstream" approaches to guidance, which largely accept the notion that a post–industrial, learning–based economy and society requires the channelling of educational and career guidance in specific directions. In other words, one way of describing what is happening in the CEECs reviewed is by claiming that practices there are attempting to make up for the "lag" in development—due to the nature of the economic and political leadership they experienced prior to 1989—and that they are now involved in a process of "catching up" with the more "advanced" practices in the EU, membership of which they have either just gained, or are aspiring to. This is indeed the perspective presented in the conclusions to the Budapest Conference on guidance in Central and Eastern Europe, where it is noted that the "career–quake" that occurred across North America, Europe and other post–industrial societies is now hitting the CEECs. The process whereby old notions of a career which, in more economically advanced countries, have been "shaken and in many cases destroyed", replaced by "a new concept of career [...], redefined as the individual's lifelong progression in learning and in work" (Budapest Conference Report 2000, 6), is now having an impact on transition societies as well.

Such a perspective is easily justified if one considers the trends that can be elicited from the ETF database, and places them along a continuum marking "origins" (or what guidance practice tended to be like) and "destinations" (or where guidance practice is trying to get to). Indeed, this would be to map each country internationally along the categorised continuum for comparative purposes. For the CEECs collectively, the continuum would capture the following flows:

### Table 1. The continuum of flows in educational and occupational guidance

| From a service that… | To a service that… |
|---|---|
| Is considered to be secondary, not central | Citizens are legal entitled to |
| Is provided mainly at key decision points | Is provided lifelong |
| Focuses on provision | Focuses on self–access and self–service |
| Is offered on institutional sites | Is available on leisure sites, community, home |
| Is exclusively provided by the state | Is also provided by private entities |
| Is delivered only by guidance staff | Includes input by stakeholders |
| In relation to students, is outside the curriculum | Permeates guidance issues through curriculum |
| In relation to adults, addresses unemployed | Also caters for within/between career moves |

Continued

| From a service that… | To a service that… |
|---|---|
| Is centrally co–ordinated | Is decentralised but monitored centrally |
| Is largely homogenous, irrespective of client | Is differentiated, responding to specific needs |
| Is segmented according to sector | Values cross–sector collaboration |
| Targets mainly individuals | Maximises effect by also working with groups |
| Tends to fail to connect education and labour market data | Uses ICTs to consolidate different data |
| Is staffed by non–specialised personnel | Requires pre– and in–service training |
| Is poorly professionalized | Has clear entry and career progression routes |
| Is unregulated | Has codes of conduct and standards of practice |
| Is under–researched | Is systematically reflexive |

The representation of guidance in terms of such flows is probably useful, in that it does capture where the field is coming from, and where it may be moving to, with different countries being able to locate themselves in that space of flows, recognising and agreeing with the general framework in relation to which those movements are taking place, and which can be simply referred to as the "learning society".

The point I would like to make in conclusion, however, is captured by the challenging question: "Is the representation of the learning society, on which much of the current conceptualisation of guidance depends, a *correct* one?" I am here using the word "correct" in two ways, i.e., first, does such a representation correspond to the economic and labour market realities that underpin it; and second, does such a representation of the learning society correspond to what we would consider the "good life", wisely and virtuously "performed"? Let us briefly consider these two issues. In doing this my intention is to take up the baton and run with the counter discourse that is becoming progressively more vociferous in relation to the mainstream representation of the learning society, and which I will here apply to the field of guidance more specifically. For it is my view that the Lifelong Guidance train, following hot on the heels of the learning society one, is being obliged to run on two divergent rather than parallel tracks, and that in hoping to respond to both the post–industrial imperative, and the democratic one, it is finding itself in quite impossible binds.

## ...But Who is Knocking at the Gates of Lifelong Guidance?

Earlier I noted that Commission agendas for both the learning society and for lifelong guidance are marked by two logics, the economic and the social. Several authors have noted how this particular blend—mirroring the attempt at developing a social economy, where market forces are given free reign, but whose excesses are tempered by a concern for the social—is appealing in post–1989 Europe, and is indeed a hallmark that sets the EU apart from the more bullish celebration of free markets in the USA, but it nevertheless creates tensions that are quite impossible to resolve.[21] One of the ways in which such tensions are managed is through the development of complex and multifaceted discourses, such as the ones surrounding notions of "lifelong learning".

This very complexity is indeed *constitutive* of the effects of the discourse—in other words, the rhetorical and policy appeal of the learning society can be explained by the way it works as a "chameleon concept", changing its ideological colours according to the context in which it is applied. The "strategic management" (Casey, 2003) of the learning society debate—though, in relation to guidance, one would be forgiven for asking: *is* there a debate?—is of critical importance as on it depends our understanding of the nature of "learners", of the process of "learning", and more specifically, of *why* "learning citizens" should require ever more "guidance" throughout their life, in what some, in Foucauldian mode, are referring to as the "counselled society" (Edwards and Nicoll, 2001). As suggested in the analysis of trends in guidance in CEECs, a consideration of the lifelong learning discourse as an "achievement", and of the learning society as a "construct", is especially appropriate for so-called "accession countries" because "entry rights" can only be gained by those countries that "buy into" a number of world-views that are keenly held and promoted by corporate Europe, with lifelong learning as a path to the "learning economy" being one of them.

The European Commission documents referred to in the first section of this chapter illustrate the points that I am making quite clearly, and they are good examples of how contradictory strands are interwoven in a way that renders the learning society discourse particularly potent. Contradictions are ignored or submerged, with the Commission discursively accomplishing that which is materially impossible: pleasing both "god" and "mammon".[22]

It is relatively easy for those involved in guidance to connect with the dominant discourse surrounding lifelong guidance, for strands of it resonate with the broadly humanistic—even empowering and emancipative—orientations of most practitioners in the field. This, after all, is a service that sets out to maximise the choices available to clients, to help them re–engage in learning despite their negative experience of schooling, to enable them to navigate in increasingly complex and stormy waters, to plan and manage fulfilling life projects despite the uncertainties and instabilities of the labour market, to lead dignified and productive lives, and even to overcome obstacles in access to such lives due to class, gender, ethnicity, or prior employment background.

What is however less immediately apparent—and rather less humanistic in tenor—in this lifelong learning/guidance discourse is the way it sets out to mobilise individuals and services around the presumed needs of the economy. Given that we have now apparently reached "the end of history" (Fukayama 1989), with no alternatives to capitalism as a way of producing, distributing and consuming wealth, present economic arrangements are the "givens" around which all social practices must gravitate. In the field of lifelong guidance, this submission to economic imperatives leads to an interpellation and mobilisation of citizens in very specific ways. Individuals must remain engaged in learning, ever flexible and ever nimble, constantly re–shaping and re–inventing themselves in line with unpredictable changes in the labour market. They must be ever ready to enter and re–enter learning, training and working routes, and, given the "European dimension", to move to wherever such training and employment opportunities exist. All this, it must be stressed, in a context where the citizen is being urged to do more for ever diminishing economic and social returns. It is indeed striking that this radically restructured context—where, for instance, rights to a minimum wage, to satisfying work, to social support, to a pension, to leisure, to graceful ageing, are slowly being eroded—has not generated strong forms of counter–hegemonic practices in the guidance field, and that the discourse revolves solely around opportunity, and not outrage (Davey 2003).

For gone, here, are considerations of life inspired by a vision of humanity that projects "an expansive view of people with a range of subjectivities that extends beyond the production–consumption nexus" (Borg and Mayo 2002, 21). Here, the learning society's primary function seems to be that of guaranteeing the availability of suitable human resources necessary for the reproduction and accumulation of capital in a knowledge–based economy, with guidance acting as the lubricant, providing skills, information, knowledge, and even the technology to reach the furthest enclaves of the personality, in order to shape it and help attain a "fit" in this brave new world.

It is part of the irony, and also power, of this discourse—which, as we have seen, is increasingly accepted within the CEECs reviewed—that the whole concept of a lifelong submission to capital is often rhetorically bathed in a bright, glowing light. Frequent job changes caused by restructuring and the redeployment of resources are seen, in the lifelong learning/guidance discourse, as realities that present exciting and stimulating opportunities in the construction of "career narratives" and life projects. Less readily acknowledged is the way the loss of lifetime employment contracts leads to precarious lives lived constantly in the shadow of insecurity, and to the demise of work–based communities as sources of solidarity, sociality, pride, and meaning. Mobility across Europe, aided and abetted by Euroguidance and other networks, and facilitated by the harmonisation of standards and qualifications, is presented as a multiplication of opportunities for the citizen/worker. Little acknowledgement is made, however, of the implications that such uprooting from community ties, in response to the needs of European enterprises for mobile labour, has on individuals and their families. Given this chapter's focus on CEECs, where the GDP per capita is less than a third to a fifth of the average in the older EU Member States, the economic logic behind the "mobility agenda" of the EU, duly transmitted via the humanistic discourses of lifelong learning and guidance, cannot be ignored: what could be more advantageous to capital, one might ask, than the availability of mobile, well–trained, suitably socialised "human resources" from hitherto economically depressed countries, who could be used either as comparatively cheap sources of labour, or/and to drive down wages for "mainstream" European workers whose "exorbitant" demands depress profit margins, making the old continent "less competitive"? And does guidance really want to be party to this, when at the heart of its mission is the good of the client?

But there are other, less normative, more "pragmatic" objections that could be brought to bear on the whole field of lifelong guidance as it is being constructed. As we have noted, the assumptions underlying much of the policy discourse here revolve around a specific understanding of knowledge–based economies, where the context and content of education, training and employment are changing. And yet, there is an increasing amount of literature that suggests that the labour market is not quite moving in the direction predicted for so–called "high–ability" societies. What empirical research is showing is quite the opposite: a preponderance of low–skilled, low–ability jobs that are not only surviving but are actually *increasing* in number. As Casey (2003, 5) notes, drawing on such authors as Gallie (1991), Felstead and Jewson (1999), and Ritzer (1996):

> Irrespective of the upward mobility enabled by education and training for some, and manifest productivity and market gains, numerous industry sectors—including the knowledge–intensive—not only retain but newly generate low–knowledge, low–skill, neo–Taylorised jobs simultaneously with knowledge–rich jobs. Importantly, the persistence, and even growth, of drudgery jobs—jobs that are dull, repetitive, intensely managerially controlled (including those requiring emotional labour: the smiley jobs)—and the wide expansion of deregulated, contingent employment practices, including zero hours contracts is widely evident. [...] A growth of low–paid and casual employment in service industries from food and entertainment services to globally marketed call centres represents a competing trajectory to that of a highly paid and over–employed technological and knowledge–rich service sector. (Casey 2003, 5)

Clearly, guidance workers cannot resolve the tensions and contradictions inherent to the lifelong learning/lifelong guidance discourse, for these are structurally induced and not easily amenable to individual shaping. Watts (1996c, 362), in his discussion of socio–political approaches to guidance, is most probably correct when, while acknowledging the ideological binds that many in the field find themselves in, nevertheless asserts that "the professional task of the guidance practitioner is to identify what is morally and pragmatically appropriate in particular contexts." It is nevertheless disquieting that the guidance field, internationally—and in CEECs as well it seems—should so readily and unreflectively accept what I have been referring to as a "mainstream"—i.e., conservative, positive economistic, neo–liberal—position in mediating transitions between education, training, and employment on behalf of its clients. My argument is that, given this privileged location, more should be done to "unmask" the presumed innocence behind the lifelong learning debate, where we examine not only the way we, as social actors, use the discourse, but more importantly, the way the discourse uses us. It is in doing so that we can rise to the challenge of intellectual work which, following Bourdieu (1998, 106), involves "...freedom from the powers, criticism of received ideas, demolition of simplistic alternatives, restitution of the complexity of problems." Such a task requires us—and anybody who would presume to "guide" citizens in the learning society—to ask such uncomfortable questions as: what kind of learning, for what kind of society, which works in whose interests?

## Notes

1. See Clarke (1980) for a review of this with reference to theories of career development in the UK.
2. Killeen (1996) identifies the following set of inter–related phenomena as having changed the face of guidance since the late 1970s: technological change, the rise (or intensification) of globalisation and regional free trade, industrial restructuring and the emergence of the service sector, the installation of mass unemployment as a regular feature of economies, the increasing participation of women in the labour market, and an ageing workforce. For the purpose of this essay, most of these phenomena are captured in a consideration of the discursive and material construction of the Learning, post–Fordist Society.
3. The critical humanistic tenor of that document is caught nicely in the following excerpt—one among many that serve to remind us how far the present discourse surrounding lifelong learning has moved from what many consider the foundational ideas of adult education: "Is this not the time to call for something quite different in education systems? Learning to live, learning to learn, so as to be able to absorb new knowledge all through life; learning to think freely and critically; learning to love the world and make it more human; learning to develop in and through creative work." Significantly, this quotation appears on the homepage announcing the year 2000 international conference on lifelong learning, held in Saskatchewan, 2426 November [http://www.usask.ca/education/edfdt/lifelong/—Accessed on 28th March 2005].
4. There have been several portrayals of the main features of the discourse, ranging from the benign (European Round Table 1995) to the highly critical (Edwards 1997; Ranson 1998; Field 2000; Jarvis 2001; Greenwood and Stuart 2002). Here we rehearse the key elements that are most often circulated within mainstream policy circles and can be found in such documents as the European Commission's *White Paper on Education and Training* (1996), its *Memorandum on Lifelong Learning* (2000), and its final Communication *Making a European Area of Lifelong Learning a Reality* (2001a).
5. And, as it will become clear by the end of the chapter, how the international research field and collaboration between such key organisations as the OECD, the World Bank, and the EU has created a specific and shared/overlapping understanding of what guidance is about, and indeed of the whole enterprise of education in the 21st century (see Akkari, Sultana and Gurner 2001; Hirtt 2001; Laval and Weber 2002).

6. The document *Recent Policy Developments in Lifelong Guidance at European Union Level* tabled at the first meeting of the European Commission's Expert Group on Lifelong Guidance on 13 December 2002, was particularly helpful in providing the overall picture in this section.
7. Many of these insights about the nature of guidance service were also reinforced recently through the White Paper *A New Impetus for European Youth* (2002) detailing youth concerns as these were obtained through a comprehensive Europe–wide consultation process. Here too young people expressed a need for flexible, user–friendly information, guidance and counselling systems that used a personalised approach, that were easily accessible in places where young people spend their time, that connected with opportunities available locally, regionally, nationally, and across Europe; and that made good use of stakeholder input to ensure more effective services.
8. The other five priorities are: (i) valuing learning; (ii) investing time and money in learning; (iii) bringing together learners and learning opportunities; (iv) basic skills; and (v) innovative pedagogy.
9. These are: (i) partnership working across the learning spectrum; (ii) creating a learning culture; (iii) striving for excellence; (iv) insight into the demand for learning; (v) facilitating access to learning opportunities; and (vi) adequate resourcing.
10. Section 3.2 of the Communication (EC 2002b, 32) highlights three strategies for strengthening the European dimension of information, guidance and counselling. These include (i) the establishment of a European Guidance Forum of policy–makers and social partners to develop common policy approaches in the field of guidance—this has in fact not been implemented in that format, but has instead been constituted as a less high profile European Commission Expert Group on Lifelong Guidance; (ii) the establishment of an Internet Portal on Learning Opportunities, providing information on lifelong learning in Member States and candidate countries (see the PLOTEUS portal on http://europa.eu.int/ploteus/portal/home.jsp maintained by the Euroguidance network); (iii) the evaluation of existing European networks for both education and training to establish a coherent and cross–sectoral learning framework for the scope and activities of those networks. Another document focusing on *Modernising Public Employment Services to Support the European Employment Strategy* (1998), highlights the way fuller integration between EURES (the European Job Mobility Portal) into the national Public Employment Services could bring a greater European dimension to the information, counselling and brokerage services offered to jobseekers and employers. The development of a EURES website would ensure that information about skills shortages and surpluses by country and by region would be easily accessible.

11. The "open method of coordination" has been considered by some to be a most promising—albeit controversial—policy instrument in the EU, and involves on-going national level experimentation, combined with EU-level monitoring, the publicizing of good practice, and the activation of civil society in policy formation, comparison and critique. Guidelines, or policy objectives, are established at the Union level, setting out quantitative or qualitative targets for Member States, and then requiring Member States to report progress in achieving those goals to the European Commission and the Council of Ministers. These may in turn use harder or softer enforcement mechanisms, require longer or shorter reporting intervals, and choose to set guidelines at the EU level or delegate responsibility to individual Member States (de la Porte and Pochet 2002). Since its use in harmonizing Member States, the open method of coordination has increasingly served as a form of policy making, particularly in the areas of employment policy and social inclusion policy (Overdevest 2002).
12. This report grouped 15 quality indicators around four main areas, i.e., (i) skills, competencies and attitudes; (ii) access and participation; (iii) resources for lifelong learning; and (iv) strategies and systems development. Guidance and counselling were considered under the latter area.
13. The same message regarding the value of guiding young and adult learners into scientific and technical careers is repeated in the *Science and Society Action Plan* (2002).
14. Launched in 1997, the European Employment Strategy rests on the so-called "four pillars", namely (i) employability, (ii) entrepreneurship (iii) adaptability, and (iv) equal opportunities. The first pillar seeks to enhance employability through a variety of measures and strategies, including improved training in appropriate skills, increased access to lifelong learning, and better access to guidance services throughout one's life.
15. Needless to say, there is much overlap between the EU agenda for guidance and the increasingly hegemonic understanding of the field internationally, and as it is promoted by such organisations as the World Bank and, given its research lead in the area, by the OECD.
16. At the macro level, scale can matter for guidance when, for instance, it comes to managing a decentralisation process, and to developing strong municipal career service structures operating within the framework of a steering national policy. At the micro level, scale can also matter in shaping occupational destinations, not least because small, close-knit societies are more likely to develop extensive personal networks where "who you know" can sometimes be more decisive in clinching a job than "what you know".
17. The countries that took part in this review are Austria, the Czech Republic, Denmark, Finland, Germany, Ireland, Luxembourg, the Netherlands, Norway, Spain, the UK, Australia, Canada, and Korea. For an account of the

process adopted for the purpose of this review, see Sweet (2001). The author of the chapter was involved as an external expert on the country reviews for Luxembourg and Spain. Material related to the OECD review can be accessed at the following website: www.oecd.org/els/education/careerguidance

18. Access to the Internet varies a great deal between CEECs. The European Innovation Scoreboard for the year 2002, basing its report on Eurostat figures of 2001, provides information regarding Internet access as a percentage for the whole population. While the average for EU Member States is 31.4%, this is only matched by Slovenia (30%), with Slovakia (16.7%), Hungary (14.8%), the Czech Republic (13.6%), Poland (9.8%), Bulgaria (7.5%), Latvia (7.2%), Lithuania (6.8%) and Romania (4.5%) being far behind. The difference between the older EU Member States and CEECs is even more in evidence when one considers home Internet access. The older EU Member State average is 37.7%, and again it is Slovenia that comes closest to that (24%). The Scoreboard only provides information for a few of the CEECs, namely Poland (8%), Latvia (3%), Lithuania (3%) and Hungary (2.6%). [For the European Innovation Scoreboard Report, see the Cordis website: ftp://ftp.cordis.lu/pub/focus/docs/innovation_scoreboard_2002_en.pdf].

19. It is clear that most CEECs are still attached to a centralist model of policy making and implementation. It must be pointed out, however, that while decentralisation may be increasingly ideologically appealing in a European context where subsidiarity is highly valued, the devolution of responsibilities within a policy vacuum can lead to costly overlap, excessive disparity that gives rise to inequalities, and a deficit in standards. In the case of Poland, the winding down of the national network of labour offices in favour of local government provision has led to a serious deterioration in the quality of provision. Decentralisation can also be a convenient mechanism to devolve responsibilities to local government without passing on the necessary funding, as is noted in the report for Latvia. Both the Polish and Latvian experiences support the view that the best way forward may very well be to have a judicious mix of centralised and decentralised models, where municipalities develop their own policy in the context of central guidelines that have been arrived at after wide consultation with stakeholders. Estonia seems to have adopted such a model, stipulating contracts between central and regional government to avoid problems of great variability between regions.

20. It may very well be that the lack of development of strong associations in the field can at least partly be explained by the "feminization" of the profession. It is mostly women that are found in guidance, and their share of the sector can be as high as 90% (Poland). This has implications for occu-

pational identity, for the status accorded to the activity by society, and consequently for the salaries and resources that the profession will be able to command. It must be added, however, that the phenomenon of feminization has also been noted in the EU and EEA countries involved in the Cedefop survey (Sultana, 2004).
21. See I. Greenwood and M. Stuart (2002) for a useful review. See also Casey (2003), and Sultana (2003a). For Europe as a normative space, see Therborn (2001) and Habermas (2002).
22. This religious imagery is not being used flippantly. There is much about the EU that revolves around religious—and more specifically, Christian—symbolism and practices, starting from the Union flag's twelve stars on a blue background taken directly from the apocalyptic imagery related to the Madonna to the notion of "subsidiarity", which Delors—a devout Catholic—borrowed from a concept developed by Pope Pius XI in his 1931 *Quadragesimo Anno* (Pakkala 1997). That the Catholic Church is keen to occupy the vacuum left by the collapse of communism is hardly news, and the lobby to inscribe "God" in the European Constitution is merely a surface sign of much deeper dynamics that mark a proselytising church keen to equate European values with Christian ones. More importantly for the purpose of this essay is the impact of the "social market" consensus that underpins the social doctrine of the Catholic Church, and which finds an echo in EU macro–economic policy.

# References

Akkari, A., Sultana, R.G. and Gurtner, J.–L. (eds). *Politiques et Stratégies Éducatives: Termes de l'Échange et Nouveaux Enjeux Nord–Sud*. Berne: Peter Lang, 2001.

Bourdieu, P. *Contre-feux*. Paris, Liber: Raisons d'agir, 1998.

Borg, G. and Mayo, P. "The EU Memorandum on lifelong learning. Diluted old wine in new bottles?" Paper presented at the 2002 BAICE Conference, *Lifelong Learning and the Building of Human and Social Capital*. University of Nottingham, 6–8 September 2002.

Brown, P. and Lauder, H. "Education, economy and social change". *International Journal of Sociology of Education*, Vol.1, 1991, pp.3–23.

Brown, P., Green, A. and Lauder, H. (eds) *High Skills: Globalization, Competitiveness and Skill Formation*. Oxford: Oxford University Press, 2001.

Budapest Conference Report "Guidance and counselling: theory and practice for the 21st century." Report of the conference held in Budapest, Hungary, 29–31 March 2002.

Casey, C. "Work and workers in the learning economy: some critical questions." Paper read at the FRP5 Accompanying Measures Project workshop *Living, working and learning in the learning society—the perspective of the learning citizen in EU funded research.* University of Bremen, 27–28 March 2003.

Clark, G. Opening address at the first meeting of the European Commission's Expert Group on Lifelong Guidance. Brussels, 12 December 2002.

Clarke, L. *The Transition from School to Work—A Critical Review of Research in the United Kingdom.* London: HMSO, 1980.

Collin, A. and Watts, A.G. "The death and transfiguration of career—and of career guidance?" *British Journal of Guidance and Counselling,* 24(3), 1996, pp. 385–398.

Company, F.J. *Rapport de Synthèse sur les Politiques et les Services d'Information, Orientation et Conseil.* Cedefop, Draft report dated 12 December 2002.

Council of the European Union *Future Concrete Objectives for Education and Training Systems in Europe.* 14 Feb. 5980/01: EDUC 23. Report of the Education Council to the European Council, 2001. [http://www.pmmc.lt/PMIT/doc/Future_objectives_report.pdf]—Accessed 28th March 2005.

Davey, J.A. "Opportunity or outrage? Redundancy and educational involvement in mid–life." *Journal of Education and Work,* 16(1), 2003, pp. 87–102.

De la Porte, C. and Pochet, P. (eds) *A New Approach to Building Social Europe: The Open Method of Coordination.* Brussels: Peter Lang, 2002.

Edwards, R. *Changing Places? Flexibility, Lifelong Learning and a Learning Society.* London: Routledge, 1997.

Edwards, R. and Nicoll, K. (2001) "Restructuring the rhetoric of lifelong learning." *Journal of Educational Policy,* 16(2), pp. 103–112.

European Commission. *Making a European Area of Lifelong Learning a Reality."* 2001a. [http://europa.eu.int/comm/education/policies/lll/life/communication/com_en.pdf]—Accessed on 28th March 2005.

European Commission. *Joint Employment Report.* 2001b. [http://europa.eu.int/comm/employment_social/index_en.html]—Accessed 28th March 2005.

European Commission. *European Report on Quality Indicators for Lifelong Learning.* Brussels, 2002a. [http://europa.eu.int/comm/education/policies/lll/life/report/quality/report_en.pdf] Accessed on 28th March 2005.

European Commission. *A European Area of Lifelong Learning.* Luxembourg: Office for Official Publications of the European Communities, 2002b.

European Commission. *Action Plan for Skills and Mobility.* Brussels, 2002c. [http://europa.eu.int/comm/employment_social/news/2002/feb/ap_en.pdf]—Accessed on 28th March 2005.

European Commission. *Increasing Labour Force Participation and Promoting Active Ageing.* Brussels 24.01.2002, COM(2002) 9, Final, 2002d. [http://europa.

eu.int/comm/employment_social/news/2002/feb/com_2002_9_en.pdf]
—Accessed on 28th March 2005.

European Innovation Scoreboard Report, 2002. The Cordis website, available at the following [ftp://ftp.cordis.lu/pub/focus/docs/innovation_scoreboard_2002_en.pdf]—Accessed on 28th March 2005.

European Round Table. *Education for Europeans: Towards the Learning Society*. 1995. Web site: [http://www.ert.be]—Accessed on 28th March 2005.

Faure, E. et al. *Learning to Be: The World of Education Today and Tomorrow*. Paris: Unesco, 1972.

Felsted, A. and Jewson, N. (eds.). *Global Trends in Flexible Labour*. Basingstoke, UK: Macmillan, 1999.

Field, J. "Governing the Ungovernable: Why Lifelong Learning Policies Promise So Much Yet Deliver So Little." *Educational Management and Administration*, 28(3), 2000, pp. 249–261.

Fretwell, D.H. and Plant, P. "Career Development Policy Models: Synthesis Paper." Paper presented at the *Second International Symposium on Career Development and Public Policy*, Vancouver, Canada, 2001.

Fukayama, F. "The End of History?" *The National Interest*, Summer, 1989, pp. 3–18.

Gallie, D. "Patterns of skill change: upskilling, deskilling or the polarisation of skills?" *Work, Employment and Society*, 5(3), 1991, pp. 319–351.

Gelpi, E. *Lifelong Education and International Relations*. London: Croom Helm, 1985.

Greenwood, I. and Stuart, M. *Restructuring, Partnership and the Learning Agenda: A Review*. Leeds: E.M. Harmer, 2002.

Greenwood, I. and Stuart, M. "Employment or Lifelong Flexibility: Unpicking the Contradictions of the European Employment Strategy." Paper read at the FRP5 Accompanying Measures Project workshop *Living, Working and Learning in the Learning Society—the Perspective of the Learning Citizen in EU Funded Research*. University of Bremen, 27–28 March 2003.

Habermas, J. "Why Europe Needs a Constitution." *New Left Review*, 11 (Sept.–Oct.), 2001, pp.5–26.

Hirtt, N. *L'École Prostituée: L'Offensive des Entrepreises sur l'Enseignement*. Bruxelles: Éditions Labor, 2001.

Jarvis, P. (ed.) *The Age of Learning. Education and the Knowledge Society*. London: Kogan Page, 2001.

Killeen, J. "The Social Context of Guidance." In: A.G. Watts, B. Law, J. Killeen, J.M. Kidd and R. Hawthorn. *Rethinkging Careers Education and Guidance: Theory, Policy and Practice*. London and New York: Routledge, 1996.

Kress, G. "A Curriculum for the Future". *Cambridge Journal of Education*, Vol.30(1), 2000, pp.133–145.

Laval, C. and Weber, L. (eds) *Le Nouvel Ordre Éducatif: OMC, Banque Mondiale, OCDE, Commission Européenne*. Paris: Nouveaux Regards, 2002.

Lê Thành Khôi. *Éducation et Civilisations: Sociétes d'Hier*. Paris: Unesco, 1995.

Madsen, B. "Occupational Guidance and Social Change." *International Journal for the Advancement of Counselling*, 9(1), 1986, 97–112.

McCarthy, J. *The Skills, Training and Qualifications of Guidance Workers*. A paper commissioned jointly by the European Commission and the OECD, prepared for the OECD review of policies for information, guidance and counselling services, 2001.

OECD. *Career Guidance and Public Policy: Bridging the Gap*. Paris: OECD, 2004.

Overdevest, C. *The Open Method of Coordination, New Governance, and Learning: towards a Research Agenda*. Department of Sociology and Rural Sociology, University of Wisconsin–Madison, Working Paper, 2002.

Pakkala, R. *Reconcilable Differences? The French and the Germans on Subsidiarity in the European Union*. Working Paper, 1997.

Ranson, S. (ed.) *Inside the Learning Society*. London: Cassell, 1998.

Ritzer, G. *The MacDonaldization of Society*. Thousand Oaks, CA: Pine Forge, 1996.

Schön, D. *Beyond the Stable State. Public and Private Learning in a Changing Society*. Harmondsworth: Penguin, 1973.

Sultana, R.G. and Sammut, J.M. (eds) *Careers Education and Guidance in Malta: Issues and Challenges*. Malta: PEG, 1997.

Sultana, R.G. *Review of Career Guidance Policies in11 Acceding and Candidate Countries: A Synthesis Report*. Turin: European Training Foundation, 2002.

Sultana, R.G. "Concepts of Knowledge and Learning in Findings of FRP 4 and 5 projects." Paper read at the FRP5 Accompanying Measures Project workshop *Living, Working and Learning in the Learning Society—the Perspective of the Learning Citizen in EU Funded Research*. University of Bremen, 27–28 March, 2003.

Sultana, R.G. *Guidance Policies in the Knowledge Society: Trends, Challenges and Responses Across Europe*. Thessaloniki: Cedefop, 2004.

Sweet, R. "Career Information, Guidance and Counselling Services: Policy Perspectives." *Australian Journal of Career Development*, Vol.10(2), 2001, pp.11–14.

Therborn, G. "Europe's Break with Itself. The European economy and the history, modernity, and the world future of Europe." In: F. Cerutti and E. Rudolph (eds.) *A Soul for Europe.* [Vol.2]. Sterling, Virginia: Peeters Leuven, 2001.

Van der Zee, H. "The Learning Society." In: S. Ranson (ed.) *Inside the Learning Society.* London: Cassell, 1998.

Watts, A.G. "International Perspectives." In: A.G. Watts, B. Law, J. Killeen, J.M. Kidd and R. Hawthorn. *Rethinking Careers Education and Guidance: Theory, Policy and Practice.* London and New York: Routledge, 1996a.

Watts, A.G. "Careers Guidance and Public Policy." In: A.G. Watts, B. Law, J. Killeen, J.M. Kidd and R. Hawthorn. *Rethinkging Careers Education and Guidance: Theory, Policy and Practice.* London and New York: Routledge, 1996b.

Watts, A.G. "Socio–Political Ideologies in Guidance." In: A.G. Watts, B. Law, J. Killeen, J.M. Kidd and R. Hawthorn. *Rethinking Careers Education and Guidance: Theory, Policy and Practice.* London and New York: Routledge, 1996c.

Watts, A.G. and Fretwell, D. *Public Policies for Career Development: Policy Strategies for Designing Career Information and Guidance Systems in Middle–Income and Transition Economies.* Washington, DC: World Bank, 2003.

Watts, A.G. and Sultana, R.G. "Career guidance policies in 37 countries: contrasts and common themes." *International Journal for Educational and Vocational Guidance,* Vol. 4, 2004, pp. 105–122.

Young, M. *The Curriculum of the Future: From the "New Sociology of Education" to a Critical Theory of Learning.* London: Falmer Press, 1998.

• BURKART SELLIN •

# Vocational Education and Lifelong Learning in Tomorrow's Europe

## Introduction

This chapter is based on the findings of the joint research project of European Centre for the Development of Vocational Training (Cedefop) and the European Training Foundation (ETF) *Scenarios and Strategies for Vocational Education and Training and Lifelong Learning in Europe* [1]. The findings and conclusions of the research project are analysed from a new angle against scenarios and strategies likely to be selected in the next ten years to adapt educational and training systems and sub–systems to meet current and future challenges. The new angle of the analysis also pays special attention to developments in Central and Eastern European countries (CEECs). Although current trends appear contradictory and divergent to an outside observer, the scenario method allows us to pick out some of the most important and most likely, shedding some light on the confusion, especially in the international and European contexts. This method is aimed, inter alia, at persuading decision–makers and players to take into account in their daily decisions not only short–term needs but also foreseeable medium and long–term consequences. At present policy–making and practice in vocational education and training, particularly in continuing training, is characterised by an apparent arbitrariness and a tendency to short–termism which sometimes borders on panic. This methodology—provided it is applied comprehensively at various decision–making levels—could help to achieve the sustainability or pro–activity that is so often called for.

# Development of Scenarios and Strategies for Policy–makers and Practitioners, Potential and Limitations of the Method, Cui Bono?

## Advantages and Areas of Application of the Method

The alternative scenarios and strategies determined by a particular method form a basis for players to make medium and long–term workable decisions. They help to clarify complex relationships within a relatively simple (but not simplistic) framework, encouraging stakeholders to reflect objectively in a team on the consequences of their routine activities and to define or evaluate the relevant day–to–day decisions of all those involved from this medium or longer term perspective. This can be done despite the players' divergent interests and conflicting positions on fundamental questions, such as undeniably exist between the interests of employees and employers. The benchmarking or Delphi–method, in contrast, gives only the picture at any particular moment. It aims to set parameters that permit conclusions as to the advantages and disadvantages of specific policies of public or private stakeholders on the basis of a number of indicators for competitiveness or social cohesion, for example. The two methods of analysis are similar, however, in that they study both qualitative and quantitative factors.

Scenarios are semi–militaristic strategic games which, in our context at least, have little to do with short–term power plays or directly winning "battles", but are targeted towards medium and long–term workable concepts and pertinent action.

In the field of education the method has been practised since the mid–1980s. It is comparable with the Delphi method, developed about the same time, which uses multiple interviews with experts to determine options for future development. It aims to find mainly short–term solutions for options already on the agenda. More recently, the scenario approach has proved its worth as a method encouraging consensus and mediation on alternative options between theory and practice, research and application. For some years it has also been used to improve our understanding of trends in an international (global) and European context.[2]

Although this approach is useful for promoting and monitoring dialogue between different players, experts and practitioners, it is difficult to really guarantee its recognition and use. As a rule this depends on a moderator or coach capable of bringing together the different interest groups and disciplines, countries and cultures, and also requires that players and participants invest considerable time, something which policy–makers do not have in abundance. Vocational education and training, and lifelong learning or continuing training is a polyvalent, interdisciplinary and/or multicultural or intercultural world, especially where questions of European and international cooperation are involved.

The scenario method allows us to collate and organise a number of factors and variables or variants in a controlled way. This is particularly important for international comparison and analysis.

## Cui Bono?

This makes the scenario method useful for some projects under certain conditions:

- to develop strategies or systematically investigate alternatives and the most important or likely trends against the background of different systematically constructed scenarios, and then to make a justifiable selection of particular actions and measures for policy–making and practice;
- to reduce the complexity of contradictory and complex or multi-variant interrelationships;
- to provide impartial support on issues which are controversial due to undeniable clashes of interest, and to integrate or at least approximate extreme positions through pragmatic decisions based on a broad consensus which is pro–active and workable in the medium and long term[3];
- to mutually support and integrate socio–scientific statistical data from quantitative surveys and factor analyses, and information from qualitative surveys, for example from interviews and secondary analyses. This means that scientists working primarily with quantitative data analyses or surveys can pool their resources with scientists whose work is primarily qualitative.

The scenario method should not, however, be mistaken for a representative opinion poll or foresight research. Although it makes no claim to be representative, it does claim a high degree of credibility and plausibility. Thus it has more affinity with applied science and action research than with fundamental research, and is closely connected with (political) practice, which sometimes makes pure scientists somewhat suspicious of it.

Since Meadows (1972) and the Club of Rome with its reports on the long–term future development of the earth, air, water and ground, and since complicated computer simulations have made it possible to successfully link huge numbers of factors and to vary their development over time, in other words since the end of the 1960s, the scenario method has proved its worth. It even seems to be more reliable than concepts from prediction research, which have recently taken a back seat. It has, however, integrated some elements of foresight research.

In times of predominating short–termism and even somewhat hysterical policy measures, decisions of questionable foundation and permanence are frequently taken in isolation or ad–hoc. They are often criticised for their arbitrariness and lack of transparency. This, together with calls for "sustainability" and "pro–active action", gives rise to a growing need for instruments or tools to clarify this complexity and help ensure a certain degree of continuity, however abstract this may sometimes be. It can effectively help decision–makers in particular, who are under constant pressure, out of the dilemma described above, and guarantee the necessary transparency in decision–making, the integration of participating institutions and thus the effective implementation of a specific (and not just any) policy in practice.

## Scenarios for European Policies in General

Before I present the approaches and findings of the project *Scenarios and Strategies for Vocational Education and Training and Lifelong Learning in Europe*, I would like to document the findings of some other groups, both to facilitate understanding and because of their European frame of reference. While their interviews and questionnaires may not have been as numerous or comprehensive, nor their socio–statistic methods as complex, their proximity to political decision–makers renders them equally important.

*The Work of the Forward Studies Unit.* On the basis of the five major topics chosen as the starting point of their work—development of institutions and governance, social cohesion, economic adaptability, expansion of the EU, and international context (Bertrand et al. 1999, 11)—this group bundled a number of variables relating to potential scenarios, allocated them to various players and then interviewed high–ranking decision–makers from the Commission and other EU institutions, brought them together in workshops and worked out alternatives with them. Finally they arrived at five scenarios, which they termed "coherent, concerted and plausible images", representing the spectrum of possibilities, factors and actors which could in future play a crucial role. Each of these scenarios has a final, corresponding image, which I summarise briefly here (Bertrand et al. 1999, 5–6):

1. "The Triumph of the Market" scenario is characterised, as its name implies, by the absolute dominance of economic liberalism and the free exchange of goods and services. Europe, whatever its standard, would hardly be different from the rest of the world, which would then be a single planetary market.
2. "A Hundred Flowers" scenario is typified by growing paralysis (and corruption) of major public and private institutions. Europeans withdraw to the local and micro level and to a primarily informal economy entailing a duplication of initiatives with no logical connection.
3. "Divided Responsibilities" scenario is based on the hypothesis of metamorphosis of the public sector against a background of positive economic development, which could engender renewed social and industrial policies.
4. "The Developing Society" scenario depicts a society undergoing extensive transformation with respect to socio–economic and political developments under the premise that ecological and human development values prevail. It includes a basically workable new form of humanism and paves the way for an "immaterial and global renaissance".
5. "The Turbulent Neighbourhood" scenario depicts a weakened Europe in conjunction with sudden and deeply disturbed geopolitical developments, both in the East and in the South, with growing tensions and conflicts causing a "European Security

Council" to be entirely concerned with questions of defence and security.

These scenarios reveal that the search for a vision for Europe, its institutions, its identity and geopolitical stabilisation is still in full swing. The process of expansion is not yet complete, and the broad–based consensus to find the socio–economic direction which Europe could take in the next ten years is still relatively open. The further stabilisation of Europe with a maximum guarantee of economic and social prosperity is, at present, regarded as a doubtful hypothesis.

***Employment, Collective Agreements, Social Protection: What Kind of Social Europe?*** One other relevant work on socio–economic development in the narrower sense exists, along with four interesting scenarios focusing on employment and social security (Maurice et al.1999).

An expert working group[4] was formed under the leadership of the Research and Education Centre for Socio–economic Analyses at the Technical College of Road and Bridge Construction[5], comprising civil servants, consultants, researchers and, not least, speakers for the employers' organisations and the trade unions, to discuss social and socio-political scenarios in preparation for the French presidency in the second half of 2000.

For some time the economic and monetary policies of Europe have been developing without reference to a "Social Europe". The work of the *Atélier*[6] focused on the following questions:

1. How can social solidarity be achieved in the new environment (i.e., Economic and Monetary Union)?
2. Which new models for industrial relations[7] will appear?
3. What will be the future role of the markets in the individual Member States and in the EU?
4. What part will the social partners play on a national and perhaps European scale?

Below we present four different development scenarios for a Social Europe on the basis of three central questions:

- Will the national social systems continue to develop in isolation?
- Will the systems of industrial (occupational) relations converge?
- Will the social security systems be complemented in future by

specific European benefits?

The current situation whereby differing national models are preserved and accumulated has engendered friction, contradictions and tension.

The process accompanying the construction of Europe may indeed have brought about a degree of approximation of the social systems during its different phases, but by and large this approximation has been limited.

Discussions between representatives of the European social partners (European Trade Union Confederation and European employers' associations), which started in Val Duchesse near Brussels in the early 1980s, led to a social dialogue and gradually to the 1989 *Charter of Basic Social Rights*, the 1991 agreement between the social partners and joint statements, and to the 1993 appendix to the *Maastricht Treaty* in the form of a protocol declared binding by eleven of the twelve states making up the Union at the time.

Finally, in 1997 the Treaty of Amsterdam made a breakthrough with important progress in social affairs: annually updated guidelines on employment policies, and the anchoring of basic social rights[8] in the Treaty with reference to the respective Council of Europe Conventions.

So what do the four scenarios presented by the working group have to offer?

**Table 1. Matrix overview of scenarios of the *Commissariat général du plan***

| Type of industrial / occupational relations | Various models retained (status quo) | Convergence in the sense of harmonisation (increasing approximation) |
|---|---|---|
| Type of social solidarity / cohesion | | |
| remains essentially different in each country (status quo) | Scenario A: Fragmented Social Europe | Scenario B: Competing Social Europe |
| develops an additional common dimension (stronger social cohesion) | Scenario C: Europe united despite its differences | Scenario D: Integrated Social Europe |

Note: The comments in brackets are by the author but are based on explanations in Maurice et al. (1999). For further details on the scenarios please refer to the source.

In the context of the two key issues—"industrial and occupational relations" and "social solidarity/cohesion"—and the added dimensions of continued divergence or increasing convergence of the former, the predominance of national authority or the added dimension of the European level for the latter, the workshop discussions with high–ranking researchers, civil servants and decision–makers resulted in the following matrix (Table 1).

These scenarios and those of the above–mentioned Forward Studies Unit of the Commission have one great advantage for our work and for evaluating the results of the Cedefop/ETF project *Scenarios and Strategies for Vocational Education and Training and Lifelong Learning in Europe*:[9] they enable us to set the scenarios of our project group, which are rather pragmatic and designed for implementation in the three different contexts:

- economy and technology,
- employment and social affairs, and
- education, training and qualifications,

as well as in a broader context of general policy–making and the construction of Europe, with their varying corresponding visions.

## The Project "Scenarios and Strategies for Vocational Education and Training and Lifelong Learning in Europe"

### Summary of the Project Findings

Three "contextual environments" were distinguished: context A "Business and Technology", context B "Employment and the Labour Market", and context C "Training, Skills and Knowledge". A number of specific trends and strategies in each of these categories were given the highest values by all the partner institutions from the participating countries. (More information on project methods and phases can be found in Annex I at the end of this chapter.)

Stakeholders and experts in participating countries received and completed identical questionnaires. They were asked to grade the trends and strategies according to their importance and/or likelihood. The results of the survey were evaluated and discussed at conferences at both national and European level.

The most significant of the trends determined show clearly that public–private partnerships and the new economic order are regarded as vital for improving competitiveness, promoting changes in the workplace, and increasing flexibility and mobility among the workforce. This necessitates corresponding flexibility in vocational training courses, a change in the frame of reference of training providers (vocational schools and training centres), greater acceptance of the social dimension as a frame of reference for policies, and individualisation and decentralisation of vocational education and training programmes. Four main scenarios were proposed, based on these factors: one scenario each for contexts A and B and two for context C (see below).

**Table 2. Matrix of scenarios in the context A "Business and Technology"**

| Partnership between public and private agencies | No/ few partnerships/ cooperation | Many partnerships between public and private agencies for economic and technological development |
|---|---|---|
| Economic restructuring to increase competitiveness | | |
| Little modernisation | **Scenario 1: Stagnation** Economic development is uncertain, little interaction with initial and continuing training | **Scenario 2: Good will but few results** In this scenario no strong economic impetus prevails, although numerous links with training providers exist |
| Comprehensive modernisation | **Scenario 3: Short–term development** Modernisation and restructuring of enterprises takes place without significant links to education | **Scenario 4: Comprehensive development** The economy is thoroughly modernised and there is a high level of interaction between education/training and enterprises |

Of the numerous strategies resulting from these trends, several can be regarded as common to all or at least as trans–national, although the details differ from one country to another. These are briefly described in the following sections. For further details and analyses, including country-specific factors, please refer to the individual reports and findings[10].

***Context A "Business and Technology".*** Tactics for improving incentives for all players to become involved in vocational education and training, to anticipate the particular needs of specific target groups, regions, sectors and enterprises (particularly SMEs)[11] and to promote the establishment of learning organisations, regions and knowledge management were generally considered important.

Here are the four scenarios for the context A "Business and Technology" (Table 2).

Table 3. Matrix of scenarios in the context B "Employment and the Labour Market"

| Modernisation/ flexibility of labour, the workplace and organisation of work  Workforce mobility (occupational and geographic) | Little modernisation or flexibility of labour | High degree of flexibility and restructuring of labour |
|---|---|---|
| Little mobility or flexibility | **Scenario 1: Immobility** Enterprises cling to traditional structures, and staff are not interested in change or innovation | **Scenario 2: Organisational change** The organisation of labour changes while the workforce clings to old practices |
| High degree of mobility/ flexibility among workforce | **Scenario 3: Flexible workers, inflexible organisation of labour** In this case employees are prepared to think in new dimensions and forms of labour, but enterprises show little innovation in their internal organisation | **Scenario 4: Synergy between labour and capital** Here there is agreement on the need for restructuring labour and its organisation and the need for the workforce to adapt: both pull together |

*Context B "Employment and the Labour Market"*. The move towards a "modern workforce" and modern employment contracts, the establishment of supporting structures and the promotion of special measures for high–risk groups were identified as common strategic trends among participating countries.

Scenarios for the context B "Employment and Labour Market" are mentioned in Table 3.

Table 4. Matrix I—scenarios in the context C
"Training, Skills and Knowledge"

| Development of the demand for social and general qualifications and competences | Little demand for social and general competences in con-nection with in-company training | Strong demand and involvement of enterprises |
|---|---|---|
| Innovative and adaptable external and group training providers | | |
| Little willingness to adapt/innovate on the part of training providers | **Scenario 1: Traditional inward-looking system** No great need for social and generic qualifications; providers uphold their usual courses and content | **Scenario 2: Clash between supply and demand** The demand for social and generic competences is great but is not being satisfied |
| (Vocational) education centres well prepared | **Scenario 3: Unproductive innovation** Education providers renew their programmes but there is no commensurate demand | **Scenario 4: Demand keeps pace with the innovative capacity of education provision** Decentralisation of the supply structure and growing demand for new kinds of qualification are commensurate |

*Context C "Training, Skills and Knowledge"*. The following strategies were commonly considered important: to improve the transparency of qualifications (national and European) and mobility (both spatial and occupational), to promote personal development (of individuals and workforces) and to combat social marginalisation, to provide more basic and general knowledge (in addition to technical and occupation–related knowledge) and to pay more attention to older employees and job seekers. Both enterprises and private individuals must be persuaded to invest more in initial training and especially in continuing (vocational) training.

Two separate matrices were needed for the context C "Training, Skills and Knowledge" because the four most important dimensions were considered almost equally important (Table 4 and Table 5).

### Table 5. Matrix II—scenarios in the context C "Training, Skills and Knowledge"

| Social cushioning of certain target groups | Vocational training policies not viewed as social policies | Vocational training is used extensively for the integration or reintegration of vulnerable target groups |
|---|---|---|
| Individual responsibility | | |
| Little individual responsibility for vocational training | **Scenario 1: Fragmentation** Hardly anyone feels really responsible for vocational training | **Scenario 2: Predominantly collective responsibility** Traditional state–based "social democratic" training predominates |
| Vocational training is primarily the responsibility of the individual | **Scenario 3: Neo–liberal approach** The market and the purchasing power of the individual or the economy dominate | **Scenario 4: Responsibility lies jointly with the individual and public or social partners** Vocational training provision as a public responsibility and individual initiative coincide |

## Evaluation of the Findings with a Special Look at Trends and Developments in CEECs

It was interesting to discover in the course of the first phase of the project that there were no significant differences between the assessment of the importance of the basic trends and the likelihood of their occurrence in the participating countries, in spite of the numerous differences in details. After joint discussion each country could add up to three specific trends to the approved list of about twenty per context. Only a few teams availed themselves of this option.

As expected, several significant differences existed between old EU Member States and the acceding CEECs, but these were not so marked that the two groups needed to be treated separately. In other words, the CEECs differ as much among themselves as they do from the old EU Member States, and the latter also demonstrated diverse structures. These differences are less noticeable in the fairly general environments of contexts A and B than in context C; and the scenarios naturally differ less than the strategies, measures, planned action and players.

It would therefore be overly simplistic to generalise that these countries were clinging to the *ancién régime* (the old system) or, at the other extreme, that they were throwing the baby out with the bath water and there was a clear trend towards neo–liberal development or a return to the Manchester capitalism of the century before last. The pressure for action and reform in the CEECs is, however, naturally much greater than in the old EU Member states, which do not have to implement this comprehensive systemic transformation.

As to mobility, freedom of movement, European standards and qualification trends, it was noticeable that the CEECs did not wish to see their newly acquired freedom of movement jeopardised, but they did fear that the emigration of highly–qualified skilled workers in particular will continue, delaying the necessary modernisation of their own economy. Many worried about a brain drain to the West.

CEECs' perception of the EU has become much more critical and sober, but their willingness to think in terms of European (i.e., EU) standards and qualification structures seems to be greater than in the participating old EU Member States.

Issues for all five CEECs were linked to the search for a right balance between individualisation and decentralisation of vocational training provisions on the one hand and cohesion and transparency of the overall opportunity structure on the other.

CEECs often noted increasing problems linked to the (in–) equality of opportunities between different target groups, regions and economic segments (small companies, sector problems etc.). They were concerned about general lack of an active employment policy with a greater share of training and lifelong learning measures (both on–the job and off–the job) more systematically.

Another concern among CEECs was the increasing polarisation between general/academic and technical/vocational education and training and a growing marginalisation of those undergoing the latter.

Mobilisation of the interviewees for the study was somewhat less in the old EU Member States than in the CEECs. The quota of participants in the questionnaire survey, the content and the form of which was admittedly not readily comprehensible, was relatively low in some of the countries. In Austria the survey was conducted just before the parliamentary elections there. This was a particular disadvantage as the elections had a polarising effect and short–term issues were perhaps given undue emphasis. Researchers confirmed a certain trend towards blocking out EU questions and especially questions regarding its expansion and the freedom of movement of labour.

These comments emphasised the need to re–examine the scenarios and principal trends, strategies, etc. during the second phase. They had to be more clearly defined and the concerns of individual countries given more consideration. The actions and measures appropriate to policy–making and practice received particular attention. Thus, in the second phase the findings were investigated in more depth and verified by more detailed interviews.

This project was intended to stimulate and foster a Europe–wide discussion on the future of vocational education and training policies. The first phase was a positive step in this direction (see more Cedefop/ETF 2002).

## Discussion of Findings

Some of the dimensions and the most important findings are underlined and evaluated here.

The question of economic renewal was the focus of attention in all countries, but especially in the CEECs, as a result of their endeavours to convert from one system to another. It was generally considered to be very important, but whether it will really succeed was of course much less clear.

A prospering economy alone, without the appropriate ecological and social backup, is neither workable nor acceptable. Integration of a region into its geographical and geopolitical environment is important, and not just since buzzwords such as globalisation and internationalisation have begun to dominate the discussion.

The one–sided dominance of economic interests has shaken value systems, especially in highly industrialised and technology–oriented countries. In the 1990s, paid labour and employees seemed to have become a tiresome evil, and many people thought they could be done away with, or that we could free ourselves from them entirely.

These views have, however, been clearly refuted in recent years. The "computer economy" or "new economy" does not function without people and "soft skills". Neither does it function just with capital or the use of hardware and machines alone. It can only fulfil its potential with the help of real people, not just temporarily available workers in the strict Fordist sense of the division of labour! Money and short–term profit are not everything. Workers have not been rendered superfluous. They are currently being rediscovered as "active and creative colleagues". They must, however, be prepared to involve themselves in the process of organisation and cannot avoid recognising that maintaining and developing qualifications has become an ongoing task. Social and general qualifications and competences rank alongside specialised qualifications. Of course this brings advantages and disadvantages: alienation from the work process may lessen, but control and the pressure to be loyal to production goals and to one's employers or enterprise increases.

In addition, the social management and organisation of modern forms of work become the focus of attention, which also raises the issues of workers' competence and qualifications in this context, ordinary people's opportunities to participate in lifelong learning, access to continuing training and retraining, etc. We need a new type of worker to reorganise work. Institutions must be modernised and new forms of time management found for hours of work, leisure time and learning time, for example, in respect of the distribution of work throughout a person's entire working life.

These are some of the most important findings of the Cedefop/ETF Scenario project.

Analysis of the findings permits some further conclusions.

The need to think in terms of processes and networks continues to grow in view of the immense increase in the range of application of new technologies, their affordability and availability. Mass production and a comprehensive supply are becoming less important than the satisfaction (just in time) of individual and local, and therefore highly diversified, requirements in the different times and regions, in which in Europe, at least, basic requirements should (soon) be met. However, the accompanying individualisation and decentralisation demands new forms of cooperation, through in–company continuing training, for example, which must guarantee the inclusion of people otherwise threatened with isolation in the new networks and increasingly complex processes.

Local and sectoral systems, largely self–managing and able to adapt to the constantly and ever more rapidly changing needs and the changing demand behaviour of participants, will replace relatively rigid "supply systems", making way for more customer and participant–friendly provision geared to the concrete needs of individuals and participants, as well as enterprises and the local or regional economy and society. A controlled and transparent individualisation and decentralisation of lifelong learning as a collective responsibility, certainly with the support of public and private partnerships, and involving the further development of the social partnership in education and continuing training, is also an important theme in all the countries studied.

The concept of "futures workshops" originated in the 1970s and 1980s, propagated mainly by the science journalist Robert K. Jungk[12], and was indeed implemented. They are a variation on the scenario method and sometimes a useful, primarily group–dynamic and socio–pedagogical, complement to and technique for the application of the latter. They could engender the necessary interaction and equally necessary solidarity in continuing training and lifelong learning itself; i.e., adult learning could be significantly improved with the aid of the scenario method and/or futures workshops. We should not leave their use solely to our "stakeholders"[13], who were the preferred interviewees and most involved in the study. Every man and woman should learn to use and apply them. They are easier to understand than the instructions for some video recorders.

The 2nd European Conference in Tallinn in October 2001 provided an opportunity for major decision–makers and players involved in education, initial and continuing vocational education and training policies in Europe to discuss the findings of this project. It helped those responsible to draw their own conclusions and to make both, findings and conclusions, available and workable among policy–makers and practitioners. It also allowed Cedefop, the ETF and the European Commission, and finally the European Parliament and Council, to use them where appropriate to discuss and determine priorities and strategies for planning the next steps towards implementing these policies, such as the development of strategies for lifelong learning (e.g., Lifelong Learning Memorandum of the European Commission). The European Employment Strategy led to a European Occupational and Continuing Training Strategy, which was defined in the meantime on the basis of the 2000 and 2001 decisions of the Lisbon and Barcelona Council. Creating an improved environment for lifelong learning, which is already well underway in some Member States, will have far–reaching consequences for initial training, which will have to be adapted and reformed. All Member States (old and new) should cooperate consistently in view of the necessary adaptation of systems and institutions, thus playing an active part in shaping the process in the light of alternative scenarios and strategies.

## Overarching Scenarios and Linked Strategies for Vocational Training and Lifelong Learning at the European Level

The scenarios in the matrix that follows (Table 6) concentrate on the extent of European cooperation and cohesion in social policy arenas (a continuum between competition and cohesion), and the extent to which European "learning systems" converge or remain divergent.

To illustrate the model, we have developed the first scenario in a little more detail than the others.

The "Divided Europe" scenario is as follows:

- geography: the dividing lines are not necessarily the same as national frontiers. Rather, they divide prosperous and competitive regions and agglomerations from regions that are increasingly lagging behind. *Mezzogiornos* spread, and most countries have their own larger or smaller disadvantaged regions;
- sectors and companies: some industrial sectors and SMEs operate only at local or regional levels. Some of these are marginalised and become less prosperous and competitive within the wider Europe;
- target groups: disadvantaged target groups (low–skilled people, ethnic minorities, ageing groups and populations in remote regions with poor infrastructures) are put at an increased disadvantage. More impoverishment of larger parts in the population follows. The digital divide goes hand in hand with an increasing social division.

**Table 6. Matrix of overarching scenarios and strategies in all three contexts at European cross–country level**

| Socio–economic development / Systemic divergence or convergence | Competition rather than co-operation | Socio–economic cohesion |
|---|---|---|
| Liberalisation, decentralisation and individualisation | **Scenario 1: Competitiveness and splendid isolation—"Divided Europe"** Systemic divergences within and between countries remain and may be growing. Education/training systems and providers are competing strongly. Polarisation and marginalisation of certain target groups, regions and sectors are increasing. | **Scenario 2: Unity in diversity—"Pick and Mix Europe"** The social and innovative role of education and training is recognised. However, no wider system development is taking place; systems and provisions develop only slowly towards mutual compatibility or transparency. |
| Increasing convergence and mutual learning | **Scenario 3: Convergence without great coherence—"Learning Europe"** Despite prevailing divergences in the economy and society, converging regulations and provision are being developed, though the links to industry and private economy are largely missing. Efforts to ensure compatible rules and procedures at European level contribute little to increasing mobility and innovation. Systems and structures compete, and see European issues as peripheral. | **Scenario 4: Balance and coherence—"Towards a comprehensive European education and training system"** The trend towards closer socio–economic cooperation among old and new EU Member States. More people (young and old) gain higher levels of education and training. Resources are available through public and private funds. Systems develop in a comparable way. Qualification structures and educational/training provisions become increasingly similar and compatible. |

In the "Pick and Mix Europe" the Member States work towards better socio–economic cohesion, although the systems do not converge very much. Training provisions stay basically different and take little account of the European dimension, cooperation is limited and competition may even be increased. Local and regional concerns, as well as individual ones (enterprises' and participants') are taken on board more efficiently.

In the "Learning Europe"[14] scenario, European Member States, institutions and stakeholders learn from each other. A culture of learning and working towards the establishment of a renewed and knowledge–based society develops. Europe, as part of the wider world, plays an increasingly important role in shaping or moderating broader, global development. Nonetheless, the cohesion and transparency of countries' internal education and training systems does not necessarily increase.

In "Towards a European education and training system" scenario European social–economic, monetary and cultural integration proceeds at a high speed and apparently successfully. The consequence is that either *de jure* or *de facto* (or both) the education and training systems in Europe become similar and coherent, despite continuing cultural and historical differences between groups of countries alongside a North–South and/or East–West borderline.

## Major Strategy

The findings of the joint Cedefop/ETF scenario project suggest that the following strategies rank high in terms of importance.

First, the strengthening of the social (and environmental) dimension of vocational education/training and lifelong learning in comparison with the economic and competition–policy dimension; combating polarisation and marginalisation, and ensuring equal opportunities in education and lifelong learning—enabling access to the highest possible qualifications for all and/or positive discrimination in favour of disadvantaged groups, regions and sectors; development of the institutions responsible for vocational education and training, and lifelong learning, including cooperation between trade and industry/companies and state authorities, schools and enterprises, etc.; promoting partnerships between public and private educational institutions and between education and vocational training, and education within and outside schools, particularly at local, regional and sectoral levels.

Second, provision of a transparent structure of qualifications and of adequate certification and accreditation systems at sectoral, national and European levels; creating a connection between qualifications obtained in initial and continuing training, and facilitating a common reference framework for different education and (continuing) training paths and contents; promotion of European standards in the development of qualifications and in certification/accreditation modes in certain sectors, and of continuing cooperation in the promotion of innovations, tools and methods for adjusting initial and continuing vocation education and training provision and qualifications.

Third, (re)organisation and modernisation of work, accompanied by improvements in the quality of work and life; improved integration of learning hours and working hours, facilitating time for education and recognition of experiential/informal learning; increased involvement of the social partners, promotion of flexible wage agreements and forms of working (e.g., job rotation) appropriate to the differing requirements and living and working conditions of employees and the self–employed; making it possible for people to combine work and learning throughout their whole working life. This may include modernisation and decentralisation, individualisation and increased flexibility of options and supply structures, accompanied by a strengthening of the "market" position of participants in vocational training and lifelong learning; combining improvements in the quality of work and quality of life, for instance through new types of collective agreements and working time/learning time combinations.

The following areas may thus provide a focus for the next 10 years' strategies:

- strengthening the social (and environmental) dimension of vocational education and training and lifelong learning;
- promoting public and private partnerships;
- agreeing compatible national and European (meta–) structures for both initial and continuing education and training qualifications, provision and promotion of European standards in some sectors e.g., in ICT– and e–Business skills;
- modernisation of work, at the same time safeguarding and improving quality of life including access to formal and non–formal learning on–the–job and off–the–job, lifelong learning during work and alongside work and employment.

Three major scenarios were discussed at the project conference in Tallinn in addition to the overarching ones:

1. "Europe on the Edge": a Europe, where everything is uncertain and major current problems are not resolved, e.g., unemployment, lack of flexibility of training provision and work, economic recession, high labour mobility, low (global) competitiveness and growth, traditional practice in companies, inequality neither increasing nor decreasing.
2. "Protective and Incremental Europe": tailor–made training programmes, individual training accounts, the State not responsible for lifelong learning, unemployment remains a problem, continuing privatisation, small businesses and remote regions have problems, not enough funding possibilities, increasing inequality.
3. "Sustainable and Competitive Europe": lifelong learning is important, networks between companies or learning organisations and training providers are common, increased need for foreign workers, reduced and low unemployment, individuals are mainly responsible for their own training, companies have well–developed training programmes which are part of their business plan, new kind of work contracts integrating training (leave), social inequalities remain.

Crucial questions were raised concerning the necessary resources and funds and their distribution across the various levels of intervention and contributors: private households, companies and public bodies, national and/or European Union funds, collective funding arrangements/ agreements[15] or solidarity funds, insurance or voucher, learning account systems and the extent of individual (funding) responsibility.

These scenarios were further refined and European level actors were consulted in the mean time. Which scenarios (and linked strategies) will become reality is not clear. Most of those involved in the European level debate appear to favour the third of these, the "Sustainable Europe" scenario. However, within this scenario the inequality issue is likely to be difficult to resolve[16].

# Annex I

## Methods and Phases of the Project "Scenarios and Strategies for Vocational Education and Training and Lifelong Learning in Europe"

A chronological list of the steps undertaken between end of 1998 and beginning of 2002 provided below clarifies the methods employed in the project.

*Phase I.* This phase lasted from the end of 1998 to the beginning of 2000 and consisted of the following stages:

a) Around two hundred written questionnaires were distributed in each of the participating countries: five old EU Member States and five CEECs, on each of the three different contextual environments: economic, social and educational or vocational training, listing around twenty trends per context for evaluation or assessment.
b) The survey was evaluated using socio–statistical methods and the findings collated in country reports and combined in a European report.
c) National seminars were held for groups of decision–makers to discuss and verify the plausibility and workability of the findings and for the final editing of the country reports.
d) The first European conference was organised in Athens (with the support of the Greek Manpower Employment Organisation— OAED) in January 2000 for the final evaluation of the first phase.
e) The full report and the country reports were published and the most important findings summarised as a synopsis. They were distributed and decisions were taken on the fundamental course of action for the following phase.

The results of Phase 1 stand alone. They were summarised again in the final report on Phase 2, but only to the extent necessary for understanding the course and results of the second phase.

*Phase 2.* The following steps were implemented:

a) The material and expertise necessary for conducting and scheduling the various tasks were acquired. They were discussed at a first working meeting among the partner institutes in Brussels in April 2000.
b) Work commenced on the complementary processing of statistics and objective fundamentals in each country, and a limited number of in–depth interviews were conducted on the basis of (European) "meta–scenarios" and country–specific scenarios from Phase 1, which had been checked and amended as necessary. The particular emphasis was on strategies, potential activities and policy or practice measures.
c) Evaluation of the interviews and drafting of the country reports on Phase 2 by countries.
d) Second working meeting of the partner institutes in Thessaloniki in January 2001; discussion of the findings from the country studies, preliminary discussion of the planned content of the European report, discussion of the organisation of national seminars and further planning.
e) Third working meeting was held in June 2001 to discuss the final report by the Max Goote Expert Centre[17] and the intentions of Cedefop and ETF for the second European conference.
f) The final report and a synopsis for the final conference were prepared and the country reports completed.
g) The second European conference was held with players and specialists in policy and practice of vocational training and lifelong learning at the beginning of October 2001. It was organised in Tallinn with the help of the Estonian Ministry of Education.
h) An additional survey among European level stakeholders was undertaken in early 2002 to verify and comment the outcome and to get their appreciation about overarching scenarios proposed by Cedefop for the European level.
i) The final report on the Phase 2 results was published.[18]

# Notes

1. The author of the chapter was a coordinator of the research project. The findings discussed here are entirely the responsibility of the author and not of the European Centre for the Development of Vocational Training (Cedefop) or of the European Training Foundation (ETF).

2. See for example the OECD International Futures Programme (IFP) or the programme Schooling for Tomorrow: see IFP homepage at http://www.oecd.org; also Bertrand, Gilles et al. "Europe 2010: cinq scénarios pour sortir du no future", in *Futuribles, analyse et prospective* 246 (October 1999); or the work of the Forward Studies Unit—a department of the European Commission reporting directly to the President, this group was set up in 1989 by Commission President Jacques Delors. See also the article by van Wieringen, Fons: "Strategies and scenarios for the development of (continuing) vocational education and training", in Cedefop (Sellin, Burkart) 1999: *European trends in the development of occupations and qualifications, findings of research, studies and analysis for policy and practice*, Vol. II, 331. The institute of the Joint Research Centre of the European Commission, the Institute for Prospective Technological Studies (IPTS), located in Seville, also uses the scenario method to analyse trends (see https://www.jrc.es).
3. Interestingly, these terms are on everybody's lips precisely in times of increasing arbitrariness and the dominance of short–termism (especially in international and global debate).
4. The group was set up by the *Commissariat général du plan* in connection with preliminary considerations on reforming the European institutions prior to the intergovernmental conference in Nice, which took place in autumn 2000. Since this brought no significant progress in the central questions on the future identity and development of Europe, a new intergovernmental conference was set for 2004.
5. This is one of the *Grandes Ecoles*, France's elite schools which educate not only "technical elites" but also management personnel for other sectors, especially the French administration and state enterprises.
6. Can be translated as "workshop discussion".
7. The original speaks of *rélations professionnelles*, i.e., occupational relations (Maurice et al.1999).
8. However, in contrast to political rights such as freedom of speech, membership of trade unions, etc. these are not legally enforceable. (See the catalogue of basic rights agreed in Nice: it is still to be decided whether its scope is valid only for the European institutions, or whether it applies to the Member States and all citizens.) This is a prominent topic in the European Constitution alongside the division of responsibility among the various levels (Member States, regions, EU institutions).
9. The following countries participated in research: Austria, Belgium, Luxembourg, Germany, Greece, United Kingdom (EU Member States at the time of the project) and Czech Republic, Estonia, Hungary, Poland and Slovenia (at the time candidates for accession to the EU).
10. See particularly Cedefop/ETF/ Max Goote Expert Center 2000, van Wieringen 2002, Cedefop/ETF 2002. National reports can be found at http://www2.trainingvillage.gr/etv/scenarios/nat_rep.asp
11. Here SMEs—small and medium–sized enterprises—were understood as those with up to 500 employees.
12. Cf. Jungk, R. and N.R. Müllert: *Zukunftswerkstätten,* Munich 1994 (4th edition), quoted from Albers and Broux (1999).

13. The term stakeholder comes from America and refers to landowning and land allocation. Until well into the 19th century applicants for the purchase or long–term lease of land received, against a certain sum of money, four stakes with which to mark the boundaries of their plot. From this time on they were responsible for this land, even though they were not always its legal owners.
14. See also Gavigan et al. 1999.
15. on sectoral, regional or company levels
16. Social inequalities do not primarily depend on vocational education and training policies, even if they may contribute to combating or increasing those inequalities.
17. The Max Goote Expert Centre is active in the field of vocational education and training, and adult education. It is part of the University of Amsterdam (http://www.maxgoote.nl). The Centre supported Cedefop and ETF in the technical and scientific coordination of the project.
18. For more information see http://www.trainingvillage.gr—look for the "Scenarios and Strategies" window under "Projects and Networks".

# References

Albers, O. and Broux, A. *Zukunftswerkstatt und Szenariotechnik, ein Methodenbuch für Schule und Hochschule,* Beltz Verlag Weinheim and Basel, 1999.

Bertrand, G., Michalski, A., and Pench, L. R. "Europe 2010: cinq scénarios pour sortir du no future". In: *Futuribles, analyse et prospective* 246 (October 1999), pp. 5–23.

Cedefop/ETF. *Scenarios and Strategies for Vocational Education and Training in Europe. Executive summary and synthesis of European level report: phase 1.* Paper for the European Conference, Amsterdam/Thessaloniki/Turin, 2002.

Cedefop/ETF/ Max Goote Expert Center. *Scenarios and Strategies for Vocational Education and Training in Europe. European synthesis report on phase I.* Thessaloniki, 2000.

Gavigan, J.P., Ottitsch, M. and Mahroum, S. "Knowledge and Learning. Towards a Learning Europe". The Futures Project. *IPTS Series* n°: 14, EUR 19034 EN, Sevilla, 1999.

Maurice, J., Brocas, A.–M., and Cadiou, L. *Emploi, négociations collectives, protection sociale: vers quelle Europe sociale?* Commissariat Général du Plan, Paris, 1999.

Meadows, D.L., Meadows, D., Zahn, E., Milling, P. *Die Grenzen des Wachstums.* Bericht des Club of Rome zur Lage der Menschheit, Stuttgart, 1972.

Wieringen, F. van, Sellin, B. and Schmidt, G. *Future Education: Learning the Future. Scenarios and Strategies in Europe.* Cedefop/ETF/ Max Goote Expert Center, Amsterdam/Thessaloniki/Turin, 2002.

# Contributors

**Adela–Luminita Rogojinaru** (PhD in Philology) holds the position of Reader at the University of Bucharest in Romania. She is Head of the Department of Communication and Public Relations Studies, and Director of the Centre for Distance Education at the Faculty of Letters. She also works as a policy development expert for the National Centre for Technical and Vocational Education and Training Development of the Ministry of Education and Research in Romania. She is a recognised expert in public communication and in various aspects of the educational reform process.

**Burkart Sellin** (Engineer in Physics Technology) began his career in research at the Technical University of Aachen focusing on engineering education and training development in Germany, France, Morocco, Tunisia and Somalia. Later, at the University Institute for European Studies in Brussels and with the European Cultural Foundation in The Hague he conducted comparative studies on behalf of the European Commission on the education and training of professional engineers and on vocational education and training systems. He joined the European Centre for the Development of Vocational Training (Cedefop) in 1976 and has worked and published on a wide variety of themes including youth training, apprenticeships, the role of social partners, the comparability and mutual recognition of vocational qualifications, and comparative research notably on trends in occupations and qualifications.

**Olga Strietska–Ilina** holds degrees in History, Sociology, and Political Sciences. She works as an independent expert in the field of training and skill needs on the labour market, mostly in collaboration with Cedefop in Thessaloniki, Greece. Starting her career teaching at the Central European University in Prague, she was then a Director of the National Observatory for Employment and Training in the Czech Republic for several years. She has published extensively in the field of education and training, employment and labour market, social exclusion, cultural minorities, nationalism and European affairs. She was a coordinator of the project domain which focused particularly on issues of countries in transition within the EURONE&T thematic network, out of which the present volume has been developed.

**Ronald Sultana** is Professor of Comparative Education and Educational Sociology at the University of Malta, where he directs the Euro–Mediterranean Centre for Educational Research. His main research interests are in the link between education and the world of work, vocational education and training, and teachers' training. His present work focuses on lifelong approaches to career guidance in both the education sector and in public employment services across Europe. He worked as a guidance counsellor in schools in Malta, the UK, and New Zealand, and researched school–work transition issues in Malta, England, France, New Zealand, and the US, where he was Fulbright Scholar at Stanford University. He is a founding editor of the *Mediterranean Journal of Educational Studies*.

**Manfred Tessaring** (PhD in Economics) specialises in the economics of education and labour market research. Until 1996 he worked at the Institute for Employment Research in Nuremberg, Germany, and since 1996 at the European Centre for the Development of Vocational Training (Cedefop) in Thessaloniki, Greece, where he is Head of Area "Developing Research". He has published extensively in the field of research into vocational education and training, and, in particular, into the identification of skills and qualification needs on the labour market. He has recently been involved in the evaluation activities concerning the progress achieved towards the Lisbon, Copenhagen and Maastricht goals for vocational education and training.

**Göran Therborn** is currently Professor of Sociology at Uppsala University and a Director of the Swedish Collegium for Advanced Study in the Social Sciences. He was previously Professor of Political Science at the Catholic University of Nijmegen, and Professor of Sociology at Göteborg

University. His temporary positions have included a European Chair of Social Policy in Budapest and Senior Research Fellowships at the University of Manchester and the University of Wisconsin, Madison. He has also held short–term appointments at UCLA, the Sorbonne, and a number of universities in Latin America.His latest books are: *Between Sex and Power: Family in the World, 1900–2000* (London, Routledge, 2004), *Inequalities of the World* (London, Verso, 2006), and *Asia and Europe under Globalization* (Leyden, Brill, 2006).

**Juraj Vantuch** is an education policy analyst at Comenius University Bratislava, Slovakia. Graduating from the teacher training programme at Comenius University, he also gained a RNDr degree from the Faculty of Mathematics and Physics at Comenius University in Probability and Statistics and a PhD in Pedagogy from Charles University in Prague. In December 2005 he finalised the habilitation procedure in Pedagogy Management and Education Policy at Comenius University. He is a lecturer at the Faculty of Education, offering courses in Methodology, Education Policy, Comparative Education, and Education and the Labour Market.

**Liliana Voicu** is a researcher in the field of education and training. She has participated in numerous European projects, within the Leonardo da Vinci programme or under the coordination of European agencies such as Cedefop, the European Training Foundation, and the European Foundation for Improving of Living and Working Conditions. Having worked as a researcher at the Institute for Educational Sciences in Bucharest from 1990 to 2001, then as a Director for Studies and Prognoses at the National Adult Training Board, since 2004 she has been Director of Research and Development at AxA Consulting, a Romanian training and consultancy company.